PALACE OR TEMPLE ON THE ISLAND OF COATI, IN LAKE TITICACA.

PERUVIAN

ANTIQUITIES.

BY

MARIANO EDWARD RIVERO,

DIRECTOR OF THE NATIONAL MUSEUM, LIMA, AND CORRESPONDING MEMBER OF VARIOUS SCIENTIFIC SOCIETIES IN EUROPE AND AMERICA;

AND

JOHN JAMES VON TSCHUDI,

DOCTOR IN PHILOSOPHY, MEDICINE, AND SURGERY, ETC., ETC., AND MEMBER OF VARIOUS SOCIETIES OF MEDICINE, NATURAL HISTORY, GEOGRAPHY, AND AGRICULTURE.

TRANSLATED INTO ENGLISH, FROM THE ORIGINAL SPANISH,

BY

FRANCIS L. HAWKS, D.D., LL. D.

NEW YORK:

PUBLISHED BY A. S. BARNES & COMPANY,

No. 51 JOHN-STREET.

CINCINNATI:—H. W. DERBY,

1855.

DEDICATION.

TO

THE SOVEREIGN CONGRESS

OF PERU.

CENTURIES have passed without the possession by Peru of a collection of such of her ancient architectural monuments, as have escaped the ravages of time, avarice, and superstition. These silent, yet eloquent, witnesses reveal the history of past successes, and demonstrate the intelligence, power, and grandeur of the nation once ruled by our Incas.

To us has fallen the honor of being the first to present them in this work (the fruit of some years' labor), though not as extensively and perfectly as we have desired; and to dedicate it to the national sovereignty, in the hope that it will be deemed worthy of a kind reception.

Will your Honorable Body accept this slight tribute of our diligence, and the respectful consideration of

Your faithful and obedient servants,

MARIANO EDUARDO DE RIVERO.

DR. JOHN JAMES VON TSCHUDI.

INTRODUCTORY NOTE,

BY THE TRANSLATOR.

In the prosecution of researches made in the preparation of a work on the antiquities of America generally, it became necessary to examine the book of which a translation is here presented to the reader. On its perusal, it was found to contain, with much that has already been placed in the hands of the English reader, by Mr. Prescott, in his History of the Conquest of Peru, much also that did not fall within the design of his admirable work, and is not generally accessible in our language. The book possessed also additional interest from the fact that it was, in part at least, the production of a native Peruvian of Spanish origin, who, it is believed, had no native predecessor in any similar work but Garcilasso de la Vega, who published the first part of his Commentaries in 1609, and finished the latter in 1616. We have then here the last account of Peru by a native, at a date as late as 1851; and a more particular description of its most ancient architectural remains than is to be found elsewhere. These circumstances led the translator to think that the book would possess an interest for his countrymen, and induced him to devote such leisure as he could snatch from more serious employments to the task of clothing the original in an English dress.

PREFACE.

THE history of nations, or of the times in which they flourished, does not interest, simply by showing the degree of power and culture to which they attained, and the means by which they were able to subjugate or aggrandize those who were ruled; but also, by instructing us in the progressive steps of commerce, arts, and sciences; those mighty agents which enlarge the understanding, develop the riches of nature, remove obstacles, and prepare a people for the enjoyment of rational liberty.

The code which governed the ancient Peruvian nation, dictated by its founder, Manco-Capac, and amplified by his successors, laid the foundations of that public happiness, of which for some centuries his descendants have been deprived: but it was not the basis of that political liberty which moves men, inspires great thoughts, diffuses light, and enlarges the limits of human knowledge.

Its theocratical government took care that the worship of the divinity which they adored, throughout the entire kingdom, should not languish; it was a means which, as in all the most enlightened monarchies of the old world, was called in, to give security to political power:—that public morality should not be relaxed by the toleration of disorder:—that agriculture and industry should be advanced:—that public works should be constructed and preserved:—and finally, that no one should be without occupation, and useless alike to the State and his fellow-men. Kings and priests at the same time, the sovereigns ruled, in the name of the Sun, with an absolute independence; but were not, on this account, placed above the laws of justice and humanity.

To study, therefore, institutions so beneficent, on the very spot where they existed; to examine their archæological monuments; to obtain an exact knowledge of their idiom, religion, laws, sciences and customs, as well as all that relates to the empire of the Andes, was the plan which we proposed to pursue, by traversing the land of the Incas.

There were many obstacles opposed to the successful accomplishment of our enterprise. 1. The political dissensions which have succeeded each other, keeping the country in constant alarm. 2. The diversities of climate, the bad, and indeed impassable roads of the coast and the Cordilleras, the dangers to be encountered and overcome in visiting long abandoned sites, the close, thick forests, in which nature with such prodigality shows her profusion and fertilizing power, presenting trees which almost seem to serve as props to the vault of heaven. 3. The total want of an itinerary, or of well-informed guides who might indicate to us localities or antiquities worthy of observation:—but nothing could prevent us from prosecuting our design of presenting to the public a work on the antiquities of Peru.

In 1841, speaking of this subject, we said: "We hope some day to have the satisfaction of communicating to our countrymen that the collection is complete and published, which, in our view, is a work of some importance." An aspiration which, after ten years, has been realized, but not without immense labor and great pecuniary sacrifices.

During some years we have studied ancient monuments, gathering, with great solicitude, all the curiosities of the dimes of the Incas which we could collect, and giving orders for the designing and painting of all those which were in the possession of individuals, whether Peruvians or foreigners. Having finished this toilsome work, we sought, of the Peruvian government, aid to publish it: not being able alone to undertake an enterprise so expensive. The sum which was granted us was so small that it did not suffice even to make copies of some of the plates, and consequently the manuscript remained in its case until 1850.

Determined that, even at the cost of some sacrifices, Peru and other nations should not be deprived of the collection we had made, which gives, to the first named at least, an accurate idea of the power of its monarchs and the industry of its subjects, we wrote to Don Francisco de Rivero, *chargé d'affaires* from the Peruvian Republic near the court of her Britannic Majesty, that it should be published on an agreement made with Dr. Von Tschudi. How great were those pecuniary sacrifices, the reader may easily determine by a glance at the beautiful volume of plates which accompanies the text.*

After the preparation of the plates had been commenced by one of the most distinguished artists of Vienna, we were informed that he could not proceed with the impression, because of the increased price both of paper and labor, arising from the political troubles of the past year, which had produced a great reaction in all the kingdoms of Europe.

* An atlas of fifty-eight large plates, most of them colored, and all beautifully executed, accompanies the original work. From this, our illustrations have been taken, in a sufficient number, we hope, to make plain the text when the aid of the pencil is required. To have copied all, would have made our English version as costly as the original, and placed it beyond the reach of most readers.—[TRANSLATOR.]

New disbursements had therefore to be made for the continuance of the work.

At all times, the government, which has watched with interest the progress of everything having for its laudable object the instruction of the masses, and the procuring of exact particulars concerning our history, commerce, arts or industry, has protected and fostered enterprises tending to these results. The larger number of administrations in the republic of Peru, having among them distinguished men, have been animated by proper sentiments and desires; and so much the more, as it was seen that the republic of Chili had ordered the publication of its natural and political history, by the indefatigable Mr. Gay; and that Bolivia had favored, to the extent of her ability, the interesting works of the naturalist, D'Orbigny; but these feelings and wishes of our successive administrations have been lamentably unproductive, because of the anarchy which has prevailed in the country for so many years. Without doubt, a beginning has now been made to supply in part the want above alluded to.

Dr. Von Tschudi, a member of various scientific bodies, and a distinguished European traveller, published in 1846 and 1848 his investigations in the Peruvian Fauna; a work in folio, of seven hundred pages, and of seventy-two illustrative plates, which treats of the quadrupeds, birds, reptiles and fishes of Peru, as well as of other topics (antiquities philology and medicine), being very valuable on the subject of the primitive races of South America. Mr. Prescott, too, with his accustomed masterly skill, has given us a history of the conquest, with documents and interesting details.

It is gratifying to us to record the interest which Don Manuel Ferreyros and Don Francisco de Rivero have shown in the publication of this work; the generosity with which Messrs. Weddel, Rugendas, and Pentlandt have freely furnished sketches and designs, and the care of Dr. Von Tschudi in the arrangement of the text which was sent to him from Peru, adding thereto observations on the Peruvian crania, Quichuan language, religion, &c., which were suggested by his own knowledge, his extensive learning, and the abundant books and manuscripts of the imperial library of Vienna, which he could freely consult—elements, alas! wanting in Peru.

It was not our sole object to give a description of the ruins of sumptuous edifices, the sad remains of the grandeur and power of the Incas, of their idols, and manufactures found in the *huacas* and mounds; but also of the fall of a nation made deeply interesting by its tragical history.

The description of its political institutions, its religious system, of its ceremonies, the arts and sciences cultivated by the Peruvians, may offer to investigators aid in their labors, by dispelling errors which are found at every step in the writings of authors, ancient and modern, who have transmitted to us the verbal relations of individuals whom they considered well informed.

We are not of the number of those blind admirers of the ancient Peruvian culture who have exaggerated the political institutions of the Incas, and the progress which their subjects had made in the arts and sciences; but as little are we to be classed with those historians who deny the development of the faculties in the primitive inhabitants of Peru, and consider the narratives of the old Spanish chroniclers on this point as mere fables.

A conscientious comparison of these narratives with the remains of Peruvian antiquity, and the deductions thence made, form the basis of this work. We know full well that we are not here offering to the public a work which exhausts the rich material in which we have labored. The difficulty of these investigations, the want of true translations of the *quippus* in which were preserved the remarkable events of Peruvian history and the particulars of its statistics, and the immense expense which works of this kind involve, can only be overcome by the joint labors of the learned, and the powerful aid of the government. We will not doubt (to recur to our work) that the Peruvian nation will appreciate our humble toils and our pecuniary sacrifices; and that they will know how to excuse some slight typographical imperfections, the unavoidable consequence of printing the book in a city where the Spanish language is a foreign tongue.*

* The original was printed in Vienna, for the sake, we presume, of Dr. Von Tschudi's supervision.—[TRANSLATOR.]

CONTENTS.

CHAPTER I.

RELATIONS BETWEEN THE TWO HEMISPHERES, PRIOR TO THE DISCOVERY BY COLUMBUS.

PAGE

Expedition of Bjarne Herjulfson to America, ... 3
Expedition of Leif Erikson, ... 4
" of Thorwald Erikson, ... 4
" of Thorstein Erikson, ... 4
" of Thorfinn Karlsefne and Snorri Thorbrandson, . . . 4
" of Helge and Finneboge, ... 5
Arc Marson in Huitramannaland, ... 5
History of Bjorn Asbrandson, ... 6
Voyage of Gudleif Gudlangson, ... 7
Hypothesis of Rabbi Manasseh Ben Israel, ... 8
Proofs of a Jewish immigration to America, ... 9
Hebrew words in the American languages, ... 10
Hypothesis of Don Pablo Felix de Cabrera, ... 11
Document of Votan, ... 12
Explanation of the document by Cabrera, ... 13
Hypothesis of M. de Guignes, ... 16
Investigations of M. de Paravey, ... 16
Analogies in religions of Buddha and Mexico, ... 17
The Peruvian Trimurti, ... 18
Analogies in Christianity and Buddhism, ... 19
Mexican priesthood, ... 20

CHAPTER II.

ANCIENT INHABITANTS OF PERU.

Conformation of Peruvian crania, ... 26
First form, ... 26
Second form, ... 27
Third form, ... 27
Proportions of the crania, ... 28
Geographical distribution of the different races, ... 31
Configuration of the crania of the present Indians, ... 34
Proof that the form is not the result of mechanical pressure, . . 36
Osteological anomaly in the Peruvian crania, ... 38
Note on the Peruvian crania in Dr. Morton's work, ... 40

CHAPTER III.

CONSIDERATIONS ON THE HISTORY OF PERU, BEFORE THE ARRIVAL OF THE SPANIARDS.

Origin of the Peruvian monarchy from Garcilasso, ... 42
Biographical notice of Garcilasso de la Vega, ... 45
The sources from which he drew as an author, ... 47
His partiality, ... 47
Catalogue of Peruvian monarchs, ... 49
Descendants of the Incas according to the canon Sahuaura, ... 50
Works of the licentiate Fernando Montesinos, ... 51
Chronological table of Peruvian Kings, by Montesinos, ... 52
Critique on the memoirs of Montesinos, ... 65
History of the conquest of Peru, by Prescott, ... 66
Considerations on the first Inca, ... 67
Fables as to the origin of the Incas, ... 68
Extent of the empire under Huayna-Capac, ... 69
Its population, ... 69
Diminution of population, ... 70

CHAPTER IV.

SYSTEM OF GOVERNMENT, OR POLITICAL INSTITUTIONS OF THE INCAS.

Authority of the Peruvian monarchs, ... 74
Form of government, ... 75

Veneration of the Monarchs by their subjects, ... 75
Concubines of the Inca, ... 76
Titles of the royal family, ... 77
Court of the Sovereign, ... 77
The Peruvian aristocracy, ... 78
Education of the blood royal, ... 79
The name of Peru, ... 80
Division of the Provinces and population, ... 80
Administrative organization, ... 81
Peruvian agriculture, ... 82
The order in which they worked the earth, ... 82
The tribute and mode of collecting it, ... 84
Laws of polity, ... 85
Civil laws, ... 87
Military system of the Incas, ... 88
Policy of Incas toward conquered provinces, ... 88

CHAPTER V.

THE QUICHUAN LANGUAGE.

The American languages, ... 92
Influence of foreign immigrations on the languages of the American aborigines, 93
Analogy of American words with those of the eastern continent, . . . 94
Number of the American languages, ... 96
Differences between neighboring idioms, ... 97
Common characteristics of all the American languages, ... 98
The conjugation of the personal object, or transition, ... 99
Particular use of the pronouns, ... 100
Composition of words by means of an affix, ... 101
Hieroglyphics among the American nations, ... 103
Chronological list of Quichua grammars, ... 104
Writing of the ancient Peruvians, ... 105
Hieroglyphics, ... 106
Quippos, ... 109
Specimens of Quichua literature, ... 112
The Lord's Prayer in Quichua, ... 113
Specimen of a sermon by Don Fernando de Avendaño, ... 114
The Peruvian poets or Haravicus, ... 115
The Haravis, ... 115
Dramatic poetry, ... 115

Specimens of the drama Ollanta, ... 116
Dialects of the Quichua language, ... 117

CHAPTER VI.

SCIENTIFIC CULTURE UNDER THE DYNASTY OF THE INCAS.

The *amautas* or sages, ... 125
Peruvian medical knowledge, ... 126
Practice of surgery, ... 126
Mathematics and astronomy, ... 126
The Peruvian year, ... 130
The months, ... 131
Navigation, ... 135
Three *haravis*, ... 137
Instrumental music, ... 143
Species of Pandean pipe, ... 143
Tunes of their songs, ... 145
Dramatic representations, ... 145
Music, ... 145

CHAPTER VII.

RELIGIOUS SYSTEM OF THE INCAS.

Primitive worship of the Peruvians, ... 146
Con, ... 147
Pachacamac, ... 152
The worship of Pachacamac, ... 153
Policy of the Incas with reference to this worship, ... 154
Sayings of the Incas as to worship of the Sun, ... 155
Deities of the ancient Peruvians, ... 156
The Sun, ... 157
Virgins of the Sun, ... 158
Selected Virgins, ... 158
The Moon, ... 160
The Stars, ... 161
Deities of the Elements, ... 161
Terrestrial deities, ... 161
Historical deities, ... 163
Viracocha, ... 163

The Incas, ... 164
The Huacas, ... 168
The worship of the Sun, ... 157
The gods of families, or individuals, ... 171
The Conopas, ... 172
Mode of examining wizards prescribed by Archbishop Villa Gomez, . 174
Divination by external objects, ... 176
Analogy of Peruvian ceremonies with Christian sacraments, . . 179
Baptism, ... 180
Confirmation, ... 181
Penance, ... 181
The Eucharist, ... 182
Extreme unction, ... 182
Holy orders, ... 182
Matrimony, ... 184

CHAPTER VIII.

RELIGIOUS CEREMONIES.

The festival, Raymi, ... 187
Sacrifices, ... 189
The *Mosoc Nina*, ... 190
The festival, Situa, ... 190
The driving out of infirmities, ... 192
The festival, Cusquie Raymi, ... 192
The festival of knighthood, or Huaracu, ... 192
The other festivals, ... 193
Offerings presented to the Gods, ... 194
Human sacrifices, ... 195
Sacrifices of animals, ... 197
" of vegetables, ... 198
" of minerals, ... 198
Mode of burying the dead, ... 199
The kings, ... 200
Rich vassals, ... 200
The common people, ... 201
Provisions buried with the dead, ... 202
Different kinds of corn, ... 202
Mode of enveloping the body, ... 203
The art of embalming, ... 204

Refutation of the opinion of Barreda on this subject, ... 205
Natural mummification, ... 207

CHAPTER IX.

STATE OF THE ARTS AMONG THE ANCIENT PERUVIANS.

Importance of a critical examination of ancient monuments, . . . 210
The art of cutting stone, ... 212
Weapons, ... 212
Knowledge of metallurgy among the ancient Peruvians, ... 213
Quantity of silver and gold exported by the Spaniards, . . . 213
Gold, ... 214
Silver, ... 215
Copper, ... 215
Quicksilver, ... 215
Cinnabar, ... 216
Artistic use of the metals, ... 216
Plating, ... 217
Gilding, ... 217
Plated works, ... 218
Riches of palaces, temples and gardens of gold, ... 218
Manufactures of copper, ... 222
The art of spinning and weaving, ... 223
Tanning, ... 224
The Peruvian Potters, ... 225
The principles of moulding, ... 226
Peruvian modelling, ... 226
Vases and Conopas, ... 227
Sacred vessels with designs, ... 228
The art of painting, ... 228
Peruvian architecture, ... 229
Stone hewing, ... 230
Stones of the fortification of Ollantay-Tambo, ... 231
Size of the stones at Tiahuanaco, ... 232
Mode of transporting the stones, ... 232
Mortar, ... 232
Particular houses, ... 233
The Tambos, ... 235
The Royal Storehouses, ... 235
The play-houses, ... 236

The Baths, ... 236
The Royal palaces, ... 237
The monasteries, ... 240
The Temples, ... 241
The Fortifications, ... 246
The Fortress of Cuzco, ... 246
The small fortress of Huichay, ... 249
Hydraulics among the ancient Peruvians, ... 250
The azequias or canals for irrigation, ... 251
The Bridges, ... 251
Opinion of Raynal on works of the ancient Peruvians, . . . 252

CHAPTER X.

ANCIENT MONUMENTS.

The Royal roads, ... 254
Description of them by Sarmiento, ... 255
" by Ciçea de Leon, ... 256
" Zarrate, ... 258
" Juan Botero Benes, ... 260
" Juan de Velasco, ... 260
" Humboldt, ... 261
Extent of these roads, ... 263
Ruins of the palaces of Chimu, ... 264
Antiquities found in these palaces, ... 266
Ruins of Cuelap, ... 272
" of Old Huanuco, ... 276
Tower of Chupan, ... 280
Ruins of fortifications, department of Lurin, ... 281
Castle of Masor, ... 281
Ruins of Chacabamba, ... 282
Ancient edifice in Chavin de Huanta, ... 282
Castle on the ridge of Posoc, ... 283
Reflections on the destruction of the empire of the Incas, . . 284
Ruins of Paramanca, ... 286
Ruins of the "coptras" about Chancaylla, ... 287
Ruins of Pachacamac, ... 288
Ruins about Huamanga and Vilcas, ... 291
Hills of Clustoni, ... 292

Ruins of Hatuncolla, ... 292
Ruins of Tiahuanco, ... 293
Gigantic head, ... 295
Monolythic gateways, ... 296
Ruins on the island of Titicaca, ... 297
" on the island of Coati, ... 298
" of Ollantay-Tambo, ... 298
Traditions concerning Ollantay, ... 299
Construction of the fortress, ... 300
Remains of antiquity in the city of Cuzco, ... 302
Conclusion, ... 304

CHAPTER I.

OF THE RELATIONS EXISTING BETWEEN THE TWO HEMISPHERES, BEFORE THE DISCOVERIES OF COLUMBUS.

AMONG all the sciences which are involved in the study of history, none exceeds in importance *archæology*, or the knowledge of the monuments of antiquity; a science which, drawn by the industrious and ingenious labor of modern times from its chrysalis state, or that period of infant weakness common to all sciences, has proceeded to tear away the veil which covered past ages, synthetically to reconstruct the events of remote periods, and to supply the scarcity or total absence of chronicle and tradition. Throughout the whole Western hemisphere, numerous works of art, like so many indelible pages, show to the observant traveller the genius, the occurrences, and the splendor of ancient America, with more truth and eloquence than all the worm-eaten manuscripts which sleep in our archives; so that, like shining torches, they conduct the philosophical historian through the darkness which involves the past centuries, in which were developed the first human associations of the New World.

When, led by that intrepid and skilful navigator, Christopher Columbus, the Spaniards first trod the shores of a world, till then, to them unknown, they supposed that the vast regions they had found were inhabited by a race of uncultivated savages only. Ere long, however, they were undeceived by further explorations, and became convinced that the nations which they had vanquished possessed a certain amount of cultivation, and of interesting memorials.

In the ten years immediately succeeding the conquest, certain zealous individuals, members for the most part of the religious orders, devoted themselves to the work of describing the physical aspect of the newly discovered regions, of recounting the acts of the Europeans in the New World, and of collecting the traditions and memorials of the subdued races; endeavoring from these to write a methodical history, which should illustrate the principal occurrences of those vast regions which had yielded to the valor and skill of the people of the Eastern hemisphere. But this undertaking was very difficult, since the history had for its sole foundation the traditions of the conquered, confused, contradictory, often mixed with fables and myths, and at times wilfully perverted and falsified, so that it was not only difficult, but in fact almost impossible to shed light on such a chaos; it is therefore not strange that but little fruit was gathered from the toilsome labors of men, however distinguished, who were necessarily lost in a labyrinth so dark and intricate. Modern effort, however, has been more fortunate; and it has been the privilege of our age to have dissipated, in part, the darkness which shrouded the antiquity of the Western hemisphere; and (thanks to the persevering researches of the learned of our times) it now appears indisputably, that before the coming of Columbus, there had been communication between the two hemispheres.

"*What were the relations between them; and what nations visited America in remote epochs?*" Such are the questions which naturally present themselves, and which we will endeavor to answer with some particularity.

It is supposed that various nations or stranger tribes have

invaded the American continent; and in support of this opinion, there have been alleged proofs founded, either on irrefutable historic dates, on inductions drawn from the religion, the monuments, the physical constitution, and the languages of the people of the New World, or on contemporaneous historical occurrences in the two hemispheres.

In discussing these proofs, alike ingenious and learned, we will begin with the northeastern part of North America, which, of itself alone, offers one irrefutable proof.

It is now some twelve years since the Secretary of the Society of Antiquaries of Copenhagen, Mr. Charles Christian Rafn, described, according to Scandinavian manuscripts, published in the "*Antiquitates Americanæ,*" the first voyages which the Scandinavians made to America in the tenth and eleventh centuries of our era: the accounts of these voyages were probably compiled in the twelfth century, by the learned Bishop THORLAK RUNOLFSON, author of the most ancient ecclesiastical code of Iceland, and grandson of THORFINN KARLSEFNE, who led one of the most considerable expeditions that sailed for the Western hemisphere. From these it appears that in the year 986, BJARNE HERJULFSON, voyaging from Iceland to Greenland, sailed along the eastern coast of America. Stimulated by BJARNE'S representations on his return, LEIF, eldest son of ERIC THE RED, purchased his ship, and in the year 1000, set out with thirty-five companions to make discoveries. LEIF reached the coast which had been discovered by BJARNE, and named it *Helluland* (at this day *Newfoundland*); sailing thence, he arrived on a mountainous coast which he called *Markland* (now known as *Nova Scotia, New Brunswick,* and *Canada*); thence proceeding, he reached a very pleasant shore, when an individual of the expedition, a German, named TYRKER, found an abundance of good grapes; and in consequence of that, LEIF named the country VINLAND (the land of the vine), a country which at this day corresponds to the coast between *Cape Sable* and *Cape Cod.* He then returned to Greenland, and in the following summer (1002) his brother, THOWALD ERICSON, undertook a new voyage in the same vessel: he visited the regions that had already been discovered by his brother, and penetrated further yet in the summer of 1004; and about Cape Cod (southeast of the present city of Boston) he had an encounter with the Skrellings (Esquimaux), in which, receiving an arrow-wound under the arm, he died, and was buried at what is now known as *Gurnet's Point*, a place which he himself had pointed out for his burial, and which, at the request of the dying man, was called KROSSANES (Point of the Cross). In the summer of 1006, THORSTEIN, the third son of ERIC, undertook an expedition to the same regions; his attempt was unfortunate, for he was not able to find even the coast, and overcome by his toils, he died in Greenland in the following winter. In the year 1007, a flotilla of three barks, with crews amounting to a hundred and sixty men, and with a sufficiency of live stock, left the coast of Greenland, under the leadership of the celebrated THORFINN KARLSEFNE and SNORRE THORBRANDSON; leaving the usual track, and inclining more to the south, they remained some time at the island of MARTHA'S VINEYARD, whence sailing westwardly, they spent two winters in MOUNT HOPE BAY, near SECONNET, a degree and a half of latitude nearer towards New York.

Unhappily, in the following winter, the good understanding which had subsisted between the Scandinavian adventurers and the Esquimaux terminated; the latter attacked them with a superior force, and would have exterminated them, had they not been delivered from entire destruction by the boldness of a woman named FREYDIS. This unpropitious event induced KARLSEFNE to abandon the plan of founding a colony on those coasts, and to return to Greenland about the beginning of the year 1011.

But still more mournful was the result of another expedition which two Norwegian brothers, HELGE and FINNEBOGE, made in the same year. These, with thirty of their companions, perished at the hands of the husband of FREYDIS, prompted to the murder by this masculine woman, who had taken part in the enterprise with thirty-five Scandinavians.

We have but few and scattered notices concerning any later communications between Greenland and the northeastern coast of America. We find, however, that in the year 1121 the Greenland Bishop ERICK passed over to Vinland; but we know nothing with certainty as to the time he remained there, and as little concerning the state of any colonies there, either as to extent, or the degree of progress. This, however, is certain, that the monuments, inscriptions, arms, utensils, tools, and remains of the dead, recently found in the States of Rhode Island, Massachusetts and elsewhere, attest an entrance of strangers into the country, much more considerable than any of those which the manuscripts we have mentioned bring to our knowledge.

Greater attention, in our opinion, is due to the notices contained in the documents communicated by Rafn, which make mention of a nation that, according to the traditions of the Esquimaux, dwelt in their neighborhood, wore white vestments, uttered cries, and made use of long rods with pieces of cloth attached to them. According to a probable conjecture, the country occupied by this nation was HUITRAMANNALAND, (the country of white men,) which lay along Chesapeake Bay, extending down into Carolina, and even still further towards the south. The story is, that a violent storm in 983 cast upon these shores the renowned Captain ARE MARSON, of REYKJANES, in Iceland; whose grandson, the learned and celebrated Icelander, ARE FRODE, certifies that certain *Irishmen* had assured his uncle that, according to the verbal relation of JARL THORFINN SIGURDSON, of the Orkneys, the name of ARE MARSON was known in Huitramannaland; that this intrepid adventurer there had authority, but that the natives would not permit him to return to his country. The more probable opinion is, that a Catholic population had cultivated these vast regions; it may be so inferred from the circumstances of men clothed in white, of the cries which they uttered, and of the long rods with pieces of cloth attached, as preserved in the traditions of the Esquimaux, and which correspond to a sacerdotal procession with hymns and standards or banners of a Catholic community. The testimony of Jarl Thorfinn Sigurdson, which confirms the presence of Are Marson in Huitramannaland, shows a communication, though at a later period, between *Ireland* and the northeastern part of North America.

In the same manuscripts there is found another relation which converts the above-mentioned conjecture into certainty. BIOERN ASBRANDSON, who bore the surname of Breidvikingakappi, a companion of the celebrated league of the heroes of Jomberg, and one of the most fearless champions in the battle of Fyrisvalle, in Sweden, had an amour with THURID, sister of the powerful chief SNORRE GODE, in Fordau, of Iceland, by reason of which he was obliged to emigrate in the year 999, embarking at Hraunhöfen in Snäfellsnes. Driven by a northeast wind, the vessel quickly left the coast, and for a long time there were no tidings of the fate of Bioern, who, his acquaintance finally supposed, was buried in the depths of the sea. At length it happened that an Icelandic merchant named GUDLEIF GUDLANGSON, a brother of Thorfinn, the ancestor of the distinguished historian SNORRE STURLUSON, desired to return from Dublin to Iceland, taking the route on the west of Ireland; but violent hurricanes proceeding from the northeast, drove him to the west, and afterwards to the southwest, carrying him, after a long and dangerous voyage, to an unknown coast, the natives of which seized him as soon as he had landed. In a short time a troop of men came to him, preceded by a standard, and speaking a language resembling that of Ireland; they were directed by an old man *on horseback*, of noble and imposing aspect, to whom it belonged to decide on the fate of the prisoners. He commanded that Gudleif should be brought into his presence, and asked him, in the Scandinavian language, who he was and whence he came; and discovering Gudleif to be a native of Iceland, the old man informed him that he himself was Bioern Astrandson, the lover of Thurid, and of the same place as she and his son Kiartan. Afterwards he set Gudleif and his companions at liberty, advising them to leave, as soon as possible, a country of so little hospitality; and, at their departure, he gave to him a ring for Thurid, and a sword for his son Kiartan. Gudleif returned to Dublin, and thence, in the following summer, to Iceland, where he delivered the presents, convincing all that Bioern Asbrandson had sent them.

This genuine story, written a little after the events, is in our view an important proof in favor of the opinion that Irish colonies were established in Huitramannaland, the present Carolinas, and probably also in Florida; and that the immigration of these colonies took place long before the first navigation of the Scandinavians to the New World, as we are enabled to fix it with certainty in the ninth century of our era.

Various other hypotheses have been presented relative to

the peopling of the regions of America by Western nations, before the discovery of Columbus; hypotheses which, if they do not offer a degree of probability as great as that presented in the one given above, still rest on reasons more or less ingenious, and foundations more or less solid. Among others there is one meriting particular notice: it is that which attributes the origin of the American races to the tribes which composed the ancient kingdom of Israel; that is, to the nine and a half tribes conquered and carried captive from Samaria, while there still remained in the kingdom of Judah, and in the cities on the opposite shores of the Jordan, the tribes of Judah, Benjamin, and the half tribe of Manasseh.

The learned Rabbi, MANASSEH BEN ISRAEL, in his celebrated work "*The Hope of Israel*," (published in Amsterdam in 1650,) was the first who treated this subject, at the request of MONTESINI, who had travelled in South America, and recognized there, in his Indian guide, an Israelite, who assured him that there lived in the Cordilleras a considerable number of Indians of the same origin with himself. Although the historical events alleged by Manasseh Ben Israel are less numerous than those of his successors, still, the proofs which they offer are plausible and not wanting in acuteness; and it is a singular fact that GREGORIO GARCIA, an ancient author, in his interesting work, "*The Origin of the Indians*," makes mention of a Spanish tradition, according to which the Americans proceeded from the nine and a half tribes of Israel, whom *Salmanezer*, King of Assyria, carried away captive.

Passing by the proofs, more or less ingenious, advanced by Heckewelder, Beltrami, De Laet,* Emanuel de Moraez, Beatty, Samuel Stanhope Smith,† William Penn, the Count

* Orbis Novus, seu Descriptio Indiæ Occidentalis.

† On the Varieties of the Human Species.

Crawford, and many others, we will make particular mention of Adair,* who lived forty years among the Indians, and who, after the most thorough examination and minute comparison, assures us that the origin of the Indians is Israelitish, founding his assertion principally on the religious rites, which plainly present many points of agreement with those of the Hebrew people.

Like the Jews, the Indians offer their first-fruits, they keep their new moons, and the feast of expiations at the end of September or in the beginning of October; they divide the year into four seasons, corresponding with the Jewish festivals. According to Charlevoix and Long, the brother of a deceased husband receives his widow into his house as a guest, and after a suitable time considers her as a legitimate consort. In some parts of North America circumcision is practised, and of this Acosta and Lopez de Gomara make mention. There is also much analogy between the Hebrews and Indians in that which concerns various rites and customs; such as the ceremonies of purification, the use of the bath, the ointment of bear's grease, fasting, and the manner of prayer. The Indians likewise abstain from the blood of animals, as also from fish without scales; they consider divers quadrupeds unclean, as also certain birds and reptiles, and they are accustomed to offer as an holocaust the firstlings of the flock. Acosta and Emanuel de Moraez relate that various nations allow matrimony with those only of their own tribe or lineage, this being, in their view, a striking characteristic, very remarkable, and of much weight. But that which most tends to fortify the opinion as to the Hebrew origin of the American tribes, is a species of ark, seemingly like that of the Old Testament; this the Indians

* History of the American Nations, pp. 15–212.

take with them to war; it is never permitted to touch the ground, but rests upon stones or pieces of wood, it being deemed sacrilegious and unlawful to open it or look into it. The American priests scrupulously guard their sanctuary, and the High Priest carries on his breast a white shell adorned with precious stones, which recalls the *Urim* of the Jewish High Priest: of whom we are also reminded by a band of white plumes on his forehead.

According to the credible testimony of Adair, the Indians of North America celebrate the feast of first-fruits with religious dances, singing in chorus these mystic words:—Yo Meschica, He Meschica, Va Meschica, forming thus, with the three first syllables, the name of Je-ho-vah, and the name of Messiah thrice pronounced, following each initial. On other occasions may be heard in their hymns the words, *Aylo*, *Aylo*, which correspond with the Hebrew word *El*, God; in other hymns occur the words, *hiwah*, *hiwah*,—*hydchyra*, "the immortal soul," and *Schiluhyo*, *Schiluhe*, *Schiluhva*, of which Adair thinks that *Schiluh* is the same with the Hebrew word *Schaleach*, or *Schiloth*, which signifies messenger, or pacificator. The use of Hebrew words was not uncommon in the religious performances of the North American Indians, and Adair assures us that they called an accused or guilty person *haksit canaha*, "a sinner of Canaan;" and to him who was inattentive to religious worship, they said, *Tschi haksit canaha*, "you resemble a sinner of Canaan." Lescarbot also tells us that he had heard the Indians of South America sing "*Alleluia*."

Those authors who attribute a Hebrew origin to the American tribes do not agree among themselves touching the coming of the Israelites into the New World: some think that they came directly from the Eastern hemisphere to the West, and established themselves in the central and southern parts of this hemisphere; but the majority are of opinion that they crossed Persia and the frontiers of China, and came in by the way of Bhering's Straits.

An ingenious author of our times considers the Canaanites as the first inhabitants of America, who, proceeding from Mauritania Tingitana, landed somewhere on the shores of the Gulf of Mexico.* "Fifteen hundred years after the expulsion of the Canaanites by Joshua, the nine and a half tribes of Israel passed over by the way of Bhering's Straits, and like the Goths and Vandals, assaulted that people [the Canaanites]. For a second time, and on another continent, the descendants of Joshua attacked the Canaanites, whose origin they had discovered, and animated by their ancient hatred, they burned their temples and destroyed their gigantic towers and cities."

At first view, the proofs produced by different authors in favor of an Israelitish immigration, may seem to be conclusive; but, if closely examined, it will be seen that this hypothesis rests on no solid foundation.

But it is time to turn to another hypothesis no less interesting, and up to this time never thoroughly examined. The author of this is Don PABLO FELIX DE CABRERA, of Guatemala, who labors ingeniously and with force to show the relations between the Phœnicians and Americans, sustaining his opinions by Mexican hieroglyphic inscriptions. This brilliant hypothesis merits a somewhat extended notice.

Don FRANCISCO NUNEZ DE LA VEGA, bishop of Chiapa,

* We meet in ancient history with three places called Mauritania, viz., Mauritania Tingitana, Mauritania Cæsariensis, and Mauritania Sitifensis. The first of these was what now constitutes Morocco; it was called Tingitana from *Tingis* its capital, afterwards corrupted into *Tanja*, and finally into *Tangier*, its present name. All the three, however, were in the northern part of Africa.—[TRANSLATOR.]

possessed, as he himself states in his "*Diocesan Constitutions*," published at Rome in 1702, a document in which a certain voyager or traveller, named VOTAN, minutely described the countries and nations which he had visited. This manuscript, it was found, was written in the *Tzendal* language; and was accompanied by certain hieroglyphics cut in stone; by order of the same Votan the manuscript was to be permanently deposited in a dark house (or cavern) in the province of Soconusco, and there confided to the custody of a noble Indian lady, and of a number of Indians, the places of all of whom, as they became vacant, were to be continually re-supplied.* Thus it continued preserved for centuries, perhaps for two thousand years, until the bishop above named, Nuñez de la Vega, in visiting the province, obtained possession of the manuscript, and in the year 1690, commanded it to be destroyed in the public square of Huegetan; so that the curious notices which it contained would have been completely lost, if there had not existed, in the hands of Don RAMON DE ORDONEZ Y AGUIAR, in Ciudad Real, according to his own statement, a copy, made immediately after the conquest, and which is in part published by Cabrera.

The title or frontispiece of this document consists of two squares of different colors, and with their angles on a parallel; one of them represents the ancient continent, and is marked with two characters, placed perpendicularly, in the form of the letter S; the other square represents the new continent, and contains two similar characters, but placed horizontally. When Votan speaks of the places of the Old World, the chapter is marked with the upright character S; but in speaking of the second, the chapter is indicated by the sign placed horizon-

* The reader should be apprised that the *Tzendals* were one of the Indian nations of Central America.—[TRANSLATOR.]

tally, ∽. Between the two squares, may be read the following, as the title, or topic of the manuscript: "*Proof that I am a serpent.*" The author says in the text, that he is the third bearing the name of Votan; that by nature, or birth, he is a serpent, for he is a *chivim;* that he had proposed to himself to travel until he should find the way to the heavens, whither he went to seek the serpents, his parents; that he had gone from Valum Chivim to Valum Votan, and conducted seven families from the last-named place; that he had happily passed to Europe, and had seen them at Rome, building a magnificent temple; that he had travelled by an open path seeking for his brothers, the serpents, and had made marks on this same path, and that he had passed by the houses of the thirteen serpents. In one of his journeys he had encountered other seven families of the Tzequil nation, whom he recognized as serpents, teaching them all that was necessary to prepare suitable sustenance, and that they for their part were ready to acknowledge him as God himself, and elected him their chief. Such is the tenor of the document.

In the ruins of Palenque, Don ANTONIO DEL RIO, a captain of artillery, sent in 1786, by the King of Spain, to examine the remains of that city, found various figures which represent Votan, on both continents, and this tradition was confirmed some years later by the discovery of divers medals.

With great diligence and labor, Cabrera availed himself of these sources, and commentaries on the history of the past, and drew from them the following conclusion, which alone we can here offer to our readers, the limits of our work not permitting an extended statement of the ingenious proofs brought forward by the author.

Cabrera thinks that a *Chivim* is the same as a Givim or Hivim, i. e. a descendant of Heth, the son of Canaan. To the Givims or Hivites (Avims or Avites), of whom mention is made in Deuteronomy, (ch. ii. v. 23,) and in Joshua, (ch. xiii. v. 3,) belonged Cadmus, and his wife Hermione, who, as we read in Ovid's Metamorphoses, were changed into serpents, and elevated to the dignity of gods. It is probably owing to this fable that in the Phœnician language the word *Givim* signifies also a serpent. The city of Tripoli, under the dependence of Tyre, was anciently called *Chivim;* and the theme or topic of Votan, "*I am a serpent because I am Chivim,*" simply means, when interpreted, "*I am a Hivite of Tripoli,*" a city which he calls *Valum Votan.* Building on a profound consideration of ancient history, Cabrera believes that the Tyrian Hercules, who, according to Diodorus, went over the entire world, was the ancestor of Votan; that the island of Hispaniola is the ancient Septimia, and the city of Alecto that of Valum, from which Votan began his journeyings. He also thinks that the thirteen serpents signify the thirteen Canary Isles, which derive their name from their inhabitants, the Canaanites, who tarried in them jointly with the Hivites, and that the marks or indications which Votan erected in the pathway, to his brothers, mean the two columns of white marble found at Tangier, with this inscription in the Phœnician language: "*We are the sons of those who fled from the robber Joshua, the son of Nun, and found here a secure asylum.*"

The journey of Votan to Rome, and the vast temple which he saw being constructed in that city, are events which, according to the foregoing conclusions, should have taken place in the year 290 before the Christian era, when, after an obstinate and bloody war of eight years with the Samnites, the Romans granted peace to that people, and the Consul Publius Cornelius Rufus commanded to be built a sumptuous temple in honor of Romulus and Remus; an event which, according to

Mexican chronology, took place in the year "*eight rabbits*" (*Toxtli*). The seven Tzequil families which Votan encountered on his return were also Phœnicians, and probably shipwrecked persons from the Phœnician embarkation mentioned by Diodorus.

According to Cabrera, the first emigration or colony of the Carthaginians in America took place in the first Punic war. The other conclusions of this author relative to the foundation of the kingdom of Amahnamecan by the Carthaginians, the emigration of the Toltecs, &c., are incompatible with the limits of our work; but we cannot do less than remark here on the opinions of many learned men, who think that the Toltecan god, Quetzalcoatl, is identical with the apostle St. Thomas; and it is observable that the surname of this apostle, *Didimus*, (twin) has the same signification in Greek that Quetzalcoatl has in Mexican. It is astonishing, also, to consider the numerous and extensive regions traversed by this apostle; for, though some confine them to Parthia, others extend them to Calamita, a doubtful city in India; others as far as Maliopur (at this day the city of St. Thomas on the Coromandel coast); others, even to China; and, as we have seen, there are not wanting those who think that he came even to Central America.

We decline making any remarks on the documents of Votan, and the interpretations of Cabrera, since, even if they are not considered fabulous, they still do not present a species of evidence perfectly free from suspicion.

Omitting many minute and useless hypotheses, more or less ingenious, we will succinctly recite certain opinions concerning the relation of the two hemispheres before the days of Columbus, which, however, in our view, offer very slight grounds of probability. According to SANDOVAL, the Western hemisphere was peopled by emigrations proceeding from

Trapobane, or Ceylon, lying south of the peninsula which has been called India from the most remote antiquity. GEORGE COLUNIO assigns a Gaelic origin to the American races. CHARRON pronounces for a Celtic root; and in the opinion of MARCO POLO and JOHN RANKING, Mango Capac, the first Inca of Peru, was the son of the great Kublai Khan, and Montezuma, the grandson of Askam, a noble Mongol of Tangut. And the celebrated HUMBOLDT thinks that the Toltecs derive their origin from the Huns.

But the hypothesis which, in importance, surpasses all these, is that of DE GUIGNES, who, relying upon the chronicles of China, attributes Peruvian civilization to emigrations proceeding from the celestial empire, or the East Indies. Recent investigations would seem to confirm this opinion. In the year 1844, the learned and ingenious Frenchman, PARAVEY, proved that the country of *Fu-Sang*, described in the Chinese annals, is the Mexican empire, which, as it appears from the same annals, was known to the Chinese in the fifth century of our era. A year later, Señor Neumann de Monaco treated of the same point as a new discovery, although he had knowledge of the works of his predecessor. Neither of these learned men, however, knew how to dispose of the difficulty which presented itself, in the difference existing between the actual Mexican Fauna, and that presented as such in the Chinese traditions. The difficulty was a seeming one only, and the supposed difference easily reconcilable by a person versed in Zoology. Monsieur de Paravey, in 1847, added an interesting appendix to his former work, in which he shows that at Uxmal, in Yucatan, there has been found sculptured the Buddha of Java, seated under the head of a Siva; and which was copied by Waldeck.

As the Icelandic documents are of great importance, in verifying the entrance of the Scandinavians on the Atlantic coast of the New Continent; so, also, of equal value are the Chinese chronicles, preserved in the work entitled *Pian-y-tien*, to prove a communication of Asia with America, from the eastern side of the first-named continent, washed by the waves of the Pacific. And, so too, if the investigations and discoveries of the future shall prove that no error has been committed in the interpretation of the document of Votan, such discovery will not, in the slightest degree, diminish the testimony of the Chinese annals; but on the contrary, will rather contribute to confirm the authenticity of the strange adventures which are related in their wonderful history.

There is no doubt that Quetzalcoatl, Bochica, Mango Capac, and other reformers of Central America, were Buddhist priests, who, by means of their superior learning and civilization, sought to rule the minds of the natives, and to elevate themselves to political supremacy.*

A remarkable analogy and numerous points of agreement present themselves as existing between the religion of Buddha and Bramah, and the Mexican worship. As among the East Indians, an undefined being, Bramah, the divinity in general, was shadowed forth in the Trimurti,† or as a God

* A prolonged struggle between the two religious sects of the Brahmins and Buddhists was terminated by the immigration of the Chamans from Tibet, in Mongolia, into China and Japan. If this Tartar race passed over to the northwest coast of America, and thence to the south and east, as far as the shores of the Gila and of Misury, as the etymological investigations of Vater would seem to prove; it will not then appear strange to find among the semi-barbarous nations of the New Continent idols and archæological monuments, a hieroglyphic writing, a knowledge of the length of the year, and traditions concerning the origin of the world, which will all recall the knowledge, arts and religious opinions of the ancient nations.—*Humboldt—American Monuments.*

† The Trimurti of the East Indies corresponds in a certain manner with the Trinity of Christianity.

under three forms, viz., *Bramah*, *Vishnu*, and *Sciva;* so also the Supreme Being was venerated among the Indians of Mexico, under the three forms of *Ho*, *Huitzilopoctli*,* and *Tlaloc*, who formed the Mexican Trimurti. The attributes and worship of the Mexican goddess Mictanihuatl preserve the most perfect analogy with those of the sanguinary and implacable KALI; as do equally the legends of the Mexican divinity Teayamiqui with the formidable BHAVANI; both these Indian deities wives of Siva-Rudra. Not less surprising is the characteristic likeness which exists between the pagodas of India and the Tcocallis of Mexico, while the idols of both temples offer a similitude in physiognomy and posture which cannot escape the observation of any one who has been in both countries.

The same analogy is observed between the oriental Trimurti and that of Peru; thus CON corresponds to Bramah, PACHACAMAC to Vishnu, and HUIRACOCHA to Siva. The Peruvians never dared to erect a temple to their ineffable GOD, whom they never confounded with other divinities; a remarkable circumstance, which reminds us of similar conduct among a part of the inhabitants of India as to Bramah, who is the Eternal, the abstract God. Equally will the study of worship in the two hemispheres show intimate connection between the existence and attributes of the *devadasis* (female servants of the Gods) and the Peruvian virgins of the Sun.

All these considerations, and many others, which from want of space we must omit, evidently prove that the greater part of the Asiatic religions, such as that of *Fo*, in China, of *Buddha*, in Japan, of *Sommono-Cadom*, in India; the *Lamaism* of Thibet, the doctrine of *Dschakdschiamuni* among

* The most interesting investigations as to this divinity are in the work of Dr. J. G. Müller—*Der Mexicanische Nationalgott, Huitzilopochtli*, 1847.

the Mongols and Calmucs; as well as the worship of *Quetzalcoatl*, in Mexico, and of *Mango-Capac*, in Peru, are but so many branches of the same trunk; whose root the labors of archæology and modern philosophy have not been able to determine with certainty, notwithstanding all the discussion, perseverance, sagacity and boldness of hypothesis, among the learned men who have been occupied in investigating the subject.

And, on the other hand, how marvellous the analogy between Christianity and Buddhism! The first Christian missionaries who visited Thibet, where Buddhism predominates, were overcome with surprise on finding religious usages in perfect accordance with those of Christian countries; so that they actually considered Buddhism as a degenerated Christianity, although it was perfectly certain that the last was much the more recent. The missionaries found among the followers of Buddha the pastoral crook or staff, the rosary, fasting, mendicant friars, temples adorned with paintings and sculpture, the burning of candles in divine worship, the short garment of the priests, the thurible or censer, the habit of singing certain hymns, the ringing of a bell as a signal for the faithful to unite in devotion, to which we may add sacrifices, the veneration of relics, holy water, pilgrimages, and indulgences granted by the Grand Lama.

Not less, however, was the surprise of the first Spanish ecclesiastics, who found, on reaching Mexico, a priesthood as regularly organized as that of the most civilized countries. Clothed with a powerful and effective authority which extended its arms to man in every condition and in all the stages of his life, the Mexican priests were mediators between man and the Divinity; they brought the newly born infants into the religious society, they directed their training and education, they determined the entrance of the young men into the service of the State, they consecrated marriage by their blessing, they comforted the sick and assisted the dying. This sacerdotal authority, so like in all things that of the Christian Church, particularly manifested itself in a species of confession which prevailed in Mexico, and concerning which the dogma obtained that a wrong or sin confessed to the priest, and expiated through the medium of a penance imposed by him, was thereby completely blotted out, and was placed beyond the reach of human justice and secular power.

Finally, we can do no less, before we conclude this chapter, than insist on this point, that Quetzalcoatl and Mango Capac were both missionaries of the worship of Bramah or Buddha, and probably of different sects. It does not, however, now fall within our purpose to present systematically the positive proofs of this assertion; we hope to give them hereafter in extenso, in a work specially devoted to the subject, which we propose to publish. We now pass on to the particular consideration of the inhabitants of Peru, viewed under several aspects.

NOTES.

To enumerate the various hypotheses which have been framed on the subject discussed in this chapter, would far transcend our limits, and, indeed, require a volume. Without here attempting such a work, we must confine our annotations at present to the statements of the text.

Of the visits of the Scandinavians, little doubt seems now to be entertained. The extent of coast explored by them is much less certain; though some have supposed, and, as we think, on insufficient testimony, that they were as far south as the shores of South Carolina. The principal testimony for the fact of their coming at all, is derived from the documents alluded to in the text, and published in the "*Antiquitates Americanæ*" of the Royal Society of Northern Antiquaries. But confirmatory evidence is supposed to exist in monuments that have been discovered in this country, and among these stands most conspicuous what is known as the Dighton Rock. This stone is about six and a half miles south of Taunton, on the east side of Taunton River, in the town of Berkley, Bristol county, Massachusetts. It is a fine-grained *gray wacke*, and, on one of its sides, is covered with marks and lines, of which many copies have been made, at different dates, from the year 1680 up to 1847. In 1830, the Rhode Island Historical Society caused an accurate copy to be made of the marks and lines, as they then appeared. In 1847, the same work was performed by the New York Historical Society. There is a general resemblance in most of these copies; though of some it may be said that one, familiar with the rock itself, would scarce recognize them as intended representations of the inscription on it. The lines seem not to have been chiselled, but to have been made by picking with the point of some iron implement. Some have supposed the characters to be, in part, at least, Phœnician, while the Northern antiquaries have (after comparing all the copies, except that of 1847,) pronounced them to be Scandinavian, and have even ventured, in part at least, on an interpretation.

Whether they be Scandinavian or not, there is one interesting fact connected with the Dighton inscription, for which we are indebted to Mr. Schoolcraft. At Michillimacinac, in 1839, this gentleman submitted several drawings of the inscription to the Algonquin chief, Chingwauk, somewhat celebrated for his skill in deciphering the pictographic delineations of his race. After an attentive study of them, Chingwauk pronounced a part of them to be the work of the New England Indians, and furnished what he conceived to be the interpretation of the characters. As to some of the characters, however, he professed his inability to decipher them, and Mr. Schoolcraft seems to think they may be Scandinavian; at all events, the visits of the Northmen to America, in the tenth and eleventh centuries, may be considered a fact generally admitted by antiquaries.

As to the opinion so confidently expressed by the author, that Irish colonies were planted in the Carolinas and Florida as early as in the ninth century of our era, all that can be said is, that we know at present of no other testimony in support of such a fact, but that which is contained in the text. There are, however, one or two particulars contained in the story which call for remark. If by the term "Esquimaux" be meant the people so designated at present, they are here placed further south on the Atlantic coast than they have generally been supposed to have reached. If Snorre Thurlusson saw a troop of *horse*, with a leader mounted on that animal, it contradicts the generally received opinion, that the horse was introduced into America by the Spanish conquerors, at a much later period. It should, however, be added that, within the last two years, the fossil remains of the horse have been said to be found in America. The report, however, was so vaguely given in a newspaper paragraph, that we have been unable to verify it. More light may possibly hereafter be thrown upon this supposed Irish colony; we confess, however, that, as at present advised, we very much doubt its existence.

As to the hypothesis of the settlement of America by the ten tribes, Adair has stated it most strongly. It is, however, much older than Adair. The Rev. Thomas Thorowgood, in 1645, published a sermon entitled, "Jews in America; or, Probabilities that the Americans are Jews;" this was answered by Sir Hamon L'Estrange in 1651, in his book, "Americans no Jews," and, as we think, conclusively answered. The hypothesis, however, has been revived at various periods since, but has not generally found favor among the best informed students of American antiquities.

The next hypothesis, of a Phœnician origin for that body of settlers who peopled Guatemala and the adjacent regions, has been ingeniously and learnedly supported by De Laet; and has, within the last two or three years, been invested with fresh interest by the new discoveries of the Abbé de Bourbourg, whose work is now (as we are informed) in the press in Paris. The text, in its very imperfect exposition of this hypothesis, refers to the work of Cabrera only. Cabrera himself knew, personally, little or nothing on the subject. His book is made up of what he could learn from the laborious researches of Ordoñez, of which, by an abuse of confidence, he availed himself. The Abbé de Bourbourg thus relates the story:— "The second work of Don Ramon de Ordoñez, and, without question, the most important, was a complete history of the ancient mythology of the Tzendals, and of the building of the first four American cities. During the stay of Don Ramon in Guatemala, where he resided for some time, he communicated a portion of the materials which he had collected for his great work to Doctor Paul Felix Cabrera, who, abusing the confidence thus reposed in him, appropriated the labors of the learned archæologist, and commented largely, in various works composed by him, on the origin of the Americans. One of these was translated into English, and published in Great Britain, in 1822. But in these works, Cabrera, who did not sufficiently comprehend the writings of Ordoñez, completely disfigured them, and hazarded some ridiculous opinions of his own. Ordoñez complained bitterly of this theft, and of the false representations which Cabrera had given of his work, and, because of them, obtained against him a decree of the Royal audience of Guatemala, in June, 1794." In fact, Cabrera has done much to render the views of Ordoñez, which are worthy of attentive study, ridiculous and incredible.

We cannot enter here particularly into the hypothesis of Ordoñez; ere long we hope it will be presented to the public by the Abbé de Bourbourg, from whom, as yet, we have nothing but his four letters from Mexico, addressed to the Duke de Valmy, and giving an outline of his discoveries. These letters are full of interest, and eminently suggestive to the American archæologist. As the whole subject, however, of Ordoñez's writings is brought under discussion by the present writer, in a larger work which will ere long be published, he will here say no more, than that the testimony to sustain the hypothesis of an early Phœnician colony in America, is by no means feeble.

As to the hypothesis, suggested by De Guignes, of emigration to the western coast of America, from the eastern coast of Asia, the testimony in support of it is very strong, and to the mind of the present writer, conclusive. Such emigration, however, took place in the latter part of the fifth century of the Christian era; and while it explains many facts in America, which long perplexed our archæologists, it by no means aids us in determining the origin of our earliest population. Baron Humboldt is entitled to the honor of having, by a suggestion of probability merely, opened the door to the discovery of the evidence which sustains this hypothesis. For a fuller view of this subject, however, the present writer must refer to the larger work already alluded to.

CHAPTER II.

THE ANCIENT INHABITANTS OF PERU.

ZOOLOGICAL and physiological investigations, the botany and geology of a country, form the foundation of its physical history, even as its oral traditions, its monuments, inscriptions, and annals are the indispensable materials for an historic synthesis of its political and moral aspect. As an historian, properly so called (whether anthropological or physical,) one is under a strict obligation not to permit himself to be carried away by any prejudice, to make a wise and impartial use of his materials, to seek sincerely for the truth, and when found, to admit it without hesitation, even though it may tend to dissipate opinions entertained from infancy and sanctioned by universal reception. The progress which various branches of science have made in our day, places them in seeming opposition to the Hebrew traditions preserved in the sacred writings; and of all these branches, anthropology is sometimes that which, at first view, seems to harmonize least with the meaning generally given to the first chapters of Genesis; as by ingenious explanations it aims to demonstrate that the whole human race did not proceed from a common source, and that the New Continent was peopled without any intervention of Eastern emigration. Declining here the examination of a subject so obscure, we will confine ourselves to an exposition of facts, by means of which each reader may form for himself such an opinion as he judges to be correct.

The singular conformation of the Peruvian crania, and the differences of structure which they present on a comparison with later American crania, have repeatedly been the subjects of particular study to naturalists. To explain these differences, recourse has been had to different hypotheses, none of which are satisfactory, because the learned men who formed them had not really sufficient materials with which to construct them. According to the recent numerous and scrupulously careful observations of Doctor J. D. Von Tschudi,* who, from his long residence in Peru, had it in his power to examine hundreds of crania of the ancient inhabitants of that country, it would appear that three distinct races dwelt there before the foundation of the kingdom of the Incas. Let us examine the exact description of these crania in each one of these three nations or races.

FIRST FORM.

The cranium, viewed from the anterior part, represents a truncated pyramid with the base turned upward; the face is small, the orbits are transversely oval, the upper jaw descends almost perpendicularly, the zygomatic processes are short, and point downward almost perpendicularly, the superciliary arches are a little protuberant, the curvature of the frontal bone scarcely perceptible, almost perpendicular up to the superciliary arch, and thence inclining gradually to the coronal suture. The frontal protuberances are very distinct, as are also the parietal protuberances, forming at the sides the most salient points of the cranium. Toward the sides and behind, both the parietals are united in a direction al-

* Ueber die Urbewohner von Peru von Dr. J. D. Von Tschudi, en Müller's Archiv für Physiologie, 1845, pp. 98-109.

most perpendicular to the temporal and occipital bones. The posterior wall of the occipital bone, up to the superior semicircular line, is perpendicular, and curves a little obliquely inward, and downward to the foramen magnum, or large occipital hole.

SECOND FORM.

Viewed from the anterior part, the cranium has an oval form, and laterally assumes the form of a vault, sufficiently regular, and somewhat elongated. The space occupied by the face is large, the orbits quadrangular, and the vertical diameter equal to the transverse, the upper jaw is slanting, the external angular processes of the frontal bone short, and directed strongly outward, the nasal process very broad and convex. The frontal bone is curved, with an inclination regular enough, but still more strongly marked than in form the first. The superciliary arches are not very distinct, the frontal protuberances almost imperceptible. The parietal bones, from their junction with the frontal bone, incline backward and downward; the protuberances of these bones are low down, and not very distinct, so that the transverse diameter of the head, measured from the upper point of one zygomatic process to the other, is not the larger. The upper portion of the occipital bone is placed vertically below the lambdoidal suture about an inch, but suddenly inclines strongly forward, and continues to incline thus horizontally to the foramen magnum, or great occipital hole.

THIRD FORM.

Viewed from the anterior part, the cranium presents the figure of a square, elongated from the lower and front parts towards the hinder and upper; the anterior side of which, from the swell to its opposite, makes the transverse the greater diameter of the head. The part of the face is very well defined, but shorter than in the second form. The orbits are somewhat oval, and their vertical diameter exceeds the transverse in length by some lines. The nasal process is broader than in the first form, but somewhat narrower than in the second. The frontal bone is narrow and long, and its inclination very great. In many crania it is concave in its middle portion, and presents, a little before its junction with the parietals, a strong frontal protuberance in the middle. Behind the coronal suture, the surface of the cranial vault is concave enough; and in this place the parietals curve a little upward, and then quickly fall in a straight line to unite with the occipital bone. This bone, between the lambdoidal suture and the superior semicircular line, inclines obliquely inward, and from this spot is suddenly doubled or folded downward and forward till it reaches the foramen magnum, or grand occipital hole.

These important anatomical proportions give rise to other relations no less interesting, which we proceed to explain:

I. In the first form, the longitudinal or true diameter of the head (from the glabella* to the opposite point of the occipital bone, a little above the superior semicircular line,) is equal to the transverse diameter. The inclination of the vertex of the head to the first diameter is 68 degrees. The inclination of the lower part of the occipital bone to the horizontal (measured from the foramen magnum to the external occipital protuberance) is 45 degrees; and of the upper part of the same bone is 82 degrees.

A line drawn from the point of junction of the parietal

* By this technical Latin term is designated that smooth part of the bones of the forehead situated between the two orbits, or cavities, in which the eyes are fixed.

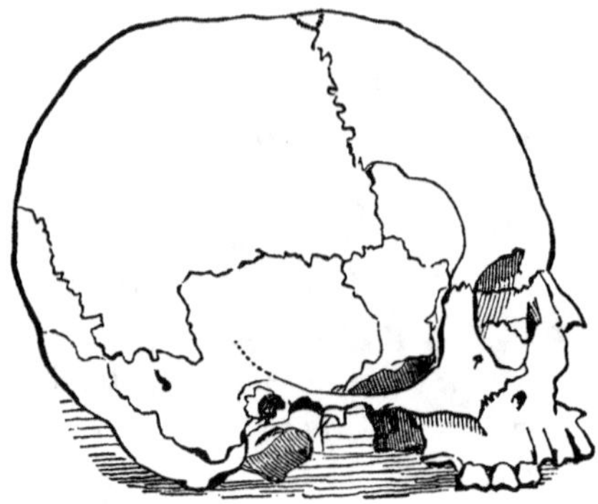

with the frontal bones, and passing outside of the cranium to its base, would almost touch the anterior edge of the external opening of the ear, and would meet a corresponding line on the opposite side forward of the anterior edge of the foramen magnum, or great occipital hole. The angle of Camper is 77 degrees.*

II. In the second form the longitudinal or true diameter (from the glabella to the junction of the third middle and parietal bones) is found to be, with respect to the transverse diameter, in the proportion of 1 to 1·3.—The inclination of the forehead to the first diameter is 45 degrees.

* By this phrase is designated an important angle in anthropology, observed and described by the distinguished Dutch anatomist, Dr. Peter Camper; an angle whose greater or less opening indicates the intellectual superiority of a race, and, up to a certain point, of individuals. One of the lines which form it (more or less oblique) is drawn from the most prominent point of the forehead to the extreme projection of the upper jaw; the other is horizontal, and passes from the entrance of the ear (the *meatus auditorius*) to the former line. The angle thus formed, sometimes called the *facial* angle, is almost a right angle in the Greek statues and in the present types of the Caucasian race.

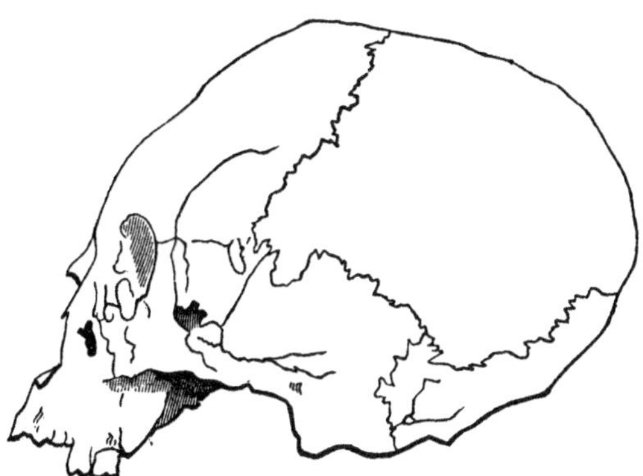

The inclination of the lower portion of the occipital bone from the foramen magnum to the upper semicircular line is only 17 degrees; from this last to the upper fifth part of the occipital bone is 55, and the inclination of the upper fifth is 85 degrees. The line before named, drawn from the junction of the coronal suture with the longitudinal to the base, will pass behind the mastoid process, and is met by its corresponding opposite in the middle of the foramen magnum. The angle of Camper is 68 degrees.

III. In the third form, the longitudinal or true diameter (from the glabella to the point of junction of the longitudinal suture with the lambdoidal) is found, in the proportion to the transverse diameter, of 1 to 1·5.—The inclination of the forehead to the first diameter reaches 23 degrees only; the inclination of the lower portion of the occipital bone is 32 degrees; that of the upper portion is 60 degrees. The line drawn from the angle formed by the coronal and longitudinal suture to the base of the cranium touches the point of junction of the parietal, temporal and occipital bones, and is met by a corresponding line on the opposite side, between

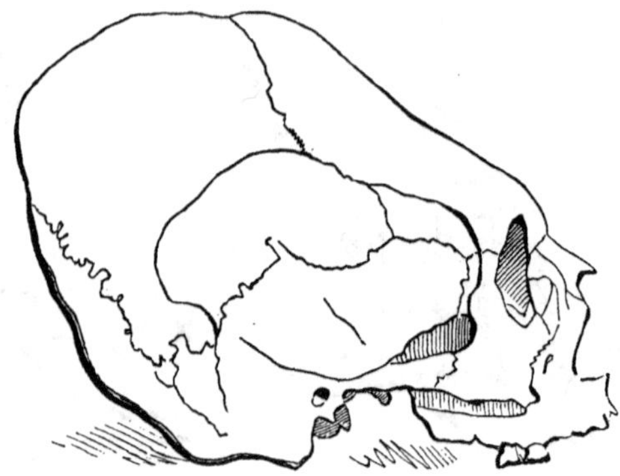

the posterior edge of the foramen magnum and the lower semicircular line. The angle of Camper is 69 degrees.

We will now examine the geographical distribution of these three races.

The first occupied the shores of the Pacific, bounded on the north by the uninhabited region of Tumbes, on the south by the immense desert of Atacama, on the east by the Cordilleras, and on the west by the ocean. This race we designate by the name of the CHINCHAS, after that of the most noted tribe that dwelt between the 10th and 14th degrees of south latitude. The crania of this race are to be met with in almost all the anthropological collections of Europe, it being very easy to obtain them in the vicinity of the Peruvian ports and harbors, where they lie scarce hidden by a light covering of sand. There are among them varieties, artificially produced, and differing according to their respective localities; sometimes the head is found very much flattened on the right side, and at other times on the left, so that the protuberance of the parietal bone on one side is little or none, while it shows itself very prominent on the other; there are some specimens in which the upper portion of the occipital bone is so much depressed that the parietal bones protrude considerably. These irregularities were undoubtedly produced by mechanical causes, and were considered as the distinctive marks of families; for in one *Huaca** will always be found the same form of crania; while in another, near by, the forms are entirely different from those of the first.

The second race inhabited the vast Peru-Bolivian elevations which raise themselves twelve thousand feet above the level of the sea. M. D'Orbigny distinguishes them by the name of the AYMARAES. In this race commenced the dynasty of the Incas, which, in the space of a few centuries, subjected to its dominion the other tribes. The crania of these people present differences equally remarkable, according to their respective localities, and particularly in the contour of the arch of the cranium.

It is proper here to remark that there is a very striking conformity between the configuration of this race and that of the Guanches, or inhabitants of the Canaries, who used also the same mode of preserving the bodies of their dead; and this resemblance is another proof which lends support to what is stated in the document or history of Votan, before referred to.

The third race, concerning which we have not so much positive information, occupied the territory comprehended between the Cordilleras and the Andes, and between the degrees of 9 and 14 of south latitude.† This race, which we

* A *Huaca* is a place of interment.—[TRANSLATOR.]

† These names are not unfrequently confounded. There are two great mountain ranges in Peru, running parallel to the Pacific. The nearest is at an average distance of 60 or 70 miles from the sea; the other is further inland. The western chain is what our author calls the Cordillera, and the eastern is the Andes. See Von Tschudi's remarks on this subject,

call the nation of the HUANCAS, after the name of the most powerful of the tribes which composed it, offers a very rare and characteristic formation, which cannot for a moment be confounded with either of the preceding, and distinguishes it also from the heterogeneous nations which we sometimes find mixed up with it.

As we have intimated, the race of the Aymaraes was the root of the Incas or Peruvian emperors, and to them is to be attributed that spreading movement from south to north (attested by the history of these vast regions), the consequences of which were the conquest of the adjacent nations, and the modifications and changes, both physical and moral, which, by reason of their conquest, the races who peopled them underwent. The Huancas, as being the nearest, were subdued first; afterwards followed the Chinchas, and both the conquered people found themselves under the necessity of yielding to the law of the strongest, and of adopting the customs, religion and laws of their conquerors; the natural result of this, in time, was a frequent mixture of the several races with each other, and a consequent mixed formation in the crania of the new generations.

It is necessary, therefore, to have at our command sufficient materials by means of which to sift out the primitive relations of these several races; and every synthesis, framed in the absence of such materials, will necessarily be erroneous, hasty and inconsistent.

And here two questions present themselves:

I. What was the cranial configuration of the primitive or real Indians?

in the very interesting and valuable account of his travels in Peru, Ch. XI. An English translation of this book was published by Putnam, in 1847.—[TRANSLATOR.]

II. Can there be found anywhere, now existing, the races above named, pure and without any mixture?

The most scrupulous investigations on these points have furnished us with the following results:

First. The true Indians, who, although dwelling in that part of Peru formerly under the power of the Spaniards, were never mingled in blood with Europeans or Africans, indicate by the formation of their crania a race very distinct from all the other tribes of South America, so that they might be considered a really primitive race, were it not that the facts brought to light incontestably prove that they proceed from the union of the *three* races already described.

Thus the cranium, in its contour, assumes the square form of the Chinchas. The size of the face is large, the upper jaw sufficiently projecting and oblique, the orbits square, the zygomatic process strongly developed and inclining backward, the nasal process near the frontal bone very strikingly convex, and then descending perpendicularly; the curvature of the forehead has, as in the Aymaraes, an inclination clearly marked from the glabella, the frontal protuberances are scarcely perceptible, the vault of the cranium is thick, the posterior part of the frontal bone and both the parietal bones are like those of the Huancas, although the point of union of these last bones with the upper part of the occipital recalls the configuration of the Aymaraes, the occipital curving from the lambdoidal suture gently at the beginning, and more rapidly afterwards to the base of the cranium.

The right diameter of the cranium passes, as in those of the Huancas, from the glabella to the point of union of the lambdoidal with the longitudinal suture; but, as in the crania of the Aymaraes, the greater transverse diameter passes from the upper root of the zygomatic process of the temporal bone to the same point on the opposite side. The proportion which it bears to the first diameter is as 1 to 1·1; consequently a greater approximation than to the proportion of the Chinchas crania, which is as 1 to 1·0.

Although the greater number of the crania of the true Indians is in accordance with these statements, yet there are numerous exceptions, and an approximation greater or less to the three primitive races; an approximation which depends on the provinces in which the Indians live, since we observe that one or the other of the primitive forms predominates more or less in those regions which have been from a remote epoch the home of one or the other of the typical races.

Secondly. The second question is of great importance, seeing that from its resolution the proof is drawn, whether the formation of the crania is or is not the result of mechanical pressure. Many physiologists, as it would seem, generally consider these forms anomalous, and as an effect produced on the heads of children entirely by pressure with small boards, or broad swathes, with which it was usual to squeeze the crania of infants. It is notorious enough that such a practice did obtain among various barbarous nations of the New World; and that it existed among the Chinchas for the sake of producing distinctive marks in families; an abuse which was forbidden by an apostolic bull in the sixteenth century. But, in our opinion, those physiologists are undoubtedly in error, who suppose that the different phrenological aspects offered by the Peruvian race were *exclusively* artificial. This hypothesis rests on insufficient grounds; its authors could have made their observations solely on the crania of adult individuals, as it is only a few years since two mummies of children were carried to England, which, according to the very exact description of Dr. Bellamy,* belonged to the tribe

* Annals and Magazine of Natural History, October, 1842.

of Aymaraes. The two crania (both of children scarce a year old) had, in all respects, the same form as those of adults. We ourselves have observed the same fact in many mummies of children of tender age, who, although they had cloths about them, were yet without any vestige or appearance of pressure of the cranium.

More still: the same formation of the head presents itself in children yet unborn; and of this truth we have had convincing proof in the sight of a fœtus, enclosed in the womb

FRONT AND SIDE VIEW.

of a mummy of a pregnant woman, which we found in a cave of Huichay, two leagues from Tarma, and which is, at this moment, in our collection. Professor D'Outrepont, of great celebrity in the department of obstetrics, has assured us that the fœtus is one of seven months' age. It belongs, according to a very clearly defined formation of the cranium, to the tribe of the Huancas. We present the reader with a drawing of this conclusive and interesting proof in opposition to the advocates of mechanical action as the sole and exclusive cause of the phrenological form of the Peruvian race.

The same proof is to be found in another mummy which exists in the museum of Lima, under the direction of Don M. E. de Rivero.

It is not possible to explain how, by means of pressure with fillets or bandages, the occipital bone can be transformed to a plane almost horizontal, without producing, at the same time, a considerable declination of the sinciput; which last is entirely wanting in the Aymaraes, and which we yet find in the Huancas, whose occiputs, notwithstanding, show no sign of pressure, not being, by any means, able to preserve their regular inclination as the points of resistance to a frontal pressure.

The considerable extension in length of the frontal bone of the parietals, and of the occipital in the last two races, might sometimes lead one to suspect pressure on the sides; but to this opinion is opposed the inclination of the frontal and occipital bone; but the most effectual proof against the use of mechanical means will, after all, be found in the actual existence of the three races in distinct though limited localities, in which there cannot be found any traces of envelopment or pressure of the head in the newly-born.

We can therefore assert with certainty:

I. That the race of the Chinchas is actually found, without any admixture, in various towns as well of the coast of Northern Peru, as of the province of the Yauyos.

II. That the tribe of the Aymaraes is still found in the sierras of Southern Peru.

III. That in some families of the department of Junin, the tribe of the Huancas is preserved pure, as we have had occasion ourselves to see.

In conclusion, it may be proper to notice an osteologic anomaly, very interesting, which is observed in the crania of all the three races; and it is this: that those of children of tender years, in the first months after their birth, present an interparietal bone (*os interparietale*) perfectly distinct; a bone which, as its name indicates, will be found placed between the two parietals, and having a form more or less triangular, whose sharpest angle is above, and is bounded by the posterior edges of the parietal bones, while its base attaches itself to the occipital bone, by a suture which runs, from the angle of union of the temporal with the occipital bone, a little above the upper semicircular line, to the similar angle on the opposite side. It follows that this inter-

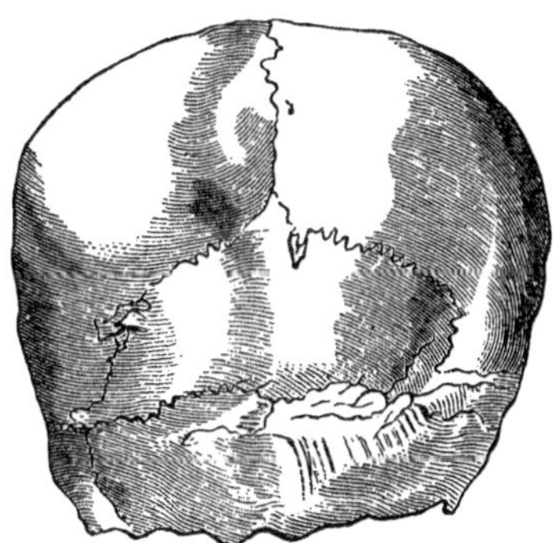

parietal bone occupies precisely that part of the occiput which in the other crania is occupied by the upper portion of the occipital, and which is connected with the parietals by the lambdoidal suture.

At four or five months this bone is regularly united to the

occipital, and the union begins at the middle of the suture, and advances by little and little towards both sides; although even after a year it is not found completely effected, but in the middle only; a furrow shows the trace of the suture; this furrow is not obliterated even at the most advanced age, and may be easily recognized in all the crania of all these races. Sometimes the union takes place very slowly, as in the cranium above, which is that of a youth of the Chinchas, of ten or twelve years old, in which the occipital suture may be seen open through its whole length. The length of the interparietal bone in this individual is four inches at the base, and an inch and ten lines high: dimensions which sufficiently prove that this singular formation is not to be confounded with that of the small supernumerary bones called *Wormiana*, which are uniformly found between the parietals in all human crania; so that this interparietal bone is a true anomaly.

Dr. Bellamy was the first who made mention of this bone, which he had occasion to remark in one of the mummies before mentioned. Among the numerous crania which we had the opportunity to examine in Peru, we have had the means of convincing ourselves that this suture is invariably found either open, or closed in part, or completely united to the occipital bone, and well indicated by a furrow very clearly marked.

It is a circumstance worthy of the attention of learned anthropologists, that there is thus found in one section of the human race a perpetual anomalous phenomenon, which is wanting in all others, but which is characteristic of the ruminant and carnivorous animals.*

* Mr. Prescott informs us that the crania of the Inca race manifest an incontestable superiority over the other races of the country on the score of intelligence; and to this intellectual superiority, announced externally

We much regret that a want of materials does not permit us to describe the formation of the crania of the barbarous Indians on the eastern side of Peru.

Enough, however, has been said to enable the reader to form a general opinion upon the physical constitution of the ancient inhabitants of Peru. We will now proceed to a history of the country before the coming of the Spaniards.

by the cranium, this eminent writer attributes the origin of that remarkable civilization and social polity which made the Peruvian monarchy superior to all the other States of South America. The work of Dr. Morton referred to by Mr. Prescott contains various drawings of the Inca cranium, and also of the common Peruvian cranium, proving that the facial angle of the first, although not very large, was much greater than that of the second, which was particularly flat, and wanting in intellectual character.—*Crania Americana.* (Philadelphia, 1829.)

We must be permitted to say that all the Peruvian crania, figured in the work of Dr. Morton, belong to those of the tribes which we have described in this chapter; doubting, as we do doubt, whether this learned anthropologist had it in his power to obtain crania of the royal family of the Incas: for with the exception of the mummies of the four emperors which were carried to Lima, and which were buried in a court or yard of Santa Anna, and the remains of which it has been impossible to discover, up to this day the sepulchres of the others are unknown, as well as of the nobility descended from them. If at this day uncertainty exists as to the remains of Francis Pizarro, deposited in the vaults of the cathedral church at Lima, how much more difficult must it be to affirm with certainty that Dr. Morton or any other person has really possessed crania of the Inca race? Besides, would they not have undergone modifications by intermixture with other noble races of different tribes existing in the capital?

NOTE.

THE subject embraced in this chapter is one admitting of, perhaps, no illustration beyond that afforded by the text itself. While more particularly attractive to the physiologist, it presents two or three important facts of interest to the general reader.

First. It shows that the crania of Dr. Morton's work are not, as he supposed, crania of the Incas; and consequently the inferences from the erroneous opinion he entertained are no longer admissible.

Secondly. It proves that *all* the peculiarities of cranial conformation, heretofore referred, without exception, to external causes, such as pressure, are not, in every instance, thus produced. In some cases they are natural.

Third. An anomaly characteristic of the ruminant and carnivorous animals would seem to exist in the ancient Peruvian crania. On this subject, we are indebted to a professional friend, from whom we sought information, for the following note.

"The *ossa Wormiana* are small bones, found occasionally in all the sutures of the skull, but most frequently in the lambdoidal, which separates the occipital from the parietal bones. These *ossa Wormiana* vary in size, from two lines to two inches in diameter. They are very variable in position and shape, as well as in size, and are mostly of an irregular form. The largeness of size, regularity of form, uniformity of shape, and position of the interparietal bones, described by the author, distinguish them from the *ossa Wormiana*, and seem to confirm his opinion that the ancient Peruvian skulls are peculiar, and mark a distinct and lower type of organization."

CHAPTER III.

CONSIDERATIONS ON THE HISTORY OF PERU, BEFORE THE ARRIVAL OF THE SPANIARDS.

THE origin of the Peruvian empire, like that of all known nations, is found involved in fables and incredible traditions, hiding thereby the truth, which it is very difficult, and, at times, impossible to disentangle. Man's inclination for the marvellous, his ignorance of its causes, the magical perspective of recollection, the intentional imposture of the priesthood, and above all individual patriotism, or the collective pride of the race, induced the majority of the people to appropriate to themselves a special protection from heaven, and to attribute a divine origin to their chiefs. The PERUVIANS believed that the SUN, a tutelar divinity of their empire, had sent his own sons to reform and instruct them, of whom the descendants were their INCAS or EMPERORS. Previous to the arrival of these children of the Sun, PERU, like the other territories of the NEW WORLD, was found, according to tradition, divided into several nations, or independent tribes, wandering or fixed, rude and ferocious, whose unteachable and warlike disposition prompted them to battle continually among themselves. Ignorant of all industry and culture, knowing no law of morality, nor any social compact, wandering through the forests, more resembling the brutes than the human race, subjected to the inclemency of the elements, and to the molestations and evils consequent upon this savage state, none teaching them that they might better their condition; such was their state, when the merciful FATHER, the SUN, placed two of his children on the lake of TITICACA, and told them "that they might go where they wished, and wheresoever they pleased; they might stop to eat and to sleep; commanded them to place in the ground a small wedge of gold, which he gave them, informing them that where that wedge should sink at one blow, and go into the earth, there the SUN wished them to stop, and make their residence and court. Arrived at the valley of CUZCO, after having vainly tried, through all the roads where they had travelled, to sink the wedge, they found themselves on the ridge of HUANANCAURI, and there endeavored anew to sink the small wedge, which went in with so much facility at the first blow, that they saw it no more. Then said the man to his sister and wife, 'In this valley, our father, the SUN, commands us to stop and make it our seat and residence, to accomplish his will. It is necessary that we take different ways, and that each should attempt to draw together and attract these people, to indoctrinate them, and accomplish the good, which our father, the SUN, commands.' "*

From the ridge of Huanancauri, the man went to the north, and the woman to the south, and harangued the multitudes, exhorting them to unite, to embrace another life, and to receive as gifts from heaven the counsels and instructions which they condescended to give by order of their father, the SUN. Fascinated by their appearance, and confirmed by the respect with which these extraordinary beings inspired them, the wandering tribes followed them to the valley of CUZCO, where they laid the foundation of a city. This region was the central

* Garcilasso de la Vega's Royal Commentaries. Vol. I., Book 1, Chap. XV. and XVI.

district of those tribes, and its name, according to GARCILASSO, in the language of the INCAS, signifies *navel;* and it is certain, according to the traditions of the natives, that as the navel is the source whence the infant receives life and growth in the womb, the plane of CUZCO was the nucleus of civilization, and the focus of light, for the State, founded by *Manco-Capac*, and *Mamá-Oello Huaco*, as the celestial couple were called.

These children of the SUN established a social union between the several Peruvian tribes, combined their united forces, enlarged their desires, and gave a new and more elevated turn to their thoughts. MANCO-CAPAC taught the men agriculture, industry, and useful arts. At the same time the wise legislator wished to give to them a more solid and enduring happiness, by means of adequate laws, a social compact, and a political system perfectly organized, a minute description of which we are compelled at present to pass by, that being the object of our latter chapters, while our present aim is solely the historical description of the Peruvian empire. On the other hand, MAMA-OELLO taught the women the art of spinning, weaving, dyeing, and, at the same time, the domestic virtues, becoming grace, chastity, and conjugal fidelity.

Such was the origin of the monarchy of the INCAS, children of the SUN, and descendants in a direct line from MANCO-CAPAC and MAMA-OELLO. Small in their origin, they extended but little distance beyond CUZCO; but within these narrow precincts MANCO-CAPAC exercised an authority without limits, and the same rights were preserved by his successors, in proportion as they augmented by arms the bounds of the empire. The authority of the INCA equalled that of the most powerful monarchs of the world.

To this unlimited power was allied, according to the traditions of the INDIANS, a tender affection for their subjects, and a great anxiety for the good of the people; not making conquests to gratify a vain ambition, but from a simple desire to make the barbarous nations whom they conquered participators in the advantages of civilization.

Thus assures us GARCILASSO DE LA VEGA, a descendant of the same INCAS, whose writings will be the first which we shall examine in the brief review which we propose making of some of the principal authors who have treated of the Peruvian history and archæology, as much for the purpose of searching to the bottom of the traditions and documents which it contains, as to guard the reader against the tone of panegyric of the author, which is quite enough of itself to cause him to be distrusted, even were there not other and greater grounds for suspicion. GARCILASSO DE LA VEGA is, of all the writers of Peruvian antiquity, the most important, and he who best deserves to fix our attention; and as being a descendant of the ancient Peruvian dynasty, none other has reached so great celebrity, nor has any been so much quoted by more recent historians.

Our author, the son of GARCILASSO DE LA VEGA, (a partisan of GONZALO PIZARRO,) and of one Ñusta, niece of HUAYNA-CAPAC, and grand-daughter of the INCA, TUPAC-YUPANQUI, was born in CUZCO in 1540. A want of culture, consequent upon the origin of his mother, and the adventurous life of the father, caused his education to be neglected until he reached the age of eighteen or twenty years. Without doubt his natural disposition, and assiduous application afterward, supplied, in part, this want of education.

The young GARCILASSO went to SPAIN in 1558 or 1560, and embraced a military career, distinguishing himself in various encounters, and reaching the rank of Captain, under the command of Don John of Austria; but the vengeful court of Spain did not forget that Garcilasso, the father, had embraced the revolutionary side, and followed in all his dangerous enterprises Gonzalo-Pizarro, and hence distrust rested upon the son, who, in consequence, despairing of ever attaining to eminence in his career, or of fixing upon any other occupation which seemed suited to his birth, threw up his commission and retired to Cordova, where he devoted himself to science and literary pursuits. At seventy years of age he published the first part of his *Royal Commentaries*, his most important work, and that which at present occupies us. This was composed of two hundred and seventy-two chapters, divided into nine books, and contains the condition of Peru before the Incas, their origin, their history, conquest and laws; the political and religious customs of the different nations which formed the vast empire of Peru; the state of science and the arts under the government of its kings, and numerous documents relative to the language, geography and natural history of the country.

The Peruvian origin of Garcilasso, an origin of which he was proud, and of which he reminds you every moment, the grave confidence with which he details the narrative of past events, whether it be concerning the history of his country, or relative to the biography of individuals, his assiduous labors and seeming impartiality, as resulting from his double European and American descent, have gained for him general approbation, a unanimous confidence in the truth of his relations, universal fame; and for his work the character of the most important monument of ancient Peruvian history; but notwithstanding all this, a scrupulous and conscientious analysis will find him defective under more than one head, and a more exacting and severe criticism will pronounce him too credulous, insufficient in his proofs, and wanting in that impartiality which a historian of modern as well as ancient events requires.

The sources of GARCILASSO's knowledge are principally the informations of his mother and one of his uncles, and his own observations relative to the customs and religion of his countrymen; all of which he began to note first, when he retired from the military service; when without delay he opened a correspondence with some friends of his, who inhabited PERU, for the purpose of acquiring additional information, and of refreshing his memory. His work was published in Lisbon, in 1609, fifty years after the author had left his country; but the manuscript was completed in 1570 or 1575, an epoch when it was natural that the descendant of the INCAS should find a difficulty in publishing it in SPAIN.

The most serious fault of GARCILASSO is his evident partiality; this is the greatest defect of a historian. Dazzled by his royal origin, he made an effort to portray his ancestors, the INCAS, as ideal monarchs, as great legislators and warriors, and to present them under the aspect or inventors and protectors of the arts and sciences; heaping encomiums upon them, the monotony of which is continued throughout, until the latest periods of his history, in which verification is more easy, and the perspective less illusive for being nearer. Arrived at the epoch of the INCA HUASCAR, Garcilasso, nearest relative of this chief, zealously took his part, and the ties of relationship blinded his judgment; and this single instance is sufficient to prove the little faith deserved by a historian who is so partial, and has always so little skill when he speaks of his parents and ancestors. Another proof is the tenacity with which he defends the illegal actions of GONZALO-PIZARRO, without other motive than that his father fought under the banner of this commander.

We must also notice that the commentaries of GARCILASSO in several places, are in direct contradiction to the statements of his predecessors, such as ACOSTA, FRAY MARCOS DE NIZA, PEDRO CIEZA DE LEON, FRANCISCO LOPEZ DE GOMARA, BALBOA ZARATE, and others, as also to several of his successors; it being easy to convince one's self, by a comparison of the text, that the tales and allegations are false, not through ignorance, and scantiness of information, but through the partiality of the author, who omits or falsifies all which tends to oppose his views. As little can it be denied that the greater part of the statements of his commentaries want a sufficient foundation, and it is necessary to recollect that the whole work is a tissue of compilations of *traditions;* and the truth of this assertion is evident, if we consider that Garcilasso inserted, or, to speak more correctly, improved the narrations, which from the lips of his parents and of ignorant and superstitious Indians he heard in his youth, when the mind is incapable of the discernment and ripeness which historical analysis requires to separate truth from the fables and stories which gather so thickly upon the current of time. Add to this that GARCILASSO published his work half a century after leaving his country, far from the scene of the events he relates; facts sufficient to make his narrations suspicious to the discerning reader. Finally, young GARCILASSO did not understand the difficult art of deciphering the QUIPOS, an important deficiency, which neither an abundance of traditions nor ingenious conjectures could supply.

Our object in inserting this notice is to make all readers and historians who consult the work of GARCILASSO, most cautious.

The arrival of MANCO-CAPAC took place in 1021, of the vulgar era, according to the current opinion, and his reign lasted forty years. GARCILASSO embraced in his narrative a space of some five hundred years, but his chronological notices want a firm foundation.

The series of the annals of the INCAS presents so much confusion and incertitude, the historical references are so defective, the traditions so contradictory, that to avoid losing ourselves in useless digressions, or in sterile and tedious investigations, we will present to our readers the following catalogue of the Peruvian Monarchs, the authenticity of which we cannot vouch for, although it seems to us the least defective that we can present under the circumstances.

I. *Manco-Capac* began to reign in the year 1021, and died in 1062, after reigning 40 years.

II. *Sinchi-Rocca* reigned 30 years, from 1062 to 1091.

III. *Lloqque-Yupanqui* reigned 35 years, from 1091 to 1126.

IV. *Mayta-Capac* began to reign in 1126, reigned 30 years, and died in 1156.

V. *Capac-Yupanqui* inherited the power in the year 1156, reigned 41 years, and died in 1197.

VI. *Inca-Rocca* began to reign in 1197, and died in 1249, after having reigned 51 years.

VII. *Yahuar-Huaccac* had a reign of 40 years, from 1249 to 1296; seven of these he passed in private life, after having renounced in 1289, in favor of his son Viracocha.

VIII. *Viracocha* occupied the throne from the year 1289, and died in 1340. This INCA predicted the ruin of the empire, and the arrival of white and bearded men. His son, *Inca-Urco*, reigned only eleven days, being deposed by the nobles of the empire, as a fool, and incapable of governing.

IX. *Titu-Manco-Capac-Pachacutec* came to the crown in the year 1340, reigned 60 years, and died in 1400, after having lived, according to tradition, 103 years.

X. *Yupanqui* inherited the regal power in the year 1400, reigned 39 years, and died in 1439.

XI. *Tupac-Yupanqui* reigned from the year 1439, and died in 1475, after 36 years' reign.

XII. *Huayna-Capac* succeeded *Tupac-Yupanqui*, in the year 1475, reigned 50 years, and died in 1525. This chief was considered the most glorious of all the Peruvian monarchs.*

XIII. *Huascar* received the crown in 1526, reigned seven years, and died in 1532.

XIV. *Atahuallpa*, or *Atavaliva*, began to reign in the year 1532, governed the whole empire for one year and four months, after having reigned six years, in Quito only, and died on the scaffold, by order of Pizarro, in the public square of Cajamarca, the 29th of August, in the year 1533.

After the conquest of the Spaniards, the brother of both the preceding monarchs was crowned as Manco-Capac II.; who reigned with a light shadow of royal dignity until the year 1553. He was succeeded by his three sons, *Sayri-Tupac*, *Cusititu-Yupanqui* and *Tupac-Amaru*. This last was beheaded in CUZCO, in the year 1571, by order of DON FRANCISCO DE TOLEDO, fifth Viceroy of PERU.

* According to the Canon, Dr. D. JUSTO SAHUARAURA of CUZCO, who pretends to spring from the INCA HUAYNA-CAPAC; by a succession of blood, the descendants of MANCO-CAPAC form the AYLLO *Ruuruhua*; those of SINCHI-ROCCA, the AYLLO *Chima-Panaca;* those of LLOQQUE-YUPANQUI, the AYLLO *Huahuanina;* those of MAYTA-CAPAC, the AYLLO *Usca-Mayta;* those of CAPAC-YUPANQUI, the AYLLO *Apumayta-Panaca-Urin-Cosco;* those of INCA-ROCCA, the AYLLO *Huicca-Qquirau-Panaca-Hanan-Cosco;* those of YAHUAR-HUACCAC, the AYLLO *Huaccaylli-Panaca;* those of HUIRACCOCHA-INCA, the AYLLO *Sucso-Panaca;* those of the INCA-PACHACUTEC, the AYLLO *Cacca-Cosco, Anahuarques;* those of the INCA YUPANQUI, the AYLLO *Inca-Panaca;* those of TUPAC-YUPANQUI, the AYLLO *Capac-Panaca;* those of HUAYNA-CAPAC, the AYLLO *Tumipampa.*

Passing by Father ACOSTA, and other authors who began the line of Peruvian monarchs, with INCA-ROCCA, we will proceed to examine the memorials of the ancient history of Peru, by the licentiate, FERNANDO-MONTESINOS, which is the second work worthy of fixing our attention. The author, a native of OSONA, in SPAIN, visited Peru a century after the conquest, at two different times, and travelled fifteen years through the viceroyalty, devoting himself with great eagerness to the ancient history of the empire of the INCAS, collecting all the traditions and songs of the natives, gathering knowledge from the most learned Indians relative to past events, profiting by the unpublished manuscripts, compiled under the direction of F. LUIS-LOPEZ, bishop of QUITO, (consecrated in 1588), and studying antiquities with so much zeal, that none equalled him in archæological knowledge. At the beginning of the second half of the seventeenth century, he completed his manuscript upon the ancient history of PERU, which was deposited in the library of the convent of SAN JOSE DE SEVILLA. Some 200 years afterward (in 1846) these memorials came to light, but in French, and only in an extract which was published in PARIS, by M. TERNAUX-COMPANS, a distinguished editor of voyages, narratives or relations, and original memorials, to serve for a history of the discovery of AMERICA. Simultaneously with the memorials MONTESINOS composed another work, entitled *Peruvian Annals*, a work which, until now, has never been published. The memorials of this author treat of the ancient history of PERU, in a mode so original and distinct from all others, that we can easily perceive it to be a production alike novel and unknown. He began with his favorite hypothesis, and devoted to it the first part of his book, i. e., that PERU was the country of OPHIR, of the time of SOLOMON, and that AMERICA was peopled by repeated emigrations coming from ARMENIA. Five hundred years after the deluge began the catalogue of the monarchs, whose names are quoted by MONTESINOS, who gives, also, the ages at which they respectively died, and the most memorable events of their reigns. The catalogue which he presents ascends to a hundred and one monarchs previous to the conquest of the country by the Spaniards.

The work of MONTESINOS being but very slightly known, we do not judge it superfluous to give here a brief extract from it, in the exposition of a chronological table of the kings, according to our author.

I. *Pishua-Manca* reigned sixty years, and died at more than one hundred years of age.

PERU, says MONTESINOS, was populated five hundred years after the deluge. Its first inhabitants flowed in abundantly towards the valley of CUZCO, conducted by four brothers, named *Ayar-Manco-Topa*, *Ayar-Cachi-Topa*, *Ayar-Auca-Topa*, and *Ayar-Uchu-Topa*, who were accompanied by their sisters and wives, named *Mama-Cora*, *Hipa-Huacum*, *Mama-Huacum*, and *Pilca-Huacum*. The eldest of the brothers mounted to the summit of a ridge, and threw with his sling a stone to each of the four quarters of the world, thus taking possession of the soil for himself and his family. He afterward gave a name to each one of the quarters which he had reached with his sling, calling that beyond the SOUTH *Colla*, beyond the NORTH *Tahua*, beyond the EAST *Antisuyu*, beyond the WEST *Contisuyu*, and for that reason the Indians called their kings *Tahuantin-Suyu-Capac*, i. e. LORDS of the four quarters of the globe. The younger of the brothers, who, according to tradition, was at the same time the most skilful and hardy, wishing to enjoy alone the plenitude of power, rid himself of two of his brothers, by enclosing one of them in a cave, and throwing the other into a deep hole and thus caused the third to fly to a distant province. The fratricide consoled his sisters, and told them that they must consider him as the only child or *son* of the SUN, and obey him as such. He commanded his kinsmen to level the ground and make houses of stone; such was the origin of the city of CUZCO.* The neighboring nations followed the example of the vassals or subjects of AYAR-UCHU-TOPA, and founded populations in the vicinity of this city. For sixty years did this first king govern, (whom Indian traditions also called *Pûhua-Manco*), leaving the throne to his eldest son, the fruit of his union with his sister, MAMA-CORA.

II. *Manco-Capac* I.

The princes of the adjacent nations dreading the power of MANCO-CAPAC, solicited his alliance, and to accomplish this object they proposed to him to take for a wife the daughter of the chief among them. The monarch consented, but while they were making preparations for the wedding feasts, they received the news that a numerous multitude were approaching CUZCO, from the side of Arica and the COLLAS, [or South.] MANCO-CAPAC marched without delay to repel the foreign invasion, notwithstanding they sent him deputies assuring him that they had no evil intentions, and only begged for land to cultivate, and pasture for their cattle. The Peruvian monarch assigned them the provinces of the NORTH; many went to POMACOCHA, QUINOA, HUAYTARA, and CHACHAPOYAS; some embarked on the APURIMAC and MARANON. Traditions call this foreign horde ATUMURUNAS.

III. *Huainaevi-Pishua* reigned 50 years, and died at the age of 90.

Having obtained possession of a son of his, together with

* Montesinos supposes that the name of Cuzco is derived from Cosca, an Indian word, which signifies to level; or, from those heaps of earth, called coscos, which were found in the environs.

his nurse, the neighboring nations wished to put him to death; the child wept two drops of blood, and the enemies, alarmed, restored him to his father, and established peace. HUAYNACAVI afterward married *Mama-Micay*, the daughter of *Huillaco*, lord of a village in the country of LUCAY. During his reign was known the use of letters, and the *amautas* taught astrology and the art of writing on leaves of the plantain tree.*

IV. *Sinchi-Cozque* reigned 60 years, and lived more than a hundred.

This sovereign, also called *Pachacuti*, because he reigned a thousand years after the deluge, was as wise as he was valiant; he conquered his enemies in a bloody battle near the village of *Michina*, fortified and adorned the city of CUZCO, and invented the species of carriage or vehicle called *Llamadores*.

V. *Inti-Capac-Yupanqui* lived more than a hundred years, and reigned more than sixty.

He was the younger son of SINCHI-COZQUE, and when young conquered, in a hard-fought battle, *Huaman-Huaroca* and *Huacos-Huaroca*, both brothers and valiant chiefs, of the nation of the ANTIHUAYLAS, who had taken possession of the provinces of CONTISUYU, TUCAYSUYU, COLLASUYU, and of the CHIRIHUANAS, and threatened the city of Cuzco.†

This monarch was no less wise in peace than powerful in war. He was also very zealous for religion and the worship of the supreme gods, *Illatici-Huiracocha* and the *Sun*. He also divided CUZCO into two parts: *Hanan-Cuzco* and *Hurin-Cuzco*, and the nation into hundreds or pachacas; each centu-

* The *amautas* are explained hereafter.—[TRANSLATOR.]

† MONTESINOS says that all that which GARCILASSO relates of this victory is false. According to GARCILASSO, CAPAC-YUPANQUI reigned from 1156 to 1197; according to Montesinos, 1100 years after the deluge.

rion commanded a hundred men, each *huaranco* a hundred centurions, one *huñu* to a hundred *huarancos*, and all were made subject to the *tocricoc*, who depended solely upon the king. Each province was obliged to distinguish itself by certain personal signals in each one of its component members, and the infants were obliged to perforate the ears and wear rings of gold or silver.

To this same sovereign did his subjects owe their *Chasquis* or couriers for posting to the most distant provinces, as also the institution of the solar year into 365 days, and the division of the years into circles of tens, hundreds and thousands, from which came at last the name *Intip-Huatan* or *Capac-Hesata* (great solar year).

VI. *Manco-Capac* II.

He commanded to be opened or made great roads of communication from CUZCO to the provinces, bridges over the largest rivers, and *tambos* or stopping-places at every four leagues for travellers. At the same time he commanded the priests of ILLIATICI-HUIRACOCHA to live in cloisters and in a state of chastity, and caused edifices to be constructed for the priestesses of the SUN.

During his reign appeared two comets, and there were two eclipses of the sun which frightened the population of PERU. Unfortunately their fears were not all idle, for a frightful plague occurred which desolated the provinces, and almost depopulated the capital of CUZCO.

VII. *Topa-Capac* I.

He retired to the Andes to escape the plague, lived for some time among the mountains, and returned afterward to CUZCO, where there was great disorder.

VIII. *Titu-Capac-Yupanqui.*

After having appeased a revolution he relinquished the throne, being already advanced in years, to his son.

IX. *Titu-Capac-Amauri*, who lived 80 years.

He conquered the provinces of COLLAS and CHARCAS.

X. *Capac-Say-Huacapar* reigned 60 years, and lived 90.

XI. *Capesinia-Yupanqui* reigned more than 40 years, and lived 90; was a religious prince, and constructed many Huacas, [sacred places.]

XII. *Ayatarco-Cupo* reigned 25 years.

Giants having entered PERU, they populated Huaytara, Quinoa, Punta de Santa Helena, and Puertoviejo, and built a sumptuous temple in PACHACAMAC, using instruments of iron. As they were given up to sodomy, divine wrath annihilated them with a rain of fire, although a part of them were enabled to escape by going to CUZCO. AYATARCO-CUPO went out to meet them, and dispersed them about LIMATAMBO.

XIII. *Huascar-Titu* reigned 30 years, and lived 64, dying at a time when it was proposed to make war with the CHIMUS.

XIV. *Quispi-Tutu* reigned three years, and lived 60.

XV. *Titu-Yupanqui*, or PACHACUTI II., died at a very advanced age. He suppressed a military revolution, and reduced the feasts and revels of the Indians.

XVI. *Titu-Capac* reigned 25 years.

XVII. *Paullu-Icar-Pirhua* reigned 30 years.

XVIII. *Lloqueti-Sacamauta*, a very wise prince, reigned 50 years.

XIX. *Cayo-Manco-Amauta* died at 90 years of age.

XX. *Huascar-Titupac* II. reigned 33 years, and died at 75 years of age.

He gave to all the provinces new governors of royal blood. He introduced in the army a species of cuirass composed of cotton and copper, and a shield of leaves of the plantain-tree and cotton, as a distinction and a protection for the bravest soldiers, to whom he gave other arms and dresses, and granted them numerous privileges. He finally established a council of twenty old men of royal blood.

XXI. *Manco-Capac-Amauta* IV.

This chief was addicted to astronomy, and convened a scientific meeting, in which they agreed that the sun was found to be at a greater distance than the moon, and that both followed different courses. At the same time he fixed the beginning of the year at the summer equinox.

XXII. *Ticatua* reigned 30 years.

XXIII. *Paullu-Toto-Capac* reigned 19 years.

XXIV. *Cao-Manco* reigned 30 years.

XXV. *Marasco-Pachacuti* reigned 40 years, and lived double that space of time. This prince conquered the barbarians recently come to Peru, in a bloody combat, and strengthened the garrisons as far as the banks of the RIMAC and the HUANUCO. Zealous in religion, he opposed the progress of idolatry, and published several decrees favorable to the worship of his predecessors.

XXVI. *Paullu-Atauchi-Capac* died at 70 years of age.

XXVII. *Lluqui-Yupanqui* reigned 10 years, and died at 30 years of age.

XXVIII. *Lluqui-Ticac* died at the same age, after having reigned 8 years.

XXIX. *Capac-Yupanqui* reigned 50 years, and died at 80 years of age. He was a celebrated jurisconsult.

XXX. *Topa-Yupanqui* reigned 30 years, and died at a very advanced age.

XXXI. *Manco-Avito-Pachacuti*, or *Pachacuti* IV., reigned 50 years.

He was a very warlike prince, and commanded them to begin the year with the winter equinox.

XXXII. *Sinchi-Apusqui* reigned 40 years, and died at 80 years of age, 2070 after the deluge. He ordered them to call the Pirhua gods *Illatici-Huiracocha*, and for this reason did the Indians give this king the name of *Huarma-Huiracocha.*

XXXIII. *Auqui-Quitua-Chauchi* reigned four years.

XXXIV. *Ayay-Manco* died at 60 years of age.

This monarch gathered together in CUZCO the *Amautas* to reform the calendar, who decided among themselves, that the year should be divided into months of 30 days, and weeks of ten days, calling the five days at the end of the year a small week. They also collected the years into decades or groups of tens, and into groups of ten decades, or one hundred years, which form one sun or century. The half of a sun, or space of 50 years, was called PACHACUTI.

XXXV. *Huiracocha-Capac* II. reigned 15 years.

XXXVI. *Chinchi-Rocca-Amauta* reigned 20 years.

He was a monarch very much devoted to astrology.

XXXVII. *Amauro-Amauta.*

He was so melancholy a prince, that none ever saw him laugh.

XXXVIII. *Capac-Raymi-Amauta.*

Celebrated for his astronomical knowledge, he knew which was the longest, and which the shortest day of the year, and when the sun reached the tropics. His vassals, in honor of their king, gave to the month of December the name of *Capac-Raymi.*

XXXIX. *Illa-Topa* reigned three years, and died at 30 years of age.

XL. *Topac-Amauri* died at the same age.

XLI. *Huana-Cauri* II. reigned four years.

XLII. *Toca-Corca-Apu-Capac* reigned 45 years, and established a University in CUZCO.

XLIII. *Huancar-Sacri-Topa* reigned 32 years.

XLIV. *Hina-Chiulla-Amauta-Pachacuti* reigned 35 years.

The 5th year of his government corresponds with the year 2500 after the deluge.

XLV. *Capac-Yupanqui-Amauta* reigned 35 years.

XLVI. *Huapar-Sacritopa.*

XLVII. *Caco-Manco-Auqui* reigned 13 years.

XLVIII. *Hina-Huella* reigned 30 years.

XLIX. *Inti-Capac-Amauta* reigned 30 years.

L. *Ayar-Manco-Capac* II.

LI. *Yahuar-Huquiz* reigned 30 years.

He was a celebrated astronomer, and intercalated a year at the end of four centuries.

LII. *Capac-Titu-Yupanqui* reigned 23 years, and died when more than a hundred years of age, of one of those malignant diseases [literally *small-pox*] which desolated the country.

LIII. *Topa-Curi-Amauta* II. reigned 39 years, and died when more than 80 years of age.

LIV. *Topa-Curi* III. reigned 40 years.

LV. *Huillca-Nota-Amauta* reigned 60 years, and died at more than 90 years of age.

This prince gained a memorable victory in HUILLCA-NOTA, over several foreign hordes from TUCUMAN, who had invaded the country.

LVI. *Topa-Yupanqui* reigned 43 years, and died at 90 years of age.

LVII. *Illac-Topa-Capac* reigned four years,

LVIII. *Titu-Raymi-Cozque* reigned 31 years.

LIX. *Huqui-Ninaqui* reigned 43 years.

LX. *Manco-Capac* III. reigned 23 years.

According to the *Amautas*, this prince reigned in the year 2950 after the deluge, and consequently at the time of the birth of Jesus Christ, an epoch when PERU had reached her highest elevation and extension.

LXI. *Cayo-Manco-Capac* II. reigned 20 years.

LXII. *Sinchi-Ayar-Manco* reigned 7 years.

LXIII. *Huamantaco-Amauta* reigned 5 years. During his reign they experienced earthquakes that lasted several months.

LXIV. *Titu-Yupanqui-Pachacuti* V.

In his reign was completed the third millenary cycle since the deluge.

There were several irruptions of foreign hordes, coming from Brazil and the Andes, which desolated the country. The INCA fortified himself in the mountains of PUCARA, and fought a bloody battle with the invading enemies, in which, after a frightful carnage, the Peruvian monarch fell by an arrow; and the air, corrupted by the miasma of the putrified corpses which remained unburied on the field of battle, generated a frightful plague, which almost depopulated PERU.

LXV. *Titu.*

Many ambitious ones, taking advantage of the youth of the new king, denied him obedience, drew away from him the masses, and usurped several provinces. Those who remained faithful to the heir of TITU-YUPANQUI, conducted him to Tambotoco, whose inhabitants offered him obedience. From this it happened that this monarch took the title of king of Tambotoco; since, like the Roman Empire in the time of Galienus, Peru counted many simultaneous tyrants. All was found in great confusion, life and personal safety were endangered, and civil disturbances caused the entire loss of the use of letters.

LXVI. *Cozque-Huaman-Titu* reigned 20 years.

LXVII. *Cayo-Manco* III. reigned 50 years.

LXVIII. *Huica-Titu* reigned 30 years.

LXIX. *Sivi-Topa* reigned 40 years.

LXX. *Topa-Yupanqui* reigned 25 years.

LXXI. *Huayna-Topa* reigned 37 years.

This monarch wished to rebuild the city of CUZCO, but by the advice of the priests, he abandoned the undertaking.

LXXII. *Huancauri* reigned 10 years.

LXXIII. *Huillca-Huaman* reigned 60 years.

LXXIV. *Huaman-Capac.*

LXXV. *Auqui-Atahuilque* reigned 35 years.

LXXVI. *Manco-Titu-Capra* reigned 27 years.

LXXVII. *Huayna-Topa* reigned 50 years.

LXXVIII. *Topa-Cauri-Pachacuti* VI.

The ninth year of his reign corresponds with the year 3500 after the deluge.

This prince began by conquering some provinces, but did not continue the enterprise, finding the inhabitants very vicious. He prohibited them, under the severest penalties, from making use of the *quellca*, (a species of parchment of plantain leaves,) to write upon, and also prohibited the invention of letters; but introduced the use of the quippos, and founded, in PACARITAMBO, a military school for knights.

LXXIX. *Arantial-Cassi* lived 70 years.

This prince commanded that in the tomb of his father should be interred his legitimate wife and favorite concubines. He also ordered the corpse of his father to be embalmed, when freed from the intestines, which by order of the monarch were preserved in golden vases.

LXXX. *Huari-Titu-Capac* lived 80 years.

LXXXI. *Huapa-Titu-Auqui* died at 70 years of age.

LXXXII. *Tocosque* lived 80 years.

During the reign of this prince the country was invaded by savage hordes, coming some from Panama, some from the Andes, and some from the Port of Good Hope. These nations were cannibals, sodomites, lived like brutes, and were found wallowing in the greatest state of degradation.

LXXXIII. *Ayar-Manco* reigned 22 years.

LXXXIV. *Condorocca.*

LXXXV. *Ayar-Manco* II. died at 24 years of age.

LXXXVI. *Amaru.*

LXXXVII. *Chinchirocca* reigned 41 years, and lived 70. At this period they began to make golden idols.

LXXXVIII. *Illa-Rocca* reigned 75 years.

LXXXIX. *Rocca-Titu* reigned 25 years.

XC. *Inti-Capac-Maita-Pachacuti* VII.

During the reign of this prince was completed the fourth millenary cycle since the deluge. Customs were so corrupted, vices so abominable, the links of society so decayed, so little were the law and the royal power respected, that the country bid fair to be destroyed little by little. In this condition a princess of royal blood, named *Mama-Ciboca*, contrived, by artifice and intrigue, to raise to the throne her son, called *Rocca*, a youth of 20 years, and so handsome and valiant that his admirers called him *Inca*, which means lord, as the Arabs gave the title of Cid, which signifies the same in their language, to the bold and handsome Rodrigo de Vivar. This title of Inca was finally adopted by the successors to the throne of Peru.

XCI. *Inca-Rocca* reigned 40 years, and died at 60 years of age.

Young *Rocca* came from the ridge of Chingana, near Cuzco, and presented himself to the Indians as a true son of the sun, endeavoring to persuade them of his heavenly origin, in which enterprise his astute mother, *Mama-Ciboca*, was of great use to him. The young prince endeavored to reform the manners, ordered sodomy to be punished with fire, and in order to give his vassals an example of conjugal virtues, he contracted nuptials with his sister, *Mama-Cora*, an example which his people so rapidly followed, that on the day after his marriage, more than 6000 persons were married.

He then declared war with the neighboring princes, who refused him obedience, and would not acknowledge him a child of the sun; conquered the King of Huancarama, of Andahuylas, subjugated the King of the Huillcas, and returned triumphant to Cuzco. He commanded them to consider the sun as the principal God, and promulgated many laws relative to religion and the military state.

XCII. *Inca-Hualloque-Yupanqui.*

He married his sister, *Mama-Chahua.*

From his brother MANCO-CAPAC, comes the family of the *Raucas-Panacas.*

XCIII. *Inca-May-Tacapaca.*

He contracted a marriage with his sister, *Mama-Tanca-Riachu.* His younger brother, *Aputaca,* was a branch of the family of the *Illochibainin,* and his second son, *Putano-Uman,* of the family of the *Uscamaytas.*

XCIV. *Inca-Capac-Yupanqui.*

He married his sister, *Mama-Corilpa-Ychaca,* and had four sons—*Sinchi-Rocca-Inca, Apoc-Colla-Unapiri, Apu-Chancay,* and *Chima-Chavin,* from whom descended the *Apu-Maytas* of Cuzco.

His brother, *Putano-Uman,* formed a conspiracy against him, but the Inca, forewarned of it, caused the traitor to be interred alive, and threw the other conspirators into a ditch filled with serpents, tigers, and lions.

XCV. *Inca-Sinchi-Rocca* lived 90 years.

He took for a wife his sister, *Mama-Micay.* He conquered, in a bloody battle, one league from *Andahuylas,* the king of the Canchas, and made a triumphal entry into Cuzco, with a splendor never before seen.

He had four sons—*Mayta-Yupanqui, Mayta-Capac, Huaman-Tacsi,* and *Huiraquira,* a branch of the *Huiraquiras.*

XCVI. *Inca-Yahuar-Huaccac* or *Mayta-Tupanqui.*

The fruits of his marriage with his sister, *Mama-Cochaquiela*, were six sons—*Huiracocha*, *Paucariali*, *Pahuac-Huallpamayta*, *Marcayutu*, *Yupa-Paucar*, and *Cincar-Rocca*, from whom descended the *Aucay-Lipaunacas*, and who was a conqueror of the Chancas.

This Inca suffered all his life from an affection of the eyes, which were always inflamed, and for this reason, his subjects said he wept blood, and called him *Yahuar-Huaccac.*

XCVII. *Inca-Topa-Yupanqui*, called *Huiracocha*, on account of his extraordinary actions; he lived 75 years, and reigned 45.

He married his sister, *Mama-Runtucay*, and made a campaign to Chili, where he installed, as governors, two of his nephews, and caused to be constructed a royal road from *Chirihuanas*, to the pass, crossing the whole country of Chili. He then passed to the north, conquered the Canar Indians, those of Quito, the Atarunos, Sichos and Lampatos, and still beyond these, the Chonos, inhabitants of the province of Guayaquil, and the Princes of the Isle of Puna, also the Chimus, on his return to Cuzco. He repaired the temple of *Pachacamac*, and during his reign were experienced great earthquakes and two irruptions of the volcanoes of Quito, one in front of Paucallo, and another in front of the mountains of Oyumbicho.

XCVIII. *Inca-Topa-Yupanqui* II. reigned 20 years, and died at 50 years of age.

He married his sister, *Caya-Mama-Ocho*, and reduced to obedience the Chimus, who had rebelled anew, forbidding the use of necessary water for the irrigation of their fields.

XCIX. *Inca-Inticusi-Huallpa*, called also *Huaynacapac*, on account of his beauty and prudence.

After having contracted a matrimonial alliance with his sister, *Coya-Rahua-Ozollo*, he marched to the province of

Chachapoyas, sent troops by the river Moyobamba, and almost entirely annihilated the nation of the Palcas. He soon afterward reduced to obedience the Indians of the river Quispe, commanded by a woman called Quilago. Finally, after a troublesome battle, he completely routed the Prince of Coyamba, on the banks of the Lake of *Yahuarcocha.*

C. *Inca-Inticusi-Huallpa-Huascar.*

Montesinos assures us that the name of *Huascar* was given to this Inca by his foster mother, and declares to be apocryphal the story of Garcilasso and other historians, touching the chain of gold which was made in honor of his birth.

CI. *Inca-Huaypar-Titu-Yupanqui-Atahuallpa.*

Montesinos deduces the surname of this prince from the words: *atahu,* virtue, strength, and *allpa,* good, gentle. (!)

From this exposition, we see that the work of Montesinos cannot stand analysis. It will be at once noticed that the foundation on which the author erects his history, *i. e.* the identity of Peru with the country of Ophir, and the continued communication of Armenia with the New World, is a gratuitous hypothesis, and simply an exposition of the historical investigations of the Spanish authors who occupied themselves, in the sixteenth and seventeenth centuries, with the subject of the discovery of America. But further, the memorials of Montesinos present so many contradictions, so many chronological errors, and such manifest incorrectness, that it is only with the utmost precaution and much distrust that such documents can be made use of at all. In spite of his erudition, and the large amount of knowledge which his earnest search could gather during his long residence in Peru, his history does not present a character worthy of credit, and the succession of Peruvian monarchs seems very arbitrary. Doubtless, in the later periods of Peruvian history, the relations of Montesinos present a degree of authenticity superior to that of Garcilasso de la Vega; and in spite of his errors and defects, these memorials form an important element in the historic literature of Peru.

It now remains for us but to mention a third work upon Peruvian antiquity, and it is the History of the Conquest of Peru, by the celebrated American writer, W. H. Prescott, who, possessing the incomparable advantage of having at his command more materials than any other historian, and making use of them with the sound judgment and exquisite elegance which characterize him, gives us, with unequalled skill, perfect system, and brilliant coloring, an animated account of the state of Peru before the conquest, of the degree of civilization to which the nation had attained under the dynasty of the Incas, and of the form of government of these monarchs. We feel it beyond measure as a great privation, that many ancient manuscripts, which throw a brilliant light upon the obscure centuries of Peruvian antiquity, should be known to us only through the quotations of Prescott, and we do not doubt, that for archæologists and antiquarians, the relations of Sarmiento, Ondegardo, Betanzos, would possess inexpressible interest, as would, also, the anonymous memorials upon the discovery and the conquest, and the documents upon the inscriptions, medals, antiquities, &c.

In the first chapter of our work, we have fully expressed our opinion concerning the great Peruvian reformer, known under the traditional name of *Manco-Capac.* It is not to be questioned that there existed in Peru, previous to his arrival, a certain degree of culture, but the problem remains to be solved (though it may be perhaps forever impossible), what was the origin of this culture? Was it a successive, progressive manifestation of the mind of the aboriginal nations, or rather transplanted from another soil? It is certain that this culture failed, and decayed rapidly before the new reforming era had begun. The acute skill, and exact knowledge of the soil in which he was going to construct his new edifice, induced the reformer to take for a foundation the previous decayed cultivation; and it is owing to this that we meet, especially in the religious worship, with heterogeneous elements, unconnected among themselves, although mixed, which attest without doubt the attentive and profound observer; which show the wisdom with which he knew how to unite them so ingeniously; while the progress which the organization of the monarchy produced, and its free advancement, argue the simplicity and perspicacity with which those political and religious laws were established.

The general opinion is that the Incas descend directly from Manco-Capac. All the traditions relate that this person was distinguished from the natives by his physiognomy and the clear color of his complexion; and although the majority of historians attribute to all the Incas these personal qualities, nothing certain do we know on this head; yet do we see that some modern travellers pretend that the descendants of the royal family were distinguished from the other Indians by their physical aspect. Our minute and recent investigations go to prove that the Incas do not derive their origin from the legislator above named (be his name Manco-Capac or any other) by a succession of blood, but from a native family established in the royal dignity by the stranger reformer. According to this hypothesis, Inca-Rocca was the first Indian autocrat and stock of the *Ayllo* of the Peruvian monarchs. We well know that on this point probably we never shall reach undoubted truth; but this opinion is the result of such a critical study of the history as does not lend a blind faith to tradition, but endeavors to penetrate into the connection of motives and historical effects.

The traditions of the Indians and the opinions of the historians relative to the origin of the Incas and their arrival at Peru, differ much among themselves; some of them there are which, by their simplicity and verisimilitude, cannot fail to satisfy, while there are others which by their silliness, arbitrary assertions, and historical improbability, do not deserve the slightest credit, and shock at first sight. Such as, for instance, the one which makes an English sailor the legislator of Peru. I deem it best to relate the origin of this opinion, in order to prove how much a want of sense or desire of originality may lead one astray. An English sailor, eight centuries ago, was shipwrecked on the coast of Peru, (so runs the story.) A prince, who chanced to be on the banks of the sea, asked him who he was, and the sailor answered in his own tongue, "*Englishman*," a word which, in his *quichua* pronunciation, the prince repeated *Ingasman*; and, the Englishman being very fine looking, the prince, in speaking of him to his companions, added *Ingasman-Capac*, (the handsome Englishman;) and thus the stranger retained the name of *Ingasman-Capac*, which in time grew into *Inga-Manco-Capac*. This apocryphal and ridiculous story suffices to show the poverty and nullity of the historical account pretended to be founded on it. According to some authors, it took place before the restoration of the government of the Incas, and was a work of the English;* since that work, a certain Don Antonio Berreo affirms† that among other prophecies

* *Walter Raleigh*, in the description of his voyage to *Guiana*, (fol. 97, page 8, of the America of Theodore Bry.) See also the prologue to the second edition of the Commentaries of Garcilasso de la Vega, written by Don Gabriel de Cardenas, 1723.

† Deum ego testor, mihi a Don Antonio de Berreo affirmatum, quemadmodum etiam ab aliis cognovi, quod in præcipuo ipsorum templo inter alia vaticinia, quæ de amissione regni loquuntur, hoc enim sit, quod dicitur fore ut Ingæ sive Imperatores et reges Peruviæ ab aliquo populo,

preserved in the principal temple of Cuzco, relative to the destruction of the empire, was one affirming that the Incas would be re-established in their empire by certain people who should come from a country called Inclaterra.

It is superfluous to add that such a prophecy never existed, and that all this relation is a clumsily forged imposture.

The most eminent period of the dynasty of the Incas is the reign of Huayna-Capac, who died seven years before the arrival of the Spaniards, after having governed half a century. The warlike and civil works of so noted a sovereign deserve to be recorded by an eloquent pen, and his biography, compiled with the necessary circumspection, would throw more light upon the ancient Peruvian history than all the memorials, relations and commentaries which embrace so many indigestible folios, filled with contradictions, errors and fables. Under the dominion of Huayna-Capac, the empire attained to its greatest height and prosperity, and extended from the river Andasmayo, at the north of Quito, to the river Maule, in Chili, *i. e.* embracing a distance of more than forty geographical degrees, or eight hundred leagues, (which surpassed by some degrees the greatest extent of Europe,) and, bounded in all its western extent by the Pacific Ocean, extended to the pampas of Tucuman, on the southeast, and to the rivers Ucayali and Marañon on the northeast. This vast empire contained of itself ten or eleven millions of inhabitants, a number which rapidly diminished after the conquest, as, in the year 1580, the general census, made by order of Philip II., by the Archbishop Loaiza, does not show more than 8,280,000 souls.*

qui ex regione quadam, quæ Inclaterra vocetur, regnum suum rursus introducantur.

* The computation of Father Cisneros, in 1579, amounted to 1,500,000 inhabitants, but only of individual tributaries; and Humboldt was doubtful in taking this number for the sum total of the inhabitants of Peru.

Nevertheless, the population diminished in the course of time to less than one half, and in the main we may admit that the valleys of the Peruvian coast contain positively but the tenth part, or even less, of what they contained in the time of the Incas. The valley of Santa, for instance, held 700,000 souls, and at the present day, the number of its inhabitants does not amount to 1200. According to Father Melendez, were found, shortly after the conquest, in the parish of Aucallama, of the province of Chancay, 30,000 individuals paying tribute or taxes—that is, men of more than eighteen or twenty years—and at present they number only 425 inhabitants, and among them 320 slaves.

We will conclude these considerations with a wish that the *ancient* history of Peru may find a historian as eminent as the history of its conquest has found in Mr. Prescott. Would that a patriotic government would aid in such an important enterprise!

NOTE.

It is a fact as gratifying as it is singular, that a work, one of the authors of which is of Spanish descent, and, as we believe, a native of Peru, should yield to our distinguished countryman, Mr. Prescott, the honor, not merely of possessing the best materials for illustrating truly the history of Peru, but the still greater honor of having so used them as justly to take precedence of all other writers on the conquest of that interesting country.

Indeed, concerning the original authorities from which the historian of Peru must take his facts, the previous chapter furnishes very scanty information; while on this head, as on every other he has touched, Mr. Prescott's work leaves nothing to be desired, and very little to be added.

As the subject of the chapter, however, is the ancient history of Peru, perhaps the best service we can render is to direct the attention of the reader to such productions, commented on by Mr. Prescott, as may enable him, if so disposed, to resort to more abundant and better materials than those suggested by our authors.

Garcilasso de la Vega. An admirably just and discriminating notice of this writer will be found in Mr. Prescott's Conquest of Peru, vol. I., p. 293. Our authors have objected to Garcilasso that he did not know how to decipher the Quippus; Mr. Prescott states expressly that he did (p. 295).

Fernando Montesinos. Our readers will probably have seen enough of this writer, in the text, to satisfy them that his account of the *early* history of Peru is of very little or no value. He had, however, opportunities of knowing something of its later history, and on that subject may sometimes be advantageously consulted. Mr. Prescott has furnished an account of him and his writings on p. 78 of the first volume of his work on Peru. *Ternaux Compans* has translated the "Memorias Antiguas."

Pedro Pizarro. He was related to Francisco Pizarro, the conqueror, and went to Peru, about 1529, at the age of fifteen, in the suite of his kinsman. He wrote "*Relaciones del Descubrimiento y Conquista de los Reynos del Peru*," of which Mr. Prescott had a manuscript copy, furnished by Navarrete, who subsequently published it in his collection. For an account of the author and his work, see Prescott's Peru, Vol. I., p. 76.

Pedro Cieza de Leon. He wrote "*Cronica del Peru*," having come to America at the age of thirteen. This is a valuable book—though part, only, of an unfinished work—for the history of which the reader may turn to Mr. Prescott's first volume, p. 327.

Gonzalo Fernandez Oviedo. He wrote "*Natural e General Historia de las Indias*," which Mr. Prescott has in manuscript. It has not been published entire. Ramusio (as Mr. Prescott states) has published a part, and so also has Barcia. See Prescott's "Conquest of Mexico," Vol. II., p. 293, and "Conquest of Peru," Vol. II., p. 326.

Augustin de Zarate. His history of Peru was published first at Antwerp, in 1555, and afterward at Seville, in 1577. An English translation by Nicholas, was published in London, in 1581. It was reprinted from the Spanish by Barcia, in his collection, Vol. III. For an account of the author, and the value of his work, see Prescott's Peru, Vol. II., p. 471.

Diego Fernandez de Palentino. He was a private soldier in Peru, but appears to have possessed an education above his station. See Prescott's Peru, Vol. II., p. 473.

Juan de Sarmiento. His work, which exists in manuscript only, is possessed by Mr. Prescott. It is entitled "*Relacion de la sucesion y govierno de las Yngas Señores naturales que fueron de las Provincias del Peru, y otras cosas tocantes á aquel Reyno.*" It is particularly valuable, Mr. Prescott states, on the institutions of the Peruvians. Prescott's Peru, Vol. I. p. 175.

Polo de Ondegardo. The work of this author, who was a jurist, like the last named, exists in manuscript only. Mr. Prescott gives it a high character. See "Peru," Vol. I., p. 177.

Antonio de Herrera. He wrote "*Historia General de las Indias Occidentales*," and drew largely, Mr. Prescott says, from the manuscript work of Ondegardo, mentioned above, as he did also from the "History of the Indies," by Las Casas, bishop of Chiapa. For a full account of Herrera and his writings, see Prescott's Mexico, Vol. II., p. 94.

Francisco Lopez de Gomara. His works are, "*Historia General de las Indias*," and "*Cronica de la Nueva España.*" Barcia has incorporated both into his collection, of which they form the second volume. The "*Cronica*" was also translated into *Aztec*, of which a copy exists in Mexico, under the title of the "Chronicle of Chimalpain." See Prescott's Mexico, Vol. II., p. 175.

To these we take the liberty of adding—

Juan Melendez. "*Tesoros Verdaderos de las Yndias del Peru.*" Printed in Rome, 1681–2. Three vols., folio.

Buenaventura de Salinas. "*Memorial de las Historias del Nuevo Mundo Piru.*" Lima, 1630. Quarto.

Francisco de Xerez. "*Verdadera Relacion de la Conguista del Peru.*" Printed in Barcia's third volume

CHAPTER IV.

THE SYSTEM OF GOVERNMENT AND POLITICAL INSTITUTIONS OF THE INCAS.

It is not our object to explain circumstantially all that belongs to the government and administration of the ancient Peruvian territory; but to give greater clearness to the chapters which are to succeed, we cannot do less than offer to our readers a brief sketch of the political organization of the empire of the Incas.

The authority of the Peruvian monarchs exceeded, as we have already hinted in our preceding chapter, that of the most powerful kings of the earth. Their will was the supreme law—no council of state, no ministry or institution whatsoever, could limit the power of the sovereign; and if some among them were accustomed to consult the wise ancients, it was only through deference, or for their own private good, and not by any organic law of the dynasty. The Inca was the master of the life and estates of his vassals, and was considered, throughout his vast empire, as the supreme arbiter of all creatures breathing the air or living in the waters. "The very birds will suspend their flight, if I command it," said Atahuallpa to the Spaniards, in his hyperbolical language.

Moreover, the monarchs of Peru, considered as children of the Sun, and descendants, in a direct line, from Manco-

CAPAC, were the high priests and oracles in religious matters. Thus uniting the legislative and executive power, the supreme command in war, absolute sovereignty in peace, and a venerated high-priesthood in religious feasts, they exercised the highest power ever known to man—realized in their persons the famous union of the Pope and the Emperor, and more reasonably than Louis XIV., might have exclaimed: "*I am the State!*"

We may characterize the form of government as a theocratical autocracy. Clothed with dignity so complex and so elevated, we cannot consider singular the blind obedience which was rendered to the sovereign by his subjects, and the profound humility with which they approached his person. Add to this that the celestial descent of the Inca caused him not only to be obeyed as absolute monarch and a venerable high priest, but also to be respected as a deity; his person was holy, his corpse was guarded sacredly, and his memory religiously respected.

This innate veneration was increased by severe laws: thus, the first magnates of the empire did not dare to appear shod in the presence of the Inca; the chief lords came to the audiences with a light bundle, in token of submission, and the masses were obliged to pull off their shoes and stockings, and uncover their heads, when they approached the street in which the royal palace stood. The other members of the royal family participated in the universal respect, but in a smaller degree than the monarch and his august spouse, who was, excepting her royal consort, the most respected person in the kingdom.

Notwithstanding all this, if we believe Garcilasso de la Vega, the government of the Incas was paternal, and all the members of the dynasty, without exception, were filled with tender solicitude for their subjects, with whom they were accustomed to mix, in spite of their hierarchy, inquiring into the condition of the inferior classes, seeing that they should want for nothing, and that, in as far as it was possible, all the members of their vast empire should enjoy contentment and abundance. They also condescended to preside at certain religious festivities, and on these occasions offered banquets to the nobility, in which, according to the usage of European nations, they pledged the health of those persons for whom they felt the greatest affection; a custom truly extraordinary, and which we are surprised to meet with among the American Indians. Moreover, they were accustomed to travel through their dominions to acquaint themselves with the complaints of their subjects, or to regulate matters which the lower tribunals had submitted to their decision. From all parts, the multitude hastened to contemplate their monarch, and when he raised the curtains of the litter or palanquin in which he travelled, to allow them to see him, the vociferations with which the multitude congratulated him, and besought Heaven's favor in his behalf, were so great, that we are told the motion of the air caused those birds which were flying over to fall to the ground*—a prodigious effect, which, with equal claim to probability, Plutarch assures us took place in Greece when the Roman herald proclaimed the liberty of the Greeks. Those places in which tho monarch condescended to stop were religiously respected, and to them the simple inhabitants devoutly resorted in pilgrimage, and treated them with the same respect that the monks of the Holy Sepulchre show to the spots consecrated by the presence of the Saviour.

Although, like the Oriental monarchs, the Inca possessed an unlimited number of concubines, he had but one legiti-

* Sarmiento, MS. Relation, Chap. X. (vide Prescott, 1st C., p.16, note.)

mate spouse or wife, called *Coya*, and chosen from among his sisters. This incest, however repugnant it may seem to our ideas of morality, was the natural consequence of the conceit in which the Peruvians held their monarch; who, supposed to be supernatural and a child of the Sun, might not be mixed up with any of the clay of which mere mortals were composed; besides, such incest, for reasons probably analogous, was the law or custom of various Oriental dynasties. Such were the Lagidas, in Egypt. This concentration of the blood of a single family, and the absence of all foreign element, must necessarily have impressed a distinction of physiognomy, a seal, typical of the royal family, and thus augmented, by its exceptional character, the idolatrous veneration of the vassals.

All the male children* took the name *Inca* when married, and of *Auqui*, when single. To designate the reigning monarch, without giving him his name, they made use of the title *Capac-Inca* (sole king). The queen was known by the name of *Coya*. The females of royal blood bore the denomination of *Pallas*, when married, and *Ñustas* when single. The name of *Mamacunas*, or *Shipa-Coyas*, was reserved for the concubines who were not of royal blood. The throne belonged to the eldest son of the *Coya* or legitimate queen; and the sceptre, according to Garcilasso, thus passed, without interruption, from fathers to sons, during the whole period in which the imperial dynasty flourished.

The court of the sovereign was composed of several persons, of a rank more or less elevated. Immediately after

* GARCILASSO says, in his Commentaries, Part I., Chap. XXXI., Book I., in the most explicit manner, that to the *female* descendants did not pertain the name of Inca; this title, therefore, was usurped by him for himself, as he was the son of a "*palla.*"

the monarchs came the royal children, the principal magnates, and the most distinguished noblemen. Afterward came the officers of the royal household, who were members of the nobility of the kingdom; these were followed by the *curacas* or governors of the conquered provinces. Besides this, there were *astrologers*, *amautas*, or learned men, poets, superior officers, adjutants, a guard of honor, servants of various classes, and moreover numerous *chasquis*, or postboys, always ready to start when ordered by the sovereign, be it on business for the State or private matters—for instance, when he wished to eat fish fresh from the sea, two hundred leagues off.* Add to this the harem of the monarch, which, during the most brilliant epoch of the kingdom, contained seven hundred women, each one of which had several servants. Garcilasso assures us that some of the Incas left more than three hundred direct descendants. Thus it is not strange that the court of Capac-Inca contained more than eight thousand persons.

As in European countries, the Peruvian aristocracy derived its origin from its personal valor and its relationship to the sovereign. It contained or consisted of five orders.

I. That of the Incas of royal blood, who came from the same stock as the sovereign. This order, the most important of all, was divided into several classes, each one of which boasted of springing from an individual of royal blood, although all terminated in the divine founder of the empire.

* Until now, but little notice has been taken of the ancient custom of the *chasqui* or postboy's receiving from his prince or curate, or alcalde, a certain number of stripes before starting—a punishment which they themselves solicited to prevent them from being delayed on the road by pleasure, or from stopping in resting-places.

II. That of the Incas by favor, *i. e.* the descendants of the principal vassals of the first Inca, to whom was conceded as a gift, or by respect, the privilege of using this title.

III. That of noblemen sprung from families distinguished for the riches, valor, science, or some other merit of their ancestors' known members.

IV. That of persons endowed with the highest dignities.

V. That of the priesthood.

The noblemen of royal blood were educated by the *amautas* and prepared for the *huaracu*, a ceremony similar to the order of knighthood of the middle ages. At the age of sixteen years, they were examined in *Cuzco*, in a house in the suburbs, called *Collcampata*—ancient and skilful Incas presiding at the examination. The candidates were obliged to be well versed in the athletic games of war, in wrestling, and other exercises which tested their strength and agility. They also fought in mock tournaments, in which, although the weapons were without edge, the contest always resulted in wounds, and sometimes in death. They were also compelled to fast many days, to go barefooted, to sleep on the ground, dress poorly, and submit to other privations, as much for the purpose of accustoming themselves to the fatigues of war, as to make them comprehend and compassionate the misery of the necessitous. The novitiates were afterward presented to the reigning Inca, who pierced the ends of their ears with pins of gold, which they wore until the aperture was sufficiently large to hold enormous pendants, peculiar to their order, which consisted of wheels of gold or silver, so massive and heavy that they prodigiously enlarged the ears, deforming the size of the cartilage; but this, among the natives, was considered a mark of beauty and distinction. The Spaniards, shocked at this deformity, gave the name of *Orejones* [great ears] to those lords who held the first offices of the State, civil or military.*

The name *Peru* was not known to the natives, and according to Garcilasso, signifies *river*, a word which, pronounced by one of the natives, in answer to a question put by the Spaniards, gave birth to an error, causing this name to be imputed to the vast empire of the Incas, the adventurous troops of Pizarro believing that thus the inhabitants called the country. Montesinos, who endeavors to persuade us that Peru is the ancient *Ophir* from which Solomon extracted so many treasures, says that this name, Peru, is a corruption of the word Ophir. Be that as it may, it is certain that the name by which the subjects of the Incas characterized all the States depending upon the sovereign was that of *Tahuantisuyu*, which signifies *the four quarters of the globe.* The whole country was divided into four provinces of equal dimensions; that of the south was called *Collasuyu*, that of the north, *Chinchasuyu*, that of the east, *Antisuyu*, and that of the west, *Cuntisuyu.* A corresponding road led to each one of these provinces. These roads started from Cuzco, the capital or centre of the Peruvian monarchy. At the head of each province was a viceroy, or governor, who ruled with the aid of one or more counsellors. Each province was divided into more or less departments, not according to their territorial extent or size, but according to the number of inhabitants. And for the better administration and easier inspection of it, the Incas invented a simple system of subdivision. According to this system, the population of the country was divided into groups of ten, each under the command of a decurion: ten decurions obeyed one centurion:

* Garcilssao de la Vega, Com., Part I., Book VI., Chap. XXIV.—XXVIII.

ten centurions, or one thousand inhabitants, had for chief a principal magistrate, and one hundred centurions, or ten thousand men, formed a department under a governor. The decurion's office was to watch over the necessities of those who were under his command, to keep the governor informed of them, and to make known the petty transgressions of his decuriates to the principal chief, who had charge of the punishment. The greater the transgression, the greater the punishment, and the higher in office was the judge upon whom the pronouncing of the sentence devolved. The chief of any section, large or small, who did not rigorously fulfil the duties of his office, suffered a severe penalty, and was deprived of his employment. In order to be certain that each one of these chiefs complied with his obligations, the Inca was in the habit of sending inspectors throughout the kingdom. The transgressors were punished almost immediately after the accusation of them, by the decurion; each cause was to be tried, within five days at the very latest, after having been carried before the judge, and the sentence once pronounced, there was no appeal from it. Each judge, from the decurion to the governor, was obliged to give, every month, to his superior in office, a circumstantial account of all that had taken place in his section, and the Inca received from the viceroys an extract of the most important. Thus the monarch, seated in the centre of his dominions, could overlook his most remote provinces, and revise and rectify whatever evils arose in the administration of justice. This system occupied a million persons, and was immensely defective, be its advantages what they may.

This administrative organization was, to a certain extent, somewhat similar to the ideas of certain European publicists of the past and present centuries, known under the name of socialists; but there is another branch which almost entirely realizes some social ideas of the day, and which to some extent sacrifices liberty, the idol of our fathers, and immolates it to a certain fraternal equality, and to the full and certain satisfaction of mere material wants. The proud, harsh selfishness, origin of so many evils, and of the universal misery which disquiets and prostrates the greater part of the human race, can alone justify these monkish systems, which operate upon men just as arithmetic does upon homogeneous quantities, and robs them of liberty, that is, of their individuality and the expansion of their being.

Only under an autocratical government, in which the chief of the State was at the same time an absolute monarch and a venerated pope, and only under a population essentially peaceable and agricultural, was it possible for this socialism to exist.

All that part of the land which was capable of being cultivated was divided into three parts—one belonged to the sun, another to the Inca, and the third to the people. Each Peruvian received a *topu* of land, which was sufficient to produce the necessary corn for the maintenance of a married man, without children; if he had children, he received for each male child one more *topu*, and for each daughter half a *topu*. Upon his marriage the son received from his father the *topu* allotted to him from his birth.

In cultivating the earth, they always followed a fixed rule; first were cultivated the lands pertaining to the protecting divinity. Afterward they attended to the lands of the aged, the sick, the widowed and the orphans, as also to those of the soldiers who were engaged in active service, whose wives were looked upon as widows. Those who were in need of grain or seed to sow, were provided by the decurion from the royal depository. After this, the people cultivated their own lands, each one for himself, but under an obligation to aid his neighbor, when the charge of a numerous family, or any other similar circumstance, required it—a fraternal custom which even at this day is practised by the Peruvian Indians. Next in order were cultivated the lands of the curacas, and finally those of the Inca, by the whole nation, with much ceremony and the greatest rejoicing, singing popular hymns resembling the Spanish romances, in which were celebrated the exploits and noble deeds of the imperial dynasty. These songs at the same time made the work most agreeable, as much by the moral excitement which they produced, as by accommodating the labor to the rhyme, even as soldiers accommodate their pace to the accompanying sound of the drum. The beginning of a song was generally the word *hailli*, which signifies triumph. *Garcilasso* assures us that many of these songs were sung by the Spaniards, who were very fond of them.

The Peruvians improved the land with manure, principally with human excrement, which they collected and dried, using it in a pulverized state, after having sowed the seed. In certain provinces they used the dung of llamas, alpacas, huanacos, and vicunas; in maritime provinces, they fertilized the earth with the remains of dried fish, and with the *huanu*, [*i. e.* guano] or dung of birds. The circumspection of the monarchs extended even to this point: "Each island," says Garcilasso, "was marked as appropriated to such or such a province; and if the island were large, it supplied two or three provinces. They placed landmarks, so that those of one province might not encroach upon the districts of the other; and dividing it particularly, they gave to each one his limits, and to each neighbor also his limits, measuring out the quantity of manure that was necessary; and under pain of death, the citizen of one place could not take the manure without his own boundary, for it was considered a theft—nor from their own boundary could they extract more than the quantity which was appraised to it, which was a sufficiency for their lands, and a wrong in this respect was punished by disgrace."

The distribution of the nation, such as we have described it, possessed very many advantages: it facilitated the administration of the whole country, knit together all the relations of the State, gave to it an unity which might be viewed at a glance, and secured an exact account of the increase or diminution of the population. By the equal distribution of the land, the Incas avoided pauperism, a terrible evil which devours the European States. Idlers could not live in the empire of Peru, since each individual possessed his necessary occupation; as little were there any needy; and the equal distribution of wealth brought profit to the industrious and skilful only.

By the above-mentioned system the mode of raising taxes was very much facilitated. From twenty-five until fifty years of age, each Indian was taxed. But all the individuals of royal blood were exempt, all the chiefs and judges, down to the centurion, the curacas with their parentage, all those filling minor offices, whilst they retained the position, the soldiers in active service, the priests and ministers of the temple of the sun, and finally all the invalids, all the lame, and really infirm.

The tax consisted simply of personal labor; each one of the taxed was compelled to work the days or weeks consecrated to the Sun or to the Inca—each one according to his calling: the husbandman ploughed the lands of the monarch, the weaver spun the cloth and garments for the court and the depositories of the government, the silversmiths made vases and idols for the temples, the potters made vessels of clay for the use of the Inca, &c. But the materials were supplied by the State, which also undertook to support the workmen while the labor lasted. All the great works and gigantic enterprises for common use were executed by the taxed. On them it devolved to build the temples, the famous royal roads, the bridges, the aqueducts, to water the cornfields, to build the inns for travellers, the palaces for governors, the storehouses for the State. It was also their charge to preserve and repair these works, to assist travellers, to wait on them at the inns, perform the office of runners or post-boys, to tend the cattle which belonged to the Inca and the Sun. The immense flocks of sheep and alpacas were distributed in the *punas* throughout the kingdom, and the officers who superintended them kept, by a particular plan, an exact account of their number.

Each young Indian was obliged to follow the profession or office of his father, and the sons of the citizens were not permitted to learn the sciences, which were reserved peculiarly for the nobility, a measure, the object of which was to prevent the lower classes from becoming proud; this profession of the father only the curacas and centurions had power to change. Neither were they allowed to change their habitation; in order to do it, it was necessary to obtain the permission of the superior, who rarely conceded it. Doubtless the Incas were accustomed to move entire populations to other distant provinces, especially those recently conquered, for the better security of the dependence of the inhabitants by their mixture; always taking care to transfer them to countries of similar climate, and devoted to the same occupations.

The political laws were concise and wise. Father BLAS-VALERA, an authentic historian whose writings are approved by Garcilasso, quotes the following (Garc. Com. I., Book V., Chap. XI., fol. 109):

I. *The municipal law* treated of the particular duties which, in its jurisdiction, belonged to each nation or people.

II. *The agrarian law*, which treated of the distribution of the lands; the dependent was called CHACRACAMAYOC.

III. *The common law*, which designated the labors which the Indians were to perform in common; for instance, to level the roads under the direction of the *Hatunñancamayoc* (superintendent of the roads), to make bridges under the command of the *Chacacamayoc* (superintendent of bridges), to construct aqueducts and canals under the direction of the *Yacucamayoc*, or superintendent of the waters, etc.

IV. *The law of brotherhood*, which treated of mutual aid in the cultivation of lands and construction of houses.

V. *The law mitachanacuy*, which regulated the periods when work was done in the different provinces, and also, the different tribes, lineages and individuals.

VI. *The economical law*, which treated of the ordinary personal expenses, and prescribed simplicity of dress and food. At the same time, this law commanded that, two or three times each month, the neighbors of each town or nation should eat together in the presence of their chief officer, and should exercise themselves in military or popular games, with a view of reconciling quarrels, extirpating all enmities, and producing peace.

VII. *The law in favor of invalids*, which required that the lame, the deaf, the dumb, the blind, the crippled, the decrepit, and the infirm should be supported at the public expense. This law also commanded that, two or three times a month, these invalids should be invited to the festivals or public feasts, so that among the general rejoicing, they might forget in a measure their miserable condition. The *Oncocamayoc*, or superintendent of the sick, was the executor of this law.

VIII. *The law of hospitality*, which prescribed the means

of ministering to the necessities of strangers and travellers at the public expense, in the inns called *Corpahuasis*, under the superintendence of the *Corpahuasicamayoc*.

IX. *The housekeeping law*, which regulated individual labor, and provided even the children of five years of age with occupations proportioned to their strength and years, as also to the infirm according to their faculties. The same law commanded that the Indians should dine and sup with open doors, so that the administrators of justice might have free entrance to visit them. There were also certain officers called *Llactacamayoc*, or superintendents of the town, who visited very frequently the temples, the public edifices, and the private houses, and who kept a general oversight, to see that order, neatness, and convenience prevailed; punishing those persons who lived in dirt and laziness, by blows on the arms and feet, and publicly applauding those who were distinguished for their excellence and cleanliness.

It cannot be denied that such institutions were a powerful means to preserve the morality and social virtues of the nation, and that they were truly paternal, since they united the citizens in one single family, whose members mutually assisted and supported each other, and very justly might the *Count Carli* say, in his American letters (Vol. I., p 215), that the *moral* man in Peru was infinitely superior to the European.

The code of civil laws was simple, and the punishments severe. The maxims were concise—*i. e. ama quellanquichu*, avoid idleness; *ama llullanquichu*, avoid lying; *ama suacunquichu*, avoid stealing; *ama huachocchucanqui*, avoid committing adultery; *ama pictapas huañuchinquichu*, avoid murder.

Idleness was severely punished, and it was ignominious to suffer the penalty for this vice. The cheat was flagellated, and sometimes condemned to death. There were grave punishments for those who destroyed landmarks, as also for those who prevented the water from fertilizing the neighboring fields by turning it upon their own; or for those who injured the harvests. The idler, the homicide, the burner of a bridge, were condemned to death, and without possible remission of the sentence. But the principal punishments were reserved for those who sinned against religion, or against the sacred majesty of the Inca, or against that which pertained to his person. The seduction of a virgin of the sun, or adultery with one of the women of the Inca, was considered a crime so abominable, that the delinquent was buried or burnt alive, as were also his wife, his sons, his ancestors, servants, his neighbors of the town, and even his cattle. At the same time the law commanded that his houses should be demolished, his trees cut down, and the place changed into a desert, that not the slightest vestige of what might recall so horrible a crime should remain. Equally severe were the punishments awarded to those provinces which rebelled against the Inca; they were almost invariably invaded, given up to the soldiery, and all the males, not excepting the boys of tender years, were put to the sword.

It only remains to speak of the military system of the Incas. Each taxed Indian was obliged to serve a certain time in the royal armies, and, when freed from the service, he returned to his people, or nation, and took part in the military exercises which were held once or twice a month under the command of the centurions. The same organization which we have explained in the civil class, reigned in the military: ten men were governed by the *Chuncacamayoc* (decurion), fifty by the *Pichcachuncacamayoc*, one hundred by the *Pachcacamayoc* (centurion), and a thousand by the *Huarancamayoc*. Five thousand men were under the command of the *Hatun-apu* (chief captain), who also had a

Hatun-apup-rantin, or second captain, under him. One half of this number obeyed an *Apu* (captain), with his *Apup-rantin* (lieutenant). The *Apusquipay* was general of a whole army, and his lieutenant-general bore the name of *Apusquip-rantin*. Each division had its *Unanchacamayoc*, or ensign, its trumpeters (*Queppacamayoc*), and drummers (*Huancarcamayoc*), and the whole army bore the royal standard. The battalions were distinguished by their arms, of which we will speak hereafter.

We are not positively told how long the soldier was obliged to serve, and it seems to have depended upon circumstances. When the Inca employed arms against a resisting enemy, or in unhealthy provinces, he permitted the soldiers to return every three months, and even oftener, to their country, and assembled another army to take the place of the licensed. The Inca provided his soldiers with uniforms of coarse cloth (*Auasca*), shoes of woven flax, and arms: which formed part of the tax of the nation.

Very admirable were the precautions and solicitude of the Inca for the soldiers in a campaign. In the greater part of the kingdom, were found on the royal roads, at convenient distances, deposits of arms and uniforms, in such abundance, that each one of these deposits was sufficient to equip an army with everything that was necessary, and care was taken that the governors of the provinces or superintendents of royal warehouses (*Coptracamayoc*) should always keep these storehouses well provided.

In crossing a friendly country, the troops dared do no injury, and the slightest excess was punished with death. How different from our armies were the armies of that day!

The conquered provinces were treated by the Incas with the greatest consideration and indulgence, unless the obstinacy of the resistance obliged them to resort to severe measures. Their endeavors were directed primarily to the incorporating into their kingdom of the conquered territories, which, with some exceptions, obtained a better position than has been granted by any conqueror, ancient or modern, of the Eastern hemisphere. The conquerors imposed upon the conquered their religion, language, and system of government, and received a number of their subjects. But in spite of this, they knew how in a short time to gain the love and veneration of their new subjects.* Hardly had they conquered a city, when the Inca caused its principal idol to be carried to Cuzco; and ordained the adoration of the Supreme God, *Ticci Huiracocha*, imposing upon the priests as a duty that they should teach the conquered the worship of this deity. He also sent *Amautas* and masters of languages to the conquered country, that they might teach them the *Quichua* tongue, if the prevailing idiom were different; commanding under the severest penalties that each child should learn only the general language of the kingdom. The sovereign also was accustomed to cause the Prince to come to the capital with all his sons, whom he overpowered with kindness and presents conferred with the greatest generosity; and at the end of a certain time he restored the father to his ancient dignity, keeping his sons as hostages in the court, but giving them an excellent education, and loading them with gifts and proofs of benevolence. In order to gain popularity with the masses of the annexed country, the Inca diminished the first year the taxes, and treated with the greatest liberality the orphans, widows, and invalids: at the same time he sent officers to the new province, that they

* Thus the Incas treated the conquered nations, with a view to prevent their destruction—a wise and conciliatory policy, which should be adopted by more refined States, instead of employing means tending to destroy them.

might tax and enroll all the inhabitants, according to their age, lineage and offices, and he then distributed them according to the system adopted in the other provinces of the kingdom. The young Indians of the conquered fought under the royal banner, and those who remained in the country were the objects of strict and continued vigilance, in order to suppress in the bud every symptom of insurrection. And for the better security of these nations, the Incas sent colonies of six or ten thousand persons from the faithful provinces, who incorporated themselves with the conquered masses, while an equal number of these were added to that province from which the colonies were sent: but always taking care, as I have before mentioned, that these colonies should be sent to lands of similar climate and products. To these colonies, called *mitimas*, the monarch granted several privileges, by means of which he secured to himself the fidelity of the conquered province.

It is certain that history has no record of any government which, by such adequate means, was able to amalgamate so intimately such different nations, and form of them a whole so compact; and the system by which they established one of the most extensive empires recorded in human memory, is as praiseworthy as it is full of interest.

CHAPTER V.

THE QUICHUA LANGUAGE.

THE pride of civilized communities applies the term 'barbarous' to all languages spoken by nations of inferior culture, that are without literature or even writing. The American languages have been considered such; all of which, as we shall see presently, have been included in the same category. Although it is generally well known that the empires of Mexico and Peru surpassed in power and civilization the other nations of the New World, yet, in our opinion, justice has not been done to those two nations; and the contemptuous apathy of Europeans has been the cause why the literary and scientific world has been left in ignorance of many treasures which would have been brought to light, by a studious resort to sources, now indeed lost, but the products of which, put forth in earlier centuries, are still visible, and, indeed, scarcely covered by the dust of time.

The strongest proof of the truth of this assertion is to be found in the little appreciation of the study of the languages of those two countries; and it is strange that even those who have most studied their archæology, have passed by, in whole or in part, the study of the idioms spoken by their independent and powerful inhabitants in earlier times. Without doubt, language is the chief archæological element, the sole monument of reconstruction, as Volney has termed it; and in it will be found disposed, and preserved, the entire essence of a people. Language is, as it were, a stratification, which reveals to the learned who study philosophically its various layers, the genius, culture, and different historic changes of the people who used it. "As long (says Mirabeau) as men are obliged to use words, it will be necessary to weigh them." The modifications of a language indicate the changes of thought, feelings, aspirations, and even of national customs and fluctuating habits. "Let no one (says Quintilian) consider as trifling or useless the alphabetic elements; since, if their wonderful enfoldings be looked into, there will spring forth a multitude of subtle questions, capable, not merely of guiding children aright, but of drawing on, and enriching, the most profoundly learned."

Impressed with these principles, we have thought it would prove of interest to our readers should we here present a short review of the relations of the American languages to each other; and particularly of the character of the Quichuan or Peruvian tongue; flattering ourselves that the present chapter, offering a compound of extended and laborious observations which we have made on this subject, will not be the least important in our work.

In our first chapter we have shown the relations of the two hemispheres to each other before the coming of Columbus; and in view of those relations, this question naturally occurs to one engaged in the study of American languages:—What influence had the immigration from the old Continent upon the aboriginal nations of America? It may safely be answered that this influence was insensible, and not in any degree capable of imprinting a mark on the language, nor of enlightening the philologist in a knowledge of the nature of the immigrant races.

Passing by the irruptions made into the very bosom of the American continent, irruptions which almost always took place from the North to the South, the greater part of the immigrations from the Eastern hemisphere presented a pacific character; and immigrations of this kind had very little or no influence on the languages of the country which received them; in support of this truth, not to mention other instances, it is sufficient to refer to the case of the United States, where the national idiom is not in the slightest degree altered by the numerous Dutch, German and French immigrations which are emptied in her ports.

Building upon the analogy of loose and exceptionable words, there have been philologists who have pretended that the American continent was peopled by East Indians, Malays, Chinese and Japanese; others, alleging with equal confidence proofs of a similar nature, think that America derived its population from the inhabitants of Caucasus, from Carthaginians, Jews, and Irish; while others still, assure us that the origin is to be attributed to the Scandinavians, the natives of Western Africa, the Spaniards and the Biscayans.* The analogy so much relied on between the words of the American languages and those of the ancient continent, have induced us to make an approximate estimate,

* Mr. *Castelneau*, in the fourth volume of his expedition to South America (Paris, 1851), in the chapter which treats of the antiquities of Cuzco, makes a division of the human species into the three races, white, red, and black, as descendants of the three sons of Adam and the three sons of Noah. After various considerations in support of his opinion, citing various authors, both ancient and modern, he concludes:

1. That the Indians of America pertain to the Semitic race.

2. That they are the descendants of the Atlantes, making part of the red race which extended, in remote times, over a great part of the ancient

as far as our means would permit, of the numerical value of the idioms of both hemispheres; and the result was, that from between eight and nine thousand American words *one* only could be found analogous in sense and sound to a word of any idiom of the ancient continent; and that in two-fifths of these words, it was necessary to violate the sound to find the same meaning; as we can illustrate by some examples cited by philologists :

Ne in the language of the Cherqueses, *nahui* in the Quichua—the eye.

Muts in the language of the Lesgos, *metztle* in Mexican—the moon.

Nane in the Coptic, *neen* in the Abipone language—good.

Hosono in the East Indies, *acsi* in the Quichua—to laugh.

Fiote in Congo, *bode* in the Otomi (Mexico)—black.

Zippen in the Celtic, *sapi* in the Quichua—a root.

Doubtless there are words, which, from the analogy both in sound and sense, invite serious reflection; and this analogy, combined with historical considerations, sometimes conducts us to important discoveries; such, for instance, (not to enumerate other examples) is the Quichua word for the sun,

3. That America never was, during a long series of centuries, cut off from communication with the Old World.

Relying on philological resemblances and on other observations, he cites among other things the relation of an Israelite whom he encountered at Santarem, on the banks of the Amazon, who assured him that in the idioms which are spoken in the adjacent regions, there may be found more than five hundred words identical with the Hebrew—an assertion which we very much doubt; and which, at this day, is not of the same importance as the one (identical with it in all respects) which the Jew made to Montesini in the seventeenth century, as we have related in the first chapter.

It is not possible from loose words, nor even from customs and particular instruments, safely to deduce conclusions so grave and important.

Inti, which unquestionably derives its origin from the Sanscrit root *Indh*, to shine, to burn, to flame, and which is identical with the East India word *Indra*, the sun. The word *inti*, which held so important a signification in the religion of the ancient Peruvians, was taken from the private language of the Incas, and permits us to see what elements were contained in the idiom of the reformers of the Peruvian worship. Still it has not been possible to trace satisfactory analogies between the languages of the barbarous Indians (particularly of South America) and the idioms of the Eastern hemisphere, because of the large number of the first named, which, according to some philologists, amounts to not less than two or three thousand, while, according to others, there are only five hundred, or even less; so that after repeated attempts, no satisfactory result has as yet been reached, in consequence of the immense difficulties presented in the examination of the subject. It is probable that the true number may be placed between the two above named. In the continent of South America, *i. e.*, from the Isthmus of Panama to Cape Horn, there may be found from 280 to 340 languages, of which four-fifths are composed of idioms radically different; and the idioms of Central and North America rise to a number more than the double of these. According to Jefferson, the radical languages of America, i. e., according to the roots from which they are evidently derived, are twenty times more numerous than the radical languages of Asia.

That many American idioms recognize the same root, admits of no doubt, although, at times, it is exceedingly difficult to give the proofs of a common origin. To attain this end, we ought above all things to consider the influence upon the formation of language of the mode of life of the natives; and from that to deduce the causes of different tongues. The wandering life of the Indians was one of the most powerful causes of the formation of dialects, which were so transformed by time as scarcely to retain a vestige of the mother tongue. The dispersion of the tribes over immense plains and almost inaccessible mountains, the sight of new objects, novel customs, the complete separation, and destruction of all kind of relation with sister tribes, were causes more than sufficient to form, in a short time, a multitude of new words, and to produce an idiom which at first view would seem to be entirely distinct from the mother tongue. But the grammatical construction remains an indestructible monument to attest the affiliation which no circumstances of time or place can obliterate.

But more frequent than these transformed languages or dialects, do we find original idioms completely distinct between two adjacent nations having constant communication, while some tribe, residing in the mountains at a distance of more than one hundred leagues, will be found speaking the language of one of these neighboring or adjacent nations, although there are interposed, between these people of a common idiom, more than twenty intervening idioms completely different. Without citing many other examples of this, it is sufficient to refer, in proof of our assertion, to the striking instance of the Quichua and the Moxa tongues. As it respects words, there are not a half dozen in the two languages alike in sense and sound; and the grammatical differences are very great; yet were they adjacent to each other. Thus, the Quichua language has a complete declension, formed by means of certain particles placed after the noun; while the Moxa language has strictly no declension, and is obliged to form the cases by a periphrasis; as for instance, in the dative, which is often formed by the aid of the future tense of the substantive verb. Again, the Quichua has primitive personal pronouns, and also possessive pronouns quite distinct from the personal; and these are always inseparable from the noun, and always placed after it; or if used in the conjugation of a verb, they take the place of a personal pronoun to the verb; the Moxa has primitive personal pronouns identical with the possessives, and always placed before the word used. The Quichua has a system of numbers so complete that any arithmetical quantity can be expressed by them, while the Moxa has but four numbers—*ete*, one, *api*, two, *mopo*, three, *triahiri*, four; for five and all beyond it, the number must be expressed by a periphrasis.

The Quichua language has a very perfect form of conjugation, and the moods and tenses are more complete than in many of the most cultivated languages of the ancient continent; while the Moxa has only a single mood, the indicative, and two forms of tenses, one for the present and past, and the other for the future, which last is at times made to serve in place of an imperative also. These few but striking differences sufficiently show that these two neighboring idioms are both primitive, and do not proceed from the same root.

All the American languages, from the most northern shores of Greenland to the most southern point of Patagonia, possess two common grammatical characteristics—one of these exists also in some of the primitive languages of the ancient continent; the other is characteristic of the American tongues, and is the link which unites them. The first relates strictly to the whole grammar, since it is not formed by any internal change of the radical sound of a word, or by *inflection*, but by the addition to the radical word, of particles or special words which convey the relation it is desired to express; or in other words, by a *mechanical affix*. On this account these idioms have received the name of polisynthetic or agglutinate languages. This mechanical connection is often so plain that it cannot be mistaken: but sometimes the affixes are found so intimately united with the radical word, that nothing short of attentive study is sufficient to show that there is not really inflection, but simply agglutination.

The second characteristic, which, as we have said, is peculiar to the American languages, consists in particular forms of the verb, by means of which the activity of the subject is transferred to a personal object: that is, if the action of a *personal* subject is directed to a person, the pronoun which indicates this person is expressed by a change of the verb, and not by the intercalation of the accusative of the pronoun, as in the European languages, but by different affixes to the pronoun, intimately united both with it and with the verbal trunk, or with the verb thus combined with its particles. There are six forms of this transfer of action: of the first person to the second, of the first person to the third; of the second to the first, and of the second to the third; of the third to the first, and of the third to the second. All the American languages, however, have not these six forms. In some are wanting those to the third person; in others, those of the third to those of the first, so that they have but two forms. The precision and care with which these relations are distinguished are particularly admirable in the Mexican tongues; for in them there is one form of the verb when the action refers to a personal object, another when the reference is to something inanimate, and another still when there is no reference to an object at all, *i. e.* when the verb is neuter. Not less artificial, in this respect, are the Quichua and the language of Greenland; but it is most developed in the idiom of the Delawares, and in the Chilidugu, in Aranca, sometimes uniting in them two verbs so completely, that both are conjugated through all their forms, so that one single word expresses three or four ideas at once. The Spanish grammarians have called this union of the pronoun and verb *transition;* Dr. Von Tschudi, in his large work on the Quichua language, calls it *the conjugation of the personal object.*

We would further invite attention to certain peculiarities of the American languages, which, if not found in all, yet exist in the greater part of them. These peculiarities relate principally to the use of the pronoun. A double form of the first person plural exists in the personal and possessive pronouns. The first is used when a person includes in the discourse himself and all others present connected either casually or necessarily with the subject; the second is used when a certain number is excluded from the action of which the speaker treats. These two forms are called the *inclusive* and *exclusive plural*, and are repeated in the verb, if not also in the substantive. Besides these two plurals, in some idioms there is an exact dual. Various species of concrete duals are formed by means of affixes, which, united to a substantive, signify the object or person designated by the substantive with the part or member which most naturally belongs to it or him; for example: in the Quichua language, *cosa* means a husband; and the affix *ntin*, including the idea of union, *cosantin* means a husband with his wife; *hacha* signifies a tree, and *hachantin* a tree with its roots.

It is a singular circumstance, too, that in some American idioms, the women use pronouns different from those used by men. Thus in the Moxa, the demonstrative *ema* means '*this*' in the mouth of a man; a woman would express '*this*' by the word *eñi; marcani* signifies '*he*,' and is used by a man; a woman would use *pocñaqui* to say '*he*.' The same difference is observed in other parts of speech, according to the difference of sexes; thus, in the Quichua, a brother, speaking of his sister, says, *panay* (my sister); while a sister, desirous of expressing the same thing, says, *ñañay* (my sister); so a sister, speaking of a brother, says, *huauquey* (my brother); while, to indicate the same person, the brother says, *llocsimasiy-huauquey* (my brother); a father says *churiy* (my son), and the mother says *karihuahuay* (my son); the father says to his daughter *ususiy* (my daughter); the mother calls her *huarma-huahuay* (my daughter). Similar differences exist if an uncle speaks, according as his relationship is on the paternal or maternal side. We find differences analogous to these in the Chilidugu, Maypuri, Tamenaki, Mexican, Chippeway, Kickapoos, Sacs and Foxes, Ottoway, Potowotamy, Wyandot, Shawnee, and other languages. That which is most surprising is, that the same difference is remarked even in the most simple parts of speech; so that the interjections of grief, for instance, used by males, are different from those used by females; the woman utters other words than the man uses to direct attention to something, and the interjections employed to animate or cheer in work are different as used by man or woman. Azara assures us that among the Mbaya Indians of Paraguay, the language varies, according as the person who speaks is married or single—a peculiarity which probably obtains in certain expressions or forms of speech only.

To all the American languages also belongs the construction of words by means of one or more affixes joined to the primitive word, thus providing for the formation of many compound words. But this compounding is not limited to the use of affixes or particles only, for sometimes various parts of speech, in whole or in part, are united with the primitive word, which, regularly, is a verb. From this process result entire phrases expressed solely by a word thus super-compounded. This faculty of composition or *polisynthesis*, as Duponceau calls it, is found in a greater degree in the languages of North America, than it is in those of the southern part of our hemisphere; and among the former, it is not a rare thing to find twelve or eighteen different parts of speech united to form a single word.

From the mere compounding of words, that is, from the union of single particles with the primitive word, is derived an immense quantity of words in the American languages, which, as we have said, may be increased *ad infinitum*. This extraordinary copiousness has astonished the philologists, who assure us that for every English or Spanish word, the Indians, in their languages, have three or four. The most exact designation of an object or an action is another characteristic of American languages. The mode of living, the immediate relations with nature, the vigilance with which it is necessary to guard, day and night, against the attacks of wild beasts, or adjacent enemies, all these force the tribes to use the greatest precision in speech. With all the auxiliary means of our cultivated languages, we are not able to describe with the definite and unmistakable precision of an American Indian, the track of a wild beast, or the footprint of an enemy.

It is scarce necessary to remark that this copious abundance of words produces an extraordinary variety in discourse; nevertheless, these languages are distinguished by energy and conciseness, exceeding in these respects the most perfect tongues in Europe. And yet such languages are called *barbarous!* It is to be lamented that so much genius and so many distinctive traits of richness and beauty as adorn the American languages, should be accompanied with an almost total want of literature; and, as to this point, certain it is that the Eastern hemisphere was two thousand years in advance of all our Indian populations. Before the coming of Europeans, there was, among our natives, a want of representative characters; or at best, they were limited to an imperfect graphic representation, or to some defective material sign of a word. The first of these existed among the Mexicans, who used hieroglyphics painted on paper, or graved on stone; the second was found among the Peruvians, who employed their *quippos*, of which we shall speak more fully hereafter. The indefatigable zeal of some among the learned has sought to find an explanation of the hieroglyphics, and it is not improbable that what is desired might be attained if we had these characters in greater abundance; but the immense collection of Mexican writings was destroyed almost entirely by the fanaticism of the Spanish conquerors, and particularly of the Dominican friars who accompanied them, so that nothing has been saved but a few isolated fragments. How great was the treasure of manuscripts may be judged of from the relation of *Torquemada*, who tells us, that even in the last days of the Mexican monarchy, five cities only delivered up to the governor sixteen thousand bundles of papers, made of the maguay plant (Agave Americana), and that the whole of these were filled with painted hieroglyphics.

Besides the two cultivated nations of Mexico and Peru, there were also others which present us with indications, though obscure, of the possession of a hieroglyphic writing, which has not been deciphered, and probably never will be. Such are the Hurons, the Iroquois, the Indians of the Rio del Norte, of Louisiana, and others. Those countries which have been taught the use of foreign characters, show us nothing but a meagre and insignificant literature, consisting principally of prayers, catechisms, sermons, and books of elementary instruction.

Among the last-named class of languages, however, an exception is to be made in favor of the *Tiroki*;* thanks to the indefatigable labor of a native, SEQUOIAH, one of the most distinguished men in America, who, within little more than the last twenty years, has invented a syllabic alphabet which so soon became familiar to the nation that the *Thiroki Phœnix*, a newspaper, has been printed in the native language, in the letters of this alphabet.

After these observations on the principles of the American languages in general, we do not think it necessary to extend them to a particular explanation of the grammar of the Quichua language; and he who wishes to be instructed in that, can refer to one of the grammars of that idiom. It may be of interest, however, to the lovers of that beautiful tongue to know at least the titles of the philological works which treat of it; and as even among the Peruvians themselves they are but little known, we here present a bibliographical and chronological catalogue of grammatical works on the Quichua language.† It is much to be wished that some truly

* Our author means the Cherokee. [TRANSLATOR.]

† The translator has transferred this from the text to the following note:

I. *San Thomas* (Domingo de). Gramatica ó arte general de la lengua de los Indios del Peru. Nuevamente compuesto por el maestro Fray Domingo de San Thomas, de la orden de Santo Domingo, morador en dichos reinos. Impreso en Valladolid por Francisco Fernandez de Cordua. Acabose a diez dias del mez de Henero, año 1560, 8vo.; y, como apendice: Lexicon ó Vocabulario de la lengua general del Peru, llamada Quichua. Valladolid, 1560.

II. *Ricardo* (Antonio). Arte y Vocabulario de la lengua, llamada quichua. En la ciudad de los Reyes, 1586, 8vo.

III. *Ricardo* (Antonio). Vocabulario en lengua general del Perú, llamada quichua y en lengua española. En la ciudad de los Reyes, 1586, 8vo.

patriotic and learned Peruvian would devote himself to the study of the Quichua language, and seek to lay the foundations of a literature in an idiom so beautiful and singular that the sons of the ancient monarchy of the Incas should not blush to be proud of it.

The ancient Peruvians had two kinds of writing: one, and certainly the most ancient, consisted in a species of hieroglyphic characters; the other, in knots made on threads of divers colors. The hieroglyphics of the Mexicans were very distinct, and graved on stone or metal. In Southern Peru there has not yet been discovered any vestige of hieroglyphics

Pertenecen estos libros á los primeros impresos en la América meridional.

IV. *Torres Rubio* (Diego de). Gramática y Vocabulario en lengua general del Perù, llamada Quichua y en lengua española. 8vo., Sevilla, 1603.

V. *Martinez* (El Padre Maestro Fray Juan). Vocabulario en la lengua general del Perú, llamada Quichua y en la lengua española. En los Reyes, 1604, 8vo.

VI. *Holguin* (Diego Gonzalez). Gramática y arte nueva de la lengua general del Perú, llamada quichua ó lengua del Inca (en cuatro libros . Impreso en la ciudad de los Reyes del Perú por Francisco del Canto, 1607, 4to.

VII. *Holguin* (Diego Gonzalez). Vocabulario de la lengua general de todo el Perú, llamada Quichua ó del Inga. Los Reyes por Francisco del Canto. 1608, 4to., dos partes en un vol.

VIII. Arte y Vocabulario en la lengua general del Perú, llamada Quichua y en la lengua española. Lima, 1614, 8vo., por Francisco del Canto.

IX. *Huerta* (Don Alonso de). Arte de la lengua quichua general de los Indios de este reyno del Perú. Impreso por Francisco del Canto en los Reyes, 1616, 4to.

X. *Torres Rubio* (Diego de) segunda edicion, en Lima por Francisco Lasso, año de 1619, 8vo.

XI. *Olmos* (Diego de). Gramática de la lengua indica, Lima, 1633, 4to.

XII. *Carrera* (Fernando de, cura y vicario de San Martin de Reque en el corregimiento de Chiclayo). Arte de la lengua yunga de los valles

painted on paper; but according to the observations of Don Mariano de Rivero, at the distance of eight leagues north of Arequipa there exist a multitude of engravings on granite which represent figures of animals, flowers, and fortifications, and which doubtless tell the story of events anterior to the dynasty of the Incas.

ENGRAVING ON ROCK, EIGHT LEAGUES NORTH OF AREQUIPA.

In the province of Castro-Vireyna, in the town of Huaytara, there is found, in the ruins of a large edifice, of similar construction to the celebrated palace of old Huanuco, a mass of granite, many square yards in size, with coarse engravings like those last mentioned near Arequipa. None of the most trustworthy historians allude to these inscriptions or representations, or give the smallest direct information con-

del obispado de Truxillo; con un confesonario y todas las oraciones cotidianas y otras cosas. Lima por Juan de Contreras, 1644, 16mo.

XIII. *Roxo Mexia y Ocon* (Don Juan, natural de Cuzco). Arte de la lengua general de los Indios del Perú. En Lima por Jorge Lopez de Herrera, 1648, 8vo.

cerning the Peruvian hieroglyphics; from which it may plausibly be inferred that in the times of the Incas there was no knowledge of the art of writing in characters, and that all these sculptures are the remains of a very remote period.

Montesinos is the only one who tells us that in the first centuries after the conquest of Peru by the Americans, under the reign of Huainacavi-Pirhua, the use of letters was known: but that it was lost afterward, under the reign of Titu, son of Titu Yupanqui V. But we know how little confidence is to be placed in the statements of this author.

In many parts of Peru, chiefly in situations greatly elevated above the level of the sea, are vestiges of inscriptions very much obliterated by time. The drawing below represents a stone, two feet broad, which Dr. J. D. Von Tschudi found in an ancient settlement, a league from Huari.

XIV. *Melgar* (Estevan Sancho de). Arte de la lengua general de Inga, llamada Qquecchua. Lima por Diego de Lyra, 1691, 8vo.

XV. *Torres Rubio* (Diego de, de la compañia de Jesus) tercera edicion, y nuevamente van añadidos los Romances, el catecismo pequeño, todas las oraciones, los dias de fiesta y ayunos de los Indios, el Vocabulario

In the last century, a European missionary among the Panos who dwell on the banks of the Ucayali, found, in the pampas of Sacramento, manuscripts, on a species of paper made of the leaf of the plantain, with hieroglyphics joined together, as well as in simple characters, containing, according to the statements of the Indians, the history of the events of their ancestors; but it remains to be ascertained whether they referred to the history of a nation who came from the North or the East, to the mountains of Ucayali, and who brought with them the knowledge of this writing, or whether it is a vestige of ancient civilization.*

añadido y otro Vocabulario de la lengua Chinchaysuyu por el M. R. Juan de Figueredo. En Lima por Joseph de Contreras, 1700, 8vo.

XVI. *Torres Rubio* (Diego de) cuarta edicion. Arte y Vocabulario de la lengua quichua general de los Indios del Perú, que compuso el Padre Diego de Torres Rubio de la compañia de Jesus, y añadió el P. Juan de Figueredo de la misma compañia. Ahora nuevamente corregido y aumentado en muchos vocablos y varias advertencias, notas y observaciones para la mejor inteligencia del Idioma y perfecta instruccion de los Parochos y Cathequistas de los Indios. Por un religioso de la misma compañia. Lima, 1754, 8vo.

This last is the most common, and many, in consequence thereof, consider it as the most ancient grammar which they can obtain; while others, principally the Grammar and Vocabulary of Antonio Ricardo, and those of Domingo San Thomas, are to be classed among bibliographical rarities.

* In the interior of South America, between the second and fourth degrees of North latitude, there extends a plain bounded by four rivers, viz., the Oronoco, the Atabasco, the Rio Negro, and Casiquiare. There are found on it rocks of granite and syenite, equal to those of Caicara and Uruana, covered with symbolical representations, colossal figures of crocodiles, tigers, likenesses of houses, and signs of the sun and moon. At this day this unfrequented region is entirely without population over a space of five hundred square miles. The neighboring tribes, exceedingly ignorant, lead a miserable vagrant life, and are not capable of drawing hieroglyphics. In South America, a belt of these rocks, thus covered

Under the reign of the Incas, in place of characters, the Peruvians used colored threads, knotted in different modes, and called *Quippus.*

It is certain that this method of writing (if so it may be called) was not original in Peru, and it is probable that it was given to the natives by the first Inca; since, in various parts of Central Asia, and particularly in China, it was the custom from a very remote period to resort to these knotted threads, as in Peru, Mexico and Canada.

The Peruvian Quippus are of twisted wool, and consist of a string or large cord as the base of the document, and of threads more or less fine, which are fastened by knots to it. These branches (if so we may call them) include the contents of the Quippo, expressed either by single knots or by artificial intertwinings. The size of the Quippus is very different; sometimes the base cord is five or six yards long, at others, it is not more than a foot; the pendant strings or branches rarely exceed a yard in length, and, in general, are shorter. In the neighborhood of Lurin, we found a Quippo which weighed twelve and a half pounds, and we doubt not there were some even more bulky still. To give some idea of the strings which form a very large Quippo that we took from a cemetery of the natives who lived about Pachacamac, we here insert the drawing of a fragment.

with symbolic emblems, may be followed from Rupunuri, the Essequibo, and the Pacaraima mountains, to the banks of the Oronoco and the Yupura, over an extent of more than eight degrees of longitude. These marks thus engraved in the rocks, may belong to several different epochs, for Sir Robert Schomberg has seen on the Rio Negro a delineation of a Spanish ship, which, of course, must be of later origin than the commencement of the sixteenth century; and this in a savage country, where the indigenous stock was probably quite as uncultivated as the present inhabitants.—*Humboldt's Ansitchten der Natur.* 3. *Ausgabe.* *Bd.* I. *pag.* 240. Views of Nature, 3d edition, Vol. I. p. 240.

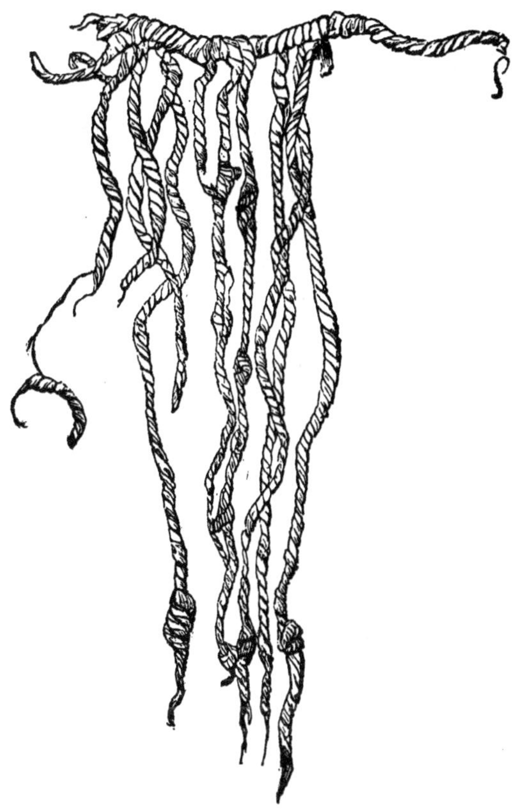

PERUVIAN QUIPPO.

The different colors of the threads have different meanings: thus, the red signifies a soldier or war; the yellow, gold; the white, silver or peace; the green, wheat or maize, &c. In the arithmetical system, a single knot means *ten;* two single knots joined, *twenty;* a knot doubly intertwined, *one hundred;* triply, *one thousand;* two of the last united, *two thousand*, &c. Not only is the color and mode of intertwining the knots to be considered, but even the mode of twisting the thread, and particularly the distance of the knot from the junction of the thread with the base cord, are of great importance to a proper understanding of the Quippo.

It is probable that these knots were, at first, applied to purposes of numeration only, but in the course of time, this science was so much perfected that those skilled in it attained to the art of expressing by knots historical relations, laws and decrees, so that they could transmit to their descendants the most striking events of the empire; and thus the Quippus might supply the place of documents and chronicles. The registers of taxes; the enrolment of tribes; distinguishing between the tax-payers, the aged, the invalids, women and children; the lists of the armies, their arms, soldiers, officers and stations; the inventories of the large quantities of wheat, maize, arms, shoes and clothing in the public magazines; the registers of deaths and births; all these matters were specified with admirable exactitude in the Quippus. In every city of any note, there was an officer called *Quippu-camayoc*, whose business it was, at all times, to knot and decipher these documents. But notwithstanding their skill, whenever a Quippu came from a distant province, it was necessary it should be accompanied by a verbal commentary, sufficient, at least, to indicate the subject matter of which it treated; as, for instance, whether it related to tribute, or the enrolment of tribes, &c. To mark the events of their respective districts, these officials had certain signs at the commencement of the mother thread, or base cord, which had a meaning intelligible to them only; and the Quippus which related to the same subject were always preserved together in certain repositories, that there might be no risk of error by changing, or mixing a military Quippu with one concerning taxes, &c.

Even at this day, in the country, Quippus are used for the purpose of numeration. Such is the case on many haciendas and cattle stations. On the first thread or branch, the herdsmen commonly place the bulls, on the second the milch-cows, on the third those which are dry, and afterward follow the calves, according to age and sex. So, too, as to animals producing wool; they are arranged in various subdivisions, as also are the number of foxes killed, the quantity of salt used, and the specification of cattle that have died.

Repeated attempts made in our day to read the Quippus, have proved failures, because of the very great difficulty of deciphering them. In effect each single knot represents some notion or thought, while there is wanting (for a meaning) a quantity of conjunctions or links. Besides, there is another and greater impediment in the interpretation of the Quippus found in the *Huacas;* and that is the want of a verbal commentary to explain the subject matter of the document; and even with this advantage, it would still require the aid of the most skilful *Quippu-camayoc.* We think that there are still, in the southern provinces of Peru, Indians who know very well how to decipher these intricate memorials, but they guard their knowledge as a sacred secret, inherited from their ancestors.

The opinion of the Prince of *San Severo,* who published in Naples a memoir, pretending to prove that the knots of the Quippus served as *letters,* is so erroneous as not to merit refutation.

Considering this defective system of writing, it ought not to cause surprise that the Quichua language wants an ancient literature, at least, any that is intelligible to us. And even though there may still exist a possibility of forming a national literature with European characters, yet even this field remains sterile, awaiting the culture of genius and patriotism. How insufficient are the translations of first lessons in the Christian religion, made by the missionaries, as specimens of the language of a nation having such a history as Peru!

A system of subjugation, and of colonization wretchedly defective, the barbarism of the epoch, and the brutality of the conquering adventurers, have made shipwreck of immense treasures which were found deposited in an idiom so rich, so elegant, so flexible and harmonious.

A short time after the conquest, at the beginning of the latter half of the sixteenth century, the Christian doctrine was translated into Quichua by the Franciscan friars; the Dominicans who came with the first conquerors, moved by religious zeal, were not occupied in converting the Indians by force of the Word alone, but, with fire and sword as accompaniments, preached the Gospel. To the Jesuits belongs the merit of having most perfectly elaborated those translations which are found, as an appendix, in almost every grammar of the general language. We here present specimens of the Quichuan literature, commencing with an elegant translation of the Lord's Prayer: *

* We transfer these specimens to a note.—[TRANSLATOR.]

LORD'S PRAYER IN THE QUICHUAN LANGUAGE.

Yayacu hanacpac hacunapi cac; sutiyqui muchhasca cachun; ccapaccayñiyqui ñocaycuman hamuchun; munayñiyqui rurasca cachun; imainam hanacpachapi, hinatac, cay pachapipas; ppunchaunincuna ttantaycucta cunan cohuaycu; huchaycuctari pampachapuhuaycu imanam ñocaycupas, ñocaycuman huchallicuccunacta, pampachaycu hina. Amatac cacharihuaycuchu huateccayman urmanccaycupac; yallinrac, mana allimantac quespichihuaycu. Amen.

We have in our possession a very rare book, printed in 1648, entitled "Sermons on the Mysteries of our holy Catholic Faith in the Spanish and general Language of the Inca; impugning the particular errors which are

But these illustrations of the language (contained in the note) are but fragments little adapted to convey an exact idea of the grammatical construction, or of the beauties and peculiarities of this interesting idiom, which is so flexible that translations of Greek and Latin odes have been made into it with great ease. Unfortunately, however, these specimens have never been published.

Among all civilized nations, poetry was the earliest form

held by the Indians; by Doctor DON FERNANDO DE AVENDANO." From these we give some passages, with a translation:

Cai checcan simi yachachisccaimantam, machuiquichiccunap lloclla pachacuti, Dilubioñisccamanta pacha, runacunap paccarinacunamanta ñisccancuna llullu simi casccanta unanchanquichic.

This truth which I have taught you, makes you to see that those things are fables which your old men have told you, of the origin of men after the deluge.

Huc machucunam ari ñincuña lloclla pachacuti yalliptinmi hanaccpachamanta quimça runtu urmamuroccan, ñaupacc ñinmi ccori runtu carccan; cai ccori runtumantam curacacuna paccarimurccan. Iscayñeqquenmi collqquerunlu carccan, caimantam ñustacuna yurimurccan. Quimzañeqquenmi ccana anta runtu carccan, caimantatacmi huaquin yancca runacuna lloççimurccan. Caihinam huc machuiquichiccuna rimancu. Cunan tapuscayquichic churicuna; curacacuna chiu chichu ccori runtumanta paccarimunancupacc? Manachu caita rimay açiccuipacc cascanta ricunquichic?

Some old men say, that after the deluge there fell three eggs from heaven: one of gold, from which the Curacas were born; another of silver, out of which were born the Nustas; and another of copper, from which came these last Indians. Tell me, my children, are the Curacas chickens, seeing they came out of an egg of gold? Can you not see that the whole story is a thing to be laughed at?

[Other passages are presented in the work we are translating; but as they are mere specimens of the Quichua language, the foregoing will suffice for the English reader.—TRANSLATOR.]

of literature; and before they found characters to perpetuate their annals and productions, they preserved in verses the acts of their ancestors, and the current of their thoughts. In all the Indian languages, even the most barbarous, vestiges of this literature are found, and it is worthy of note that triumphal songs, and songs of war, are the most ancient poetical productions of the American nations. Of the ancient Peruvian poetry but few remains have come to our knowledge, although among the Indians are preserved many beautiful songs of past times, and worthy of being gathered into a printed collection.

The *amautas*, or philosophers, were the poets who composed festive songs, comedies and tragedies; and the *Haravicus* (inventors) formed another class of poets who composed elegiac verses. It cannot be denied that the poetry reached a certain degree of perfection, by using in the amorous songs either four-syllable verses only, or by alternating them with trisyllabic lines; in the triumphal songs, six-syllable verse, or the less roundelay, was used; in the comedies, and in the larger part of the *Haravis*, the greater roundelay, or eight-syllable verse, was used. In all these forms of verse, rhyme may or may not be used.

The *Haravis*, or elegiac songs, form the most interesting part of the Quichuan poetry; the subject is usually unhappy love, and it is hard to say which most to admire in them, the harmonious mechanical composition, or the expression of the effects of despairing, overwhelming grief.

It would seem that dramatic poetry was highly esteemed and much cultivated in the time of the Incas. According to Garcilasso, those of the Inca lineage, and others of noble blood, were accustomed, on solemn days and festivals, to act comedies and tragedies before the monarch and the nobility at court. The subjects of the tragedies were military achievements, triumphs and victories, the exploits and grandeur of former kings and other heroic men: the topics of the comedies were derived from agriculture, from the farm, and familiar household affairs. To such performers as distinguished themselves presents were made of jewels and gifts of value. Happily, we have one specimen of this species of composition, consisting of a tragic drama in three acts, which we consider the most important literary production to be found in any of the American languages. We know nothing with certainty of its author, nor of the period of its production ; and it does not appear certain whether it has descended to us by tradition from the times of the Incas, or whether it is the work of a more modern genius. Some believe that it was composed in the latter half of the fifteenth century, and represented in the plaza of Cuzco, before the Incas; others, on the contrary, think that it is the work of a skilful author of a more recent date. The first of these opinions has many circumstances in its support, since the language of the piece is not as corrupt as it was in the later periods of its use: a few Castilian words found in the existing copy, and certain unskilful phrases, are easily seen to have been made or added by copyists. It is, however, certain that copies of this work, written in the sixteenth or seventeenth century, are preserved in various private libraries of Cuzco.

This drama bears the title of *Ollanta, or the Severity of a Father and the Generosity of a King.* The first act is laid at the close of the fourteenth century, the other two cover the first ten or twelve years of the fifteenth. The hero of the piece is the celebrated chief *Ollanta*, whose name is still preserved in a bridge, a fortress and a palace, and whose deeds are to this day well known among the Indians of Peru. His love for Cusi Coyllur, daughter of the Inca Pachacutec, the harshness of this monarch toward his child, her imprisonment, the rebellion of Ollanta, with its success at first, his final ruin and subjection by Rumiñahui, the general of the Inca Yupanqui, son of Pachacutec, and the generosity of this Inca toward Ollanta and Cusi Coyllur, form the substance of the drama, which is written in a masterly manner.*

The Quichua language has various dialects strongly marked. In the north is the *Quiteño*, the most impure, full of words of other idioms, and with very corrupt grammatical forms; the *Lamana*, spoken in various parts of the department of Libertad; the *Yunca*, in the bishopric of Truxillo; the *Chinchaysuyu*, in the department of Cerro de Pasco; the *Cauqui*, in the province of Yauyos; the *Calchaqui*, in Tucuman; the *Cusqueño*, in the departments of the south. This last named is the pure Quichua, which alone should be taken as the standard by the student.

The *Aymara* language, spoken in Bolivia, is very much like the Quichua, and doubtless came from the same root. Very many words in the two idioms are identical, and even in the grammatical structure there is a very striking resemblance. The German Jesuit, W. Bayer, published, in the Aymara and Latin languages, a sermon on the passion of our Lord, which was printed in one of the scientific periodicals of Germany.†

The *Puquina* language, spoken in some of the valleys of the coast, and also of the mountains of Peru, is radically different from all the rest, and indeed has no affinity with any other American idiom.

According to Garcilasso, the Incas had a private language

* Dr. Von Tschudi, in his work on the Quichua language, has given at length this curious literary production.

† *Murr* Journal für Kunst und Literatur. Vol. I., pp. 112—121; Vol. II., pp. 297—334; Vol. III., pp. 55—100.

which no one save those belonging to the royal lineage dared to learn. Unhappily, we are without data on which to form an opinion about it.

We hope that the preceding observations will serve to stimulate the zeal of the Peruvians, and lead them to cultivate the beautiful primitive language of their native land, by establishing in their colleges chairs devoted to instruction in it.

NOTE.

* *Walter Raleigh*, in the description of his voyage to *Guiana*, (fol. 97

NOTE.

There is, we think, much in this chapter calling for remark, not to say correction. We are constrained to believe our author did not possess the latest sources of information as to the languages of North America particularly. In speaking of the radical languages, he copies the statement of Mr. Jefferson, who probably had never studied one of them, and who, at any rate, was exceedingly inaccurate, as the labors of subsequent philologists, like Pickering and Gallatin, have shown.

In fact, he who has studied most carefully our American languages, will be most cautious in making general conclusions. A scholar now engaged upon them, (Professor William W. Turner) and who, at least in the view of the present writer, has probably no equal, certainly no superior in this department of letters, would have told our author that the materials are as yet too scanty to justify sweeping, general assertions; while such a declaration from such a source would have been quite enough for every American philologist, who has seen the recent publication of Mr. Riggs' Grammar and Dictionary of the Dakota language, by the Smithsonian Institute, and knows the part which Mr. Turner bore in its preparation.

What is said in the text must be taken with large allowances. It is not true that *all* the languages of North and South America are characterized by what Duponceau called *polisyntheticism.* Mr. Gallatin has already stated that the Otomi and others are not so; and some of the best of our philologists entertain more than a suspicion that future investigations are likely, from present indications, to show that such a characteristic is not universal, though it doubtless exists in many instances.

Neither are we prepared, after some study of the South American languages, to admit that four-fifths of them are *radically* different. Tested both grammatically and lexically, such has not proved to us to be the case. The fact is, that the number of families into which the South

American idioms may be resolved, is small; smaller, indeed, than in North America; and one single language, the Guarani, is the root of a very large number, spread over a very large surface. We believe we speak the opinion of the best American philologists when we say that, the further researches are made, the more do we reach the probability that here, as in the other hemisphere, a comparatively few parent tongues will finally be found to have furnished in their offshoots the various dialects of both North and South America. But, as has already been intimated, the want of sufficient material compels the candid ethnologist to suspend his judgment.

There is to the present writer something extraordinary in the assertion of the text that among eight or nine thousand American words, there is but *one* to be found "'analogous in sense and sound to a word of *any* idiom of the ancient continent;" and that in two-fifths of these eight or nine thousand, "it was necessary to violate the sound to find the same meaning." We are quite sure that if the examination be made by one at all acquainted with the canons of comparative philology, a very different result will appear. The resemblances may not justify, indeed, a general conclusion of common origin, but they are more numerous than our author represents.

As to the word *inti*, which our author states "unquestionably derives its origin from the Sanscrit root *Indh*, to shine," &c., and which he declares to be "*identical* with the East India word *Indra*, the sun," we know not whether this be the *one* word to which he alludes, but we do know that it is not "identical;" and further, that when he says it was a word that belonged to the secret vocabulary of the Incas, he states that of which neither he nor any man living can speak with absolute certainty. Where at this day is the secret language of the Incas to be found? He himself states that "unhappily we are without data on which to form an opinion about it."

As to the remarks of our author on the grammatical structure of the Quichua and Moxa languages, according to the grammars in our possession, they are in general correct. The singularity to which he alludes, of these languages (which we believe to belong to different families) being spoken by two neighboring nations, while beyond the Moxas, the Quichua was again found in another tribe, is one that is seen more than once in our American languages. Velasco states that the Peruvians found the Quichua, or a dialect of it, spoken at Quito, when they conquered it, although it was generally unknown in the intermediate country; and Mr. Prescott remarks on it as a singular fact if true. (Conq. of Peru, Vol. I. p. 124, note.) It is, we think, probably true; several such instances occur. Mr. Turner has recently discovered, for instance, that the language of our Apaches belongs to that of the Althapascas. Parallel cases have been met with in the Eastern hemisphere.

The verb is not, as our author states, uniform in possessing the peculiarities which he describes as belonging to *all* our languages. They are found in some only. Neither is he correct in supposing that the "inclusive and exclusive" plural are universal, nor that all our languages have a dual number.

As to writing, we are not aware that the "Hurons, Iroquois and Indians of Louisiana" ever had anciently a system of undecipherable hieroglyphics; which our author seems to think is now lost. They had, and still have, the usual rude pictorial representations of most, if not all, of our North American tribes; and they are by no means undecipherable to an Indian. Our author imputes the want of a literature among our natives to the absence of representative characters; by which we suppose he means an alphabet. We are not sure that there are not alphabetic characters on some of our Central American monuments; but we leave the result of our researches on that head to the larger work to which we have alluded in our prefatory note. Our author himself refers to the Panoes, and from his statement it might be inferred that they possessed an alphabet, for he speaks of "single characters." Few subjects have more interested American antiquarians than these writings among the Panoes. These were a tribe of Indians who lived on the Ucayali River, and a short time before Baron Humboldt was there, a Franciscan missionary, as Humboldt states, found among them bundles of their paper resembling our volumes in quarto, and an old man, sitting at the foot of a palm-tree, read from one to several young persons sitting around him. They were very reluctant to permit the white man even to approach, but at length he succeeded in procuring one of the books, which he sent to Lima. What became of it does not appear. We are disposed to think, from Humboldt's account, that the leaves contained *paintings;* perhaps there were also alphabetic characters.

As to the Cherokee language, and the alphabet formed by the native *Sequoiah* or *Guess*, as he is called, it must be recollected that this very clever Indian did not so much invent as apply what was already known. His first effort was prompted by the fact he had observed, that the English or Anglo-Americans about him could express the sounds of their speech by written marks; he accordingly tried (in conformity with the Chinese mode, by the way) to make a distinct character for each Cherokee *word.* This, however, required so many different characters that he soon abandoned the plan; and then, with singular ingenuity, he devoted himself to a minute observation of the various *sounds* employed in the Cherokee, and found that they amounted to but eighty-five. This was not an unmanageable number, and he readily made a mark to express each one of these sounds: nearly all of his marks, however, were adopted from forms supplied by our alphabet. Thus it will be seen that what he made was a *syllabic* alphabet of eighty-five sounds, each represented by its own character. Now, it is to be remarked, that the Cherokee possesses a peculiarity, but for which Guess could not have made his alphabet. It has very few double consonants in it, and, as in the Polynesian languages, *every syllable terminates in a vocal sound. Sequoiah,* doubtless, in what he did, manifested unusual cleverness for one of his race, but we have not been accustomed to call him, as our author does, "one of the most distinguished men of America."

CHAPTER VI.

SCIENTIFIC CULTURE UNDER THE DYNASTY OF THE INCAS.

The political institutions and the imperfect means used to supply the art of writing, were two powerful obstacles which impeded all scientific progress among the ancient Peruvians.

As we have already seen in the fourth chapter, the stems of the royal stock only fully enjoyed the advantages of education; while, supported by a humiliating protection, the common masses were denied an entrance into the sanctuary of science, obliged to follow the profession of their fathers, to prevent them from becoming proud and dazzled by the light of truth, and from refusing obedience to the constituted authorities.

There prevailed, under the sceptre of the Incas, the system of increasing the importance of the empire, more by extending the territory than by an increase of the intellectual culture of the inhabitants; military tactics were among them the chief object of education. For this purpose, there were in Cuzco and other principal cities, academies under the superintendence or direction of ancient Incas, to instruct the young disciples in all military and knightly exercises, as well theoretical as practical, and from them came the chiefs for the different armies.

The representatives of the other sciences did not belong to the priesthood, as in Europe during the barbarous centuries of the Middle Age, but formed the separate class of the *Amautas* or sages who lived in those establishments of learning (Yachahuasi), in which the pupils were under the severest inspection, instructing them in the deeds of their forefathers; explaining to them the laws and principles of the art of governing; teaching them astronomy, arithmetic, and the art of the Quippus, and initiating them in the mysteries of religion. Some of the Incas, particularly Inca-Rocca, Pachacutec, and Tupa-Yupanqui, favored these schools to such an extent, that they ordered to be constructed in their immediate neighborhood sumptuous palaces; as in Cuzco, that of Cora-Cora and of Casana, that they might visit the schools with the greater facility, and, according to Garcilasso, to them the Inca Pachacutec resorted to compile his laws and statutes.

We will now examine the intellectual character of the Peruvians, under a scientific aspect, and the knowledge which the *Amautas* had treasured up, and which they transmitted to their pupils.

Of all the branches which compose abstract philosophy, the only one which was cultivated was the moral duties arising from religious belief. It does not appear that they devoted themselves to the deep and thorny branch of metaphysics, nor did they permit their pupils to inquire into what they maintained as theocracy; and it is probable that their knowledge was limited to the scanty and confused ideas supplied to them by the priesthood.

Neither did they excel in jurisprudence. The simplicity of the Peruvian code required few commentaries, the judges were obliged to determine all law-suits in less than five days; the penal laws were similar to those in Europe, the military laws short and sanguinary, penal justice was rapid and implacable, after the Turkish manner, nay, more than this, at times arbitrary.

The medical art pertained also in part to the sphere of

the Amautas, from whom came such of the faculty as had in charge the person of the Inca. Where the common masses were concerned, they consulted for their rare and slight maladies their herbalists and old women. In either case the curative knowledge was a quackery and limited, and they endeavored to mitigate the most alarming symptoms of the malady without any nosological or thereapeutic system. Of all the means of discovery used by our physicians to form a diagnosis, they knew of but one, i. e., the state of the mucous membrane of the tongue. If this presented a white or yellow appearance, they supposed the existence of gastric difficulties, and had recourse to one of their universal medicines, i. e., the root of the Huachancana, a plant of the family of the Euphorbia, whose drastic and emetical effect is very similar to that of tartar-emetic. Studying the medicinal herbs, which are at present used among the Indians, without consulting physicians, but looking to their ailments, an accurate knowledge of the pharmacy of the ancient Peruvians may be obtained, as the medicaments, with their beneficial effects, have passed from generation to generation. Thus, in this day, as in the time of the Incas, they use the Peruvian bark, the Checasoconche, the Chenchelcome, the Chillca, the Chinapaya, the Chucumpu, the Huacra-huacra, the Huarituru (*Valeriana Coarctata*), the Llamapñahui (*Negretia-inflexa*), the Maprato or Rataña (*Krameria-triandria*), the Masca, the Matecllu, the Moho-moho, the Mulli, the Parhataquia (*Molina-prostrata*), the Panqui, the Tasta, and many other medicinal plants. They also used balsams; also a piece of the navel-string of a child, which they deemed an efficacious remedy in many of the diseases of children; the skull of the *Anta*, or great beast (*Tapirus Americanus*), against the *gutta rosacca.**

* Even at the present day, the Camatas Indians traverse almost every

The Amautas had begun to learn that in certain cases it was necessary to diminish the quantity of blood in the human frame, and to this effect they practised bleeding, but always in the vicinity of the diseased part. The instrument which they employed was a small stone, very sharp, fastened in a cleft stick; this they placed over the vein, which, by means of a slight blow, they opened, producing a flow of blood, which, more than our mode of bleeding, was similar to local depletion, or to scarifying and cupping.

The chirurgical operator was entirely unknown to the Peruvian faculty. Wounds, bruises, contusions, in one word, all external hurts were cured with balsams and medicinal leaves, without the least idea of the amputation of limbs, the opening of abscesses with cutting instruments, the sewing up of serious wounds, the application of fire, or many other chirurgical operations practised in Europe. The fracture of bones was cured, in the interior of the country, with an herb called Huarituru; and on the coast by wrapping the fractured limb up in several species of marine plants. The branch of obstetrics was not practised by the faculty; the ancient matrons assisted women in that critical situation.

The knowledge of the Amautas in mathematical sciences was almost nothing. Notwithstanding their excellent system of numeration, the graphic process of the Quippus was so rudimental and insufficient that none could go much beyond the first elements of arithmetic. Neither did they know theoretical geometry, although they were obliged to make a frequent use of the application of it, in that which concerned their own extensive territory, which they represented by means of maps, with protuberances, indicating limits and

year Southern America with collections of medicines, from their mountains, which they sell at high prices.

localities; also in the distribution of lands, in stone-cutting, and, finally, in their admirable architecture, resolving very difficult problems with the greatest ease and most perfect exactitude.

In spite of the boasted relation of their monarchs to the Sun, the Peruvians had made but small progress in astronomy, and in this respect the Amautas were very inferior to the Mexican priesthood. The almost total want of mathematical knowledge did not permit them to deduce by calculation the annual movements of the sun, and they were obliged to resort to mechanical means in order to determine the principal variations of its course, by the aid of which they fixed the times of the solstices and the equinoxes. The method by which they discovered the exact time of the solstices is described by Garcilasso (Comment. I., Book II., Chap. XXII.) in the following manner:—

"The times of Summer and Winter solstices they determined by the large characters of Eight Towers, which they had erected to the east, and as many to the west, of the city, Cuzco; being ranked four and four in several positions, those two in the middle being higher than the other two at each end, and were built much in the form of the watch-towers in Spain: when the sun came to rise exactly opposite to four of these towers, which were to the east of the city, and to set just against those in the west, it was then the summer solstice; and in like manner when it came to rise and set just with the other four towers on each side of the city, it was then the winter solstice."

As the same author relates, "to denote the precise day of the equinoctial they had erected pillars of the finest marble in the open area before the temple of the sun, which, when the sun came near the time, the priests daily watched and attended to observe what shadow the pillars cast; and to make it more exact, they fixed on them a gnomon like the pin of a dial, so that so soon as the sun at its rising came to dart a direct shadow by it, and that at its height, or mid-day, the pillar made no shade, they then concluded that the sun was entered the equinoctial line, at which time they adorned these pillars with garlands and odoriferous herbs, and placed upon them the seat or chair of the sun, saying that on that day he appeared in his most glittering throne and majesty, and therefore made their offerings of gold and silver, and precious stones, to him with all the solemnities of ostentation and joy usual at such festivals. Thus the Incas and Amautas having observed that when the sun came to the equinoctial these pillars made little shadow at noon-day, and that those in the city of Quito and those of the same degree to the sea-coast made none at all, because the sun is then perpendicularly over them, they concluded that the position of those countries was more agreeable and pleasing to the sun than those on which, in an oblique manner only, he darted the brightness of his rays."*

The Amautas noted the movements of Venus, the only planet which attracted their attention, and which they venerarated as a page of the sun. They knew some few of the constellations, such as the Hyades, which they called *Ahuaracaqui*, or jaw-bone of the tapir, and the Plyades, *Oncoy Coyllur.* As all the nations were not versed in the course of the heavenly bodies, they were frightened at the eclipses of the sun and moon, principally at those of the latter planet, believing that it threatened to burst or explode upon the earth; and to avoid

* We have here followed the old translation of Garcilasso by Sir Paul Rycaud, which, though far from literal and often inaccurate, yet in this instance conveys the meaning of the original with sufficient distinctness to make it intelligible, and with more brevity than was possible in a literal translation.—[TRANSLATOR.]

the danger, they broke forth in a frightful shouting, endeavoring to make all the noise possible from the time that the eclipse began, with instruments of all descriptions, also beating the dogs to make them howl and augment the general confusion.

The phases of the moon (*Quilla*) they explained by saying that the planet was sick when it began to decrease, and for this reason they called the decline *huañuc-quilla*, or dying moon: they gave the name of *mosoc-quilla* to the new moon; to the crescent, *puca-quilla*, or colored moon, and *quilla-huañuy*, or dead moon, to the moon in conjunction. The entire lunation they divided into four equal quarters, beginning always with the first day of the new moon: thus the first section or period lasted until the day of the fourth crescent, the second until the opposition, the third until the fourth decline, and the fourth until the conjunction. They counted the months by moons, but the year from one winter solstice to another; this they subdivided into twelve equal parts, forming thus a solar year, by which they regulated their husbandry. The time which remained from the end of the lunar year until the completion of the solar was called *puchuc-quilla*, or residue of the moon, and was devoted to leisure. They distributed the solar year into four seasons: the spring, or *panchin*,* from the vernal equinox to the summer solstice: the summer, or *rupay-mitta*, from the summer solstice to the equinox of autumn: the autumn, *uma-raymi*, from the equinox of autumn to the winter solstice; and the winter, or *para-mitta*, called also *casac-puchu*, from the winter solstice to the vernal equinox. At each one of these four seasons they celebrated a general, solemn feast.

Montesinos tells us that the king Inti-Capac renewed the computation of the time, which was being lost, and that they counted the years in his regin by 365 days and six hours,

* Or *tuctu*, from the bud or stem of the corn flower.

and the years he computed by decades of ten years: each ten decades made a century of a hundred years, and each ten centuries made a *capac-huata*, (powerful year), or *Intiphuata*, which is one thousand years, that is, the great year of the sun. Thus they counted the periods or memorable deeds of their kings.

The same author assures us that the king Yahuar-Huquiz, a skilful astronomer, discovered a necessity for intercalating a day every four years, to form a bissextile or leap-year; but he renounced this plan in favor of another, which seemed more advantageous, and which his better judgment decided should be arranged by the Amautas, and so one year was intercalated at the end of four centuries. In memory of this king, the Indians called the leap-year *Huquiz*, which was previously called *Allca-Allca*, and for the same reason they gave to the month of May the name *Huar-Huquiz*. Such is the assertion of Montesinos, an assertion very erroneous, if we may judge from the silence of other historians, from the absence of all monuments which prove the existence of such a calendar, and from the little credit to be given to the above-mentioned author. The wise Peruvians did not divide the day into hours, and could not keep an exact astronomical account, possessing, as they did, an arithmetical knowledge so scanty, and so badly supplied with graphic means. Notwithstanding, it is possible that the Amautas counted the years by the decimal system.

The year (*Huata*) was divided, as we have seen, into twelve months, and began, according to some authors, in the summer solstice, at the end of June; according to others, in the winter solstice, at the end of December. It is certain that in Cuzco it began with this latter month, and in Quito, according to the laws of Inca-Huayna-Capac, in the summer solstice.

We will now explain the division into the months, with

an enumeration of the principal occupations and feasts which took place in each. We follow, in the names, the etymology derived from the Quichua language, but as there is another set of names whose origin is less clear, not being the pure Quichua, nor belonging to any neighboring language, we have thought it best to place at the end of each month these names also.

I. *Raymi* (December, from *raymi*, a solemn dance). This first month of the year, as it began with the day of the winter solstice, was celebrated with general balls, music and singing. In that month was held one of the four principal feasts with solemn dances, preceded by a day of fasting.—(*Sassippunchau*).*

There was an assemblage of the military chiefs with chosen troops, in Cuzco, for military exercises.—*Camayquiz.*

II. *Huchhuy-poccoy* (January, from *huchhuy*, *small*, and *poccoy*, *to ripen*). Thus called because the corn began to form small ears.

Continuing the military exercises, they exercised the soldiers, by competition principally in races. They rewarded the most dexterous and skilful.—*Pura-Opiayquiz.*

III. *Hatun-poccoy* (February, from *Hatun*, *great*, and *poccoy*, to ripen). Thus called on account of the increased size of the corn.—*Cac-Mayquiz.*

IV. *Paucar-huaray* (March). As regards the etymology of this name, says the presbyter, *Don Juan de Velasco*, (Hist. of the Kingdom of Quito, Vol. II. p. 40): "*Paucar-Huaray* signifies the month of spring, which unites the beginning with the end of the solar year; since *paucar* signifies the beauty

* It is as well to observe that they counted the months from the 20th, 21st, or 22d, according to the solstice, until the same day of the following month, so that the month which we call December—Raymi—included twelve days of January.

of the colors which the flowers display during this time, and *huatay* signifies binding together. Historians write this name in various ways, erring from its having become corrupted, or through mis-information, saying: *pacar-huaruy*, *pacar huaray* and *pacar huatuy*, finding for each, different etymologies, without foundation, and without discovering the true meaning in these corrupted words."

In our opinion, the true name of this month is *Paucar-hauray*, from *paucar*, *flowery place*, *beautiful meadow*, and from *Huaray*, to place baskets under, and figuratively to unfold a carpet, since this month spreads itself upon the ground like a magnificent carpet.

In it occurred the second principal feast of the year, preceded by three days of fasting, and it was the memorable feast of the renovation of the sacred fire, or *mosoc-nina.* On the day of the equinox, the Inca waited, accompanied by all the priests and chief lords of the court, at the entrance of the chief temple for the rising of the sun, and by means of a metallic mirror, called *Inca-rirpu*, concentrated its first rays, setting fire with them to a piece of sacred cotton picked and prepared for this purpose. This substance was carried while burning to the temple, where the sacrifice and offerings to the sun were made, and afterward it furnished fire to all the houses. The Inca was also accustomed to distribute to all the assistants bread and sacred *chicha.* Finally, the feast was concluded with dancing, music, and general rejoicing. How similar is this ceremony to that which takes place on Easter day in the Christian worship!—*Pacar-Ruarayquiz.*

V. *Agrihuay* (April). This word signifies an ear of corn with grains of divers colors.

In this month began the harvest of this cereal, accompanied with dancing, music and copious libations, which degenerated into intoxication. There were premiums proposed for those who met with certain colors, determined beforehand, in the grains of the full ears. He who deserved the premium (*missac*) was celebrated throughout the nation.—*Arihuaquiz.*

VI. *Aymuray* (May). Thus called because of the conveying of the corn to the public depositories and granaries, which took place in this month. The end of the harvest they celebrated clothed in gala dress, with music, chicha, dancing, and sportive games. They began to pull up the stubble preparatory to digging the earth.—*Aymurayquiz.*

VII. *Inti-Raymi* (June, from *Inti*, sun, and *Raymi*, dance). In this month was celebrated the third solemn feast, preceded by a fast. They rested from labor, giving themselves up to pleasure and enjoyment.—(*Aucay-Cuxqui.*)

VIII. *Anta-Asitua* (July, from *Anta*, copper, and *Asitua*, great dance). This month, which many authors call simply *Asitua*, began at the summer solstice, and was the epoch of the military balls. Dressed in court robes, they made the troops perform splendid exercises, celebrated their feasts, and went through the streets with noisy music, accompanied by the people inebriated and dancing.

They cultivated the land and prepared it for sowing, emptied chicha into the aqueducts and rivers, hoping to gain by this liberal sacrifice sufficient water for their fields. —*Chahuar-Huayquiz.*

IX. *Capac-Asitua* (August, from *Capac*, powerful, and *Asitua*, great ball).

They continued the feasts of the preceding month, and even with still greater splendor and solemnity. They also called this month *Yapay-Asitua*, the month of supplementary balls. They began at this time to sow corn, potatoes, sweet-root of Peru, and practise singular ceremonies, in order to expel beforehand all epidemical diseases.—*Cituaquiz.*

X. *Umu-Raymi* (September, from *Umu*, head, and *Raymi*, dance). In this month took place the enrolling of those liable to be taxed in the empire, and the verification of the prior register, celebrating for this purpose large feasts.

They also denominated it *Coyaraymi*, because they married at that time the *Coyas* or royal princesses, to whose connections succeeded those of the rest of the empire.

The women wore gala dresses, and at this time was celebrated the fourth principal feast, or *Asitua-raymi*, preceded by a day of fast.—*Puscuayquiz.*

XI. *Aya-Marca* (October). We are not positively told the etymology of this word. The majority of historians write the name of this month, *Ayarmaca*, but in our opinion it should be written *Ayamarca*, from *Aya*, corpse, and *Marca*, carry in arms, because they celebrated the solemn feast of the commemoration of the dead with tears, lugubrious songs and plaintive music, and it was customary to visit the sepulchres of relations and friends, and leave in them food and drink. It is worthy of remark, that this feast was celebrated among the ancient Peruvians at the same period and on the same day that the Christians solemnized the commemoration of the dead (2d of November).

At this period the potters made large bottles for the chicha, and in each house was this beverage devoted to the feasts of the following month.—*Cantarayquiz.*

XII. *Capac-raymi* (November, from *capac* and *raymi*).

This was the last month, or that of the solemn balls to conclude the year. The feasts and dances possessed at times a character of excessive joy, which degenerated into intoxication and licentiousness. In this epoch they finished sowing. In the public square of Cuzco, they were in the habit of representing comedies and tragedies composed by the Amautas. At the same time the Peruvians amused themselves with different games, such as the *huayrachina*, or game of ball, the *huayru*, a species of dice, the *chunca*, a game of ball with sticks, the *huatucay*, a game of enigmas, etc.

They held reunions and numerous assemblies in the capital and in the cities, under the direction of the princes. —*Laymequiz.*

Their limited knowledge of astronomy did not permit the Peruvians to make any progress in the art of navigation. In their feeble vessels, constructed from the trunks of trees, a *balsa*, or raft with a mast, and skins of sea-wolves or mats of rushes for sails, fitted to explore the coasts of their territory and interior lakes, they did not dare to launch out into the open sea, but contented themselves with the knowledge which they possessed of their own dominions on land, acquired by their conquests; nevertheless they must have had some knowledge, from what is said by *Huaynacapac* (to which Garcilasso refers): "I suspect that those who have gone round by the coast of our sea, will prove to be a people we know; they will be a brave people, and, at all events, will prove an advantage to us." It is also worth while to notice that which is referred to by Sor. Castelneau, that the mat or rush sails which they made use of in the lake of Titicaca, and the mode of taking them in, is identical with that which is seen upon the sepulchre of *Rameses* III. in Thebes. The construction of these weak floating machines, known by the name of *balsas*, and floats of rushes in actual use on the coast, and the small lakes of the Cordilleras, has been taken for a model for steamboats, and life-boats in cases of shipwreck, made of gum-elastic and gutta-percha. These rafts serve commonly the purpose of smuggling through the ports and coves with much facility, and it is easy to transport them without difficulty by land; and as their cost is small, they attach so little value to them that they burn or destroy them when they have concluded this immoral traffic.

In speaking of the Quichua language in our preceding chapter, we have already related all that was told us of the progress made by the Amautas in poetry, and especially in the dramatical line, which was the branch they cultivated from choice. We can easily recognize in the succinct explanation which we have given of the rural tasks, feasts and solemnities of the twelve months of the Peruvian year, the wise institutions of the Incas, whose skilful wisdom and benevolent perspicacity knew always how to combine the useful with the agreeable, as much to conduce to the public good as to advance individual welfare, rendering labor less heavy by means of an adequate combination of accompanying recreations. After the fatigue of sowing for the monarch was over, which took place after having done what was required for the lands belonging to the 'Sun' and the nation, the Indians enjoyed representations of comedies, the object of which was the illustration of the social virtues, now of one member of the family for the others, now of the vassal for his monarch; again, of an individual for the state, or of a private gentleman for his fellow-citizen. In the month of October, after the feast of the dead, they assisted in dramas or tragedies which represented scenes of the patriotic virtues of their ancestors; and in the months of the military exercises, it was customary to perform comedies alluding to celebrated warlike deeds.

We do not know the greater or less degree of perfection attained in the dramatic art, but there is no doubt that in the repeated representations of comedies, the actors reached great perfection. Without doubt the applause of the assistants, and the rich rewards which distinguished those who excelled, stimulated them to make progress in that branch.

Oratory was patronized by the Incas, and a gift highly esteemed among them was a pure and soft pronunciation, as well in public speaking as in the theatres.

All the compositions in verse, except the dramatic, were destined to be sung, and it is very probable that the same poets composed the music for the poems. There existed several ancient tunes very melodious, which might serve to test the musical knowledge of the ancient Peruvians. In order to form a correct idea of this music, we will insert here three *haravis*.

I.—Haravi in Sol Minor.

tr

II.—Haravi in La Minor.

III.—Haravi in Re Minor.

Although, naturally, the Indians possessed much fondness for music, we are forced to confess that this art was in its infancy before the arrival of the Spaniards.

Rude and noisy instrumental music was liked in proportion to the disturbance it created. The greatest noise proceeded from the *chhilchiles* and *chanares*, certain timbrels and bells, and from the *huancar* or drum. Among the stringed instruments we know of none but the *Tinya*, a species of guitar, of five or six chords. Their wind instruments were the *cqueppa*, or trumpet: *ccuyvi*, or whistler, of five sounds: the *pincullu*, or flute: the *huayllaca*, or the flageolet: the *chhayna*, a certain coarse flute, whose lugubrious and melancholy tones filled the heart with indescribable sadness and brought involuntary tears into the eyes. They attained to the greatest perfection with the *huayra-puhura*, an instrument which consisted of a species of sirinx or flute of Pan, made of canes attached by a thread, each one of which contained a note higher than the preceding one; this was the only instrument on which musicians could play in concert, all the others lacked in harmony. The *huayra-puhura* was made of reeds of cane or stone, and adorned sometimes with needlework. The French General Paroissien found in a *huaca*, over a corpse, one of these instruments, made of stone, (a species of talc); and in the Museum of Berlin is preserved a plaister mould of this interesting object, which the celebrated Humboldt sent to the English physician Stewart Traill, with a letter, from which we extract the following notices, (vid. Minutoli, Description of an ancient city in Guatemala, etc., Berlin, 1832, notes, page 53, plate XII., fig. I.)

The holes of the canes are cylindrical and regularly bored, and are three-tenths of an inch in diameter to the bottom of the bore. Their length is,

Nr. 1, 4.90 inches,	Nr. 5, 2.45 inches,
Nr. 2, 4.50 "	Nr. 6, 2.85 "
Nr. 3, 4.12 "	Nr. 7, 2.00 "
Nr. 4, 3.50 "	Nr. 8, 1.58 "

The canes Nrs. 2, 4, 6, and 7 contain small lateral holes, which, being open, give no sound, but closed give the following:

This tetrachord is perfect and easy of touch. By means of these holes this diapason is divided into very distinct tetrachords. One of them is, for instance, the key of *mi* minor, the other of *fa* major. Open these holes, and the instrument produces the following:

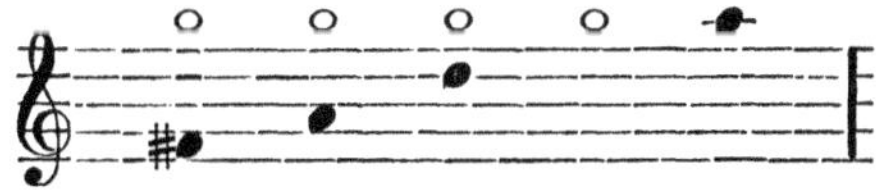

This tetrachord is perfect and also simple of touch; it was probably the favorite key of the Peruvians, and has, without doubt, produced a melodious sound.

The second tetrachord is produced by touching only the above notes, which give a complete major key:

But in this key the instrument possesses half a note more than the violin, which changes the *Fa* ♮ into *Fa* ♯ and the *Ut* ♮ into *Ut* ♯.

The holes permit an arbitrary variation of the diapason, which is modified, according to Mendelssohn, into an instrument of this description.

According to Garcilasso, (Comment. II., Chap. XXVI.) "each poem or song had its appropriate tune, and they could not put two different songs to one tune, and this was why the enamored gallant, making music at night with his flute, with the tune which belonged to it, told the lady and all the world the joy or sorrow of his soul, the favor or ill-will which he possessed, so that it might be said that he spoke by the flute." According to the same author, they did not play the songs which contained their wars and deeds, but they sang them at their great festivals and in their victories and triumphs, in memory of their valiant deeds.

7

CHAPTER VII.

RELIGIOUS SYSTEM OF THE ANCIENT PERUVIANS.

RELIGION opens a wide career to human hope, and traces a distinct route for the will; of the many subjects with which the mind is occupied, there is none which so deeply interests it, since none bears so close a relationship to the most sublime portion of human nature. Thus we may say that it is, at the same time, the strongest and most elevated of all feelings, and the exponent of the strength of a generation or people. "Give me the idea which exists of God among a nation (says Descartes), and I will give you their strength."

Thus there is no monument which so distinctly discloses the disposition, genius, tendencies, and extent of civilization in the shipwrecked empire of Peru as its worship, at once poetical and pompous, emanating from dogmas and legends, conforming to nature, sanctifying agriculture, and forming the basis of all policy, and shaping the condition even of the theocratical government of the dynasty of the Incas.

The Peruvian religion, as is generally admitted, was founded upon the worship of the Sun, was introduced by the Incas, and superseded an anterior worship, by means of one of those overturns or religious deluges, more than one instance of which is furnished us in the Asiatic annals. Previous to this reform and the establishment of the political institutions described in this work, the ancient inhabitants of Peru professed a creed which, however grossly disfigured it may have been by puerile superstitions, still attained to the conception of a Supreme Being, Creator of all that existed, to a system which contains vestiges of the dogmas of the fall of man, and of the redemption. Some historians of the earlier times of the conquest relate to us what they have succeeded in learning on this point, and upon their accounts we must rely; as all traces of the traditions of remoter times, preceding the government of the Incas, have been effaced from the memory of the nation.

According to these accounts, the Supreme Being was called *Con*, and had no human form or material body, but was an invisible and omnipotent spirit which inhabited the universe. By his word alone he created the world, elevated the mountains, excavated the valleys, filled with water the rivers, lakes and seas; and gave life to man, peopling with the race the plains and mountains, and providing them with all things necessary to their well-being and happiness. Thus overflowing with the gifts of Providence, the human race remained for a long time happy, until mankind gave themselves up to vice and crime, disregarding the respect and worship due to *Con*, and entangling themselves more and more in sin.

Under the existence of so much disrespect and corruption, *Con*, becoming enraged against ungrateful man, converted the fertile regions into sterile deserts, and depriving man of what was necessary for his subsistence, converted the race into black cats, and other horrible animals, leaving the earth uncultivated and deserted, until *Pachacamac*, son of *Con*, taking charge of the government of the world, recreated all which had been destroyed by his father, and gave new life to man, taking special care of all. More grateful than their predecessors, the new generation raised in honor to *Pachacamac* a sumptuous temple on the banks of the sea, worshipping, with the greatest idolatry, a deity so beneficent, without venturing to make a corporeal image, while, as to *Con*, they judged him to be incorporeal, and consequently invisible, although they conceived him to be an inhabitant of the temple. His worshippers never ventured to invoke the name of the Deity without prostrating themselves on the ground, kissing the earth, and making manifest demonstrations of abasement; and when they offered sacrifice they entered the temple, barefooted and silent, throwing themselves on the ground before the sacrificial altar.

The temple of Pachacamac, the immense ruins of which are still visible, near the town of *Lurin*, to the south of Lima, was the only one throughout the whole country which was dedicated to the Supreme Being, and for this reason pilgrims from distant territories directed their steps to present their offerings and worship the Deity. Thus do the historians speak of them: "The pilgrims passed with safety even through the inimical provinces, against which they had declared war without other condition than that they should go in small parties unarmed, under which condition they were entertained and supported in all parts, according to the mutual convenience of all parties." So powerful was the feeling of gencral vcncration for thc Suprcmc Boiug.

They do not tell us positively whether in that epoch the Peruvians worshipped any other Deities, but according to vestiges long prior to the introduction of the religion of the Incas, it is not probable that their religion was limited to the single worship of *Con* and *Pachacamac;* and studying attentively the worship of the Peruvian Inca dynasty, we find many vestiges of a heterogeneous system, which we must view as the remains of a primitive religion. Its analogy with the other nations of the old and new continent is a new proof which operates in favor of the supposition of a polytheistical system among the ancient Peruvians.

It cannot be denied, that the above tradition of the creation of the world, by the invisible and omnipotent *Con*, the primitive happy state of men, their corruption by sin, the destruction of the earth, and its regeneration, bears a distinct analogy to the Mosaic chronicle of the earliest epoch of the history of the human race, and we readily distinguish in this system the primitive monotheistic religion, common to all the nations of the world, a simple and exalted worship, which was soon, however, corrupted by the material personification of the Supreme Being, and the introduction of new Deities.

Upon the introduction of the new worship, the Inca, its founder, incorporated it, with cunning artifice, into the prevailing religion. He declared to the nations that the Supreme Divinity was the *Sun*, without whom nothing could exist in the world; that the Gods, *Con* and *Pachacamac*, were sons of the Sun; that he himself, the revealer of this doctrine, was a brother of these others, and consequently a son also of the *Sun;* that his omnipotent father permitted him to incarnate himself, and descend to the earth in order to teach men the arts and sciences, and instruct them concerning the will of the Supreme Being.

For a skilful and cunning man it was not difficult to exercise his intellectual superiority, to his own profit and to the general good also, as the docile and submissive diposition of the Peruvians induced them easily to adopt a religion which, without being detrimental to the established faith, enriched it and gave it a character more distinct and better adapted to their pleasures and tastes. Thus it is not strange that the new doctrine should spread rapidly throughout the principal States, and that from thence it should extend and connect itself with the progress which the imperial dynasty was constantly making.

Upon examining attentively the religious system introduced by the Incas, we do not find in it one of those profoundly metaphysical and sublime ideas which are so prominent among the Asiatic religions, and which the polytheistical worship also reveals to us. The base of their religion was the private interest of the royal family, whose authority was by this means rendered more firm and illimitable than that of the most powerful autocrat of the East.

The *Sun* was the Supreme Being whom the nation respected by erecting sumptuous temples wherein they offered most exquisite and costly sacrifices; but the Inca, as a son of the god, was considered as a personified deity—the immediate organ of the Supreme Being, and entitled to the same homage with him. A worship like this, whose illusory dogmas could not bear the slightest analysis, was only possible among a credulous people, whose faculties, suppressed by political institutions and absorbed by war, labor and feasts, did not permit them to give the slightest thought to things superior to their trivial occupations. Well did the Incas know the weakness of their doctrine, and for this reason they preserved on one side the ancient worship of *Pachacamac*, whilst on the other they inculcated in a most rigorous manner the worship of the *Sun*.

We will not enter into imaginary hypotheses relative to the result of the fusion of the religion of the Incas with the previous prevailing religion; it being almost impossible to distinguish, throughout all its extent, the elements which have been preserved, and those which were lost or added to this ancient worship, by that which superseded it, and the influence of which we cannot define.

The most important works upon this subject, for those

who desire to penetrate as profoundly as possible into it, are the "Natural and Moral History of the Indians," by *Father Acosta;* the "Chronicle of the Great Kingdom of Peru," by *Pedro Cieza de Leon;* the "Natural History of the West Indies," by *Don Francisco Lopez de Gomara;* a part of the "Commentaries" of *Garcilasso de la Vega;* and, above all, the "Extirpation of the Indians from Peru, (Lima, Hieronimo de Contreras, 1621, 4to.), written by the Jesuit *Pedro Jose de Arriaga.* The author, charged by order of Don *Francisco de Borja y Aragon*, Prince of Esquilache, sixteenth Viceroy of Peru, and by the Archbishop *Bartolomé Lobo Guerro*, with the office of visiting, with several other commissioners, the provinces of the archbishop, to inform themselves of the worship used by the natives, and to destroy their idols, traversed the assigned territory between February, 1617, and July, 1618, and afterward published the narrative of his journey, filled with most important accounts. This work, which is exceedingly rare in European libraries, gives more information concerning the Peruvian mythology than all the others of the same nature, containing a summary of the auricular confessions of more than five thousand persons, participators in the Peruvian idolatry, and also an account of the examination of numerous idols,* information which has aided us much in treating of the idols in the following pages.

Faith in the immortality of the soul was one of the fundamental ideas among all the Peruvian nations. They believed that after death the just went to a beautiful and pleasant place, unknown of the living, where they received the

* The author quoted in the text says that he confessed in eighteen months 5,624 persons, discovered and imposed penance on 679 ministers of idolatry, removed 603 principal *huacas*, 3,418 *conopas*, 45 *mamazaras*, 189 *huancas*, and 617 *mallquis*.

reward for their virtue; whilst the souls of the malicious were tormented in a doleful place, filled with sorrow and fright; and that after a certain time, not exactly determined, they should return to their bodies, beginning a new terrestial life, continuing the same occupations, and making use of the same objects which they had left at the time of their death. This belief induced them to preserve the corpses with great care, and to bury the dead with a part of their clothes, their utensils, and sometimes with their wealth.

The judge of the human race was, according to the belief of the Indians, *Pachacamac* himself, and in some provinces *Con;* the Indians not being willing to believe that the *Sun* was to be considered as the supreme judge, notwithstanding the efforts made by the Incas to familiarize the Indians with this opinion. As in the first age of the world, *Con* punished the human race with a frightful barrenness, so in the second *Pachacamac* vented his wrath in a deluge; and there was among the Peruvians a tradition analogous to the narrative of Genesis, as to the construction of an ark, and the preservation of a small portion of the human family from total ruin. There also prevailed the belief that the end of the world would come after a frightful famine, that the sun would be obscured and the moon fall into our planet, and that everything would be left enveloped in thick darkness.

In opposition to the Supreme Being, and therefore, as the Peruvian religion considered, to *Pachacamac*, who was the infinite essence, endowed with ineffable and innumerable attributes, the Indians also believed in the existence of another being, of evil disposition and very powerful, animated with an inextinguishable hatred against the human race, and disposed to injure them as much as possible. This being, who, by the character attributed to him, reminds one of the Ahreman of the Persians, or the Satan of the Jews and Christians, was called *Supay*, and in some places was worshipped in temples wherein were sacrificed to him children of tender years; an abominable worship, which reminds one of the horrible offerings to *Moloch* and *Tiphon*. But *Supay* was subordinate to *Pachacamac*, and none could injure those who were protected by this beneficent divinity, the invocation of whose name alone was sufficient to appease all malignant spirits.

The worship of Pachacamac was much more widely extended than historians suppose, and we may safely say that he was the Deity most populai and most respected by the Peruvian people generally; whilst the religion of the sun was that of the court, a worship which, although generally recognized by the Indians, never succeeded in eradicating their faith in and devotion to the primary divinity.

In fact, in all the accounts of the life of the Indians there may be seen that profound respect which they paid Pachacamac. Upon the birth of a child, they raised him in their arms, offering him to this Deity, and imploring his protection for the new-born infant. When a poor Peruvian ascended a hill or elevation, he unburdened himself of his load upon reaching the summit, made the usual reverences preceding the invocation of the name of Pachacamac, and bowing himself repeated three times the word "*Apachicta*," which was the abbreviation for *Apachicta muchhani;* which means, "I adore him who enables me to endure—I give thanks to him who has given me strength to endure thus far;" and at the same time he presented to the *Apachic* or *Pachacamac* an offering, which consisted either of a hair which was drawn from the eye-lash, and blown into the air, or of the *Coca* which they chewed, or of a small twig or little straw, or of a small stone or a handful of earth. Even at the present day the traveller observes, in the roads near the top of the

Cordilleras, *Pachetas*, heaps of stones or of earth, the result of these offerings; and the Indians even now continue the custom of leaving similar tokens in the same places, although with a very different signification.

The primitive worship not quadrating with the new one established by the Incas, or uniting itself with difficulty to the former, was always a perplexity to the imperial dynasty, which attempted to alter its various features, without, however, accomplishing its object until later days. The Inca Pachacutec having conquered the King Cuyusmancu, lord of the valleys of *Pachacamac*, *Rimac*, *Chancay* and *Huaman*, the sumptuous temple of Pachacamac fell into the hands of the conqueror. Well did the Peruvian monarch know how imprudent it would be to pursue openly the worship of this Deity, and for this reason he succeeded, with his customary cunning, in indirectly undermining it and in amalgamating it with the Sun-worship; now by corrupting the priests of PACHACAMAC, and now by causing to be constructed, in the suburbs, another temple no less magnificent, dedicated to the Sun, which was adorned in the most ostentatious manner, and which became eventually a monastery of virgins consecrated to that Deity. His successors followed the same policy, reminding us of the Sultans of *Delhi* and *Misora*—zealous Islamites, who ordered to be constructed mosques near the Brahminical pagodas—and in a few years the worship of *Pachacamac* fell almost into disuse. Finally, the *Cushipatas* or priests constructed a horrible idol of wood with a human face, thus personifying, in the most profane manner, the divinity who for so many centuries had embodied the sublime thought and ideal conception of the Peruvian worship; and they abused the idol to subserve their purposes, causing it to pronounce feigned oracles and enriching themselves at the cost of the nation's credulity.

Upon examining the worship prevailing in Peru upon the arrival of the Spaniards, it is natural to propose the question as to the Incas—Did they, its founders and protectors, so distinguished for their wisdom and prudence, believe themselves in those dogmas of the religion which they attempted to plant in their vast empire, and to introduce into the provinces which they conquered? Without pretending to solve this difficult question, we will merely quote the words of two sovereigns, which are very significant. One of them, *Tupac-Inca-Yupanqui*, says (according to the account of *Father Blas Valera*, Garcilasso de la Vega, Royal Commentaries, Part I., Book VIII., Chap. VIII.): "Many say that the Sun lives, and that he is the maker of all things: consequently that which makes anything must assist that which he has made; but many things are made during the absence of the Sun, therefore he is not the maker of all things; and that he does not live is proved, because his trips do not tire him. If he were a living thing he would grow weary like ourselves, or if he were free he would visit other parts of the heavens where he has never been. It is like a tied bullock which always makes the same circuit, or like the arrow, which goes where it is sent and not where it wishes."* The second extract is from the learned *Inca-Huayna-Capac*, and is referred to by Father Acosta (Hist. of the New World, Chap. V.): "The Indians relate that on one day of the nine during which the principal feast of the Sun, called *Raymi*, lasted, the Inca took the liberty of gazing upon the sun (which was prohibited, as it savored of disrespect). He cast his eyes upon it as long as it was possible, and remained thus for some time, gazing at it. The chief priest, who was one of

* The learned Humboldt, in his remarkable work entitled *Ansichten der Natur*, II., p. 384, erroneously attributes this saying to the Inca Huayna-Capac.

his uncles, and stood by his side, said to him, 'What are you doing, Inca? Do you not know that it is not lawful to do this?'

"The king then cast down his eyes, but after a short time took the same liberty and fixed them again upon the sun. The chief priest said, 'Consider, my lord, what you are doing; for besides being prohibited, as we are, from looking with freedom upon the sun, as it is deemed disrespectful, see the bad example given to your court, and to the whole empire, here assembled to celebrate the worship and adoration due to your father as the supreme and only lord.' *Huayna-Capac*, looking at the priest, said to him, 'I will propose to you two questions in reply to what you have said. I am your King and universal Lord; are any of you rash enough to order me, for your own pleasure, to leave my throne, and thus make the way clear?' The priest replied, 'Who would be mad enough to do thus?' The Inca replied, 'And is there any noble among my subjects, however rich and powerful he be, who would not obey me if I ordered him to go by post from here to Chili?' The priest replied, 'No, Inca, there are none who would not obey thee to the death, in all that thou commandest.'

"The King then said, 'Well, then, I tell thee that this our father, the sun, must have another lord or master more powerful than himself, who commands him each day to make the circuit that he makes without stopping; because, were he the supreme lord, he would sometimes leave off travelling and rest for his own pleasure, even though there might be no necessity for so doing."

The Peruvian deities are divided into deities of this world, and these again into *stellar* and *terrestrial* deities; into *historical* deities, deities of the *nation*, or of the *people*, and finally into deities of *families* or *individuals*, similar to the *lares* and *penates* of the Romans. To the stars belonged the *Sun*, the *Moon*, his wife or *coya*, *Venus*, the *Pleiades*, the *Hyades*, a star called *Mamanmircue-Coyllur*, and the constellation of the Southern Cross.

The *Sun* (*Inti* or *ppunchau*), as we have already said, was the god *par excellence*, the protecting deity, he who presided over the destinies of man—the origin of the royal family. To the *Sun* belonged the magnificent temples which existed in all the cities and in almost all the villages of the vast Peruvian territory—temples resplendent and ornamented with gold and jewels, upon the altars of which they kindled their sacrifices. They were only surpassed by that of Cuzco, of which we will treat more extensively in another chapter, as celebrated for its marvellous construction as for its riches. Each year the four principal feasts, corresponding with the four astronomical epochs of the year, were held in it. In these temples was sacrificed the wealth of the empire, such as precious metals, finely woven cloth, cattle, corn, gum, fruits, and even children of tender years. Numerous were the priests destined for the service of God, and by day, as well as by night, a certain number of them were obliged to watch in turn in the temples, and to fulfil the prescribed offices.

These chosen priests were held in great esteem among all the members of the priestly society; they also had to master most difficult studies, pass through severe examinations, and give high proofs of capacity. As they formed a privileged caste, the youths who were destined to occupy the sacerdotal rank in the temples were educated from their most tender years. They were obliged to observe great penances and to fast rigorously, especially before the four principal feasts. The fast, which sometimes continued a year and more, consisted in the total privation of food, if it lasted but a few days, and in the total abstinence from salt and garlic when it lasted a longer time: and sometimes so rigorous was it, that they did not venture to touch their bodies with their hands while it lasted. In some parts of the empire the *Cushipatas*, or priests, maintained a perpetual celibacy; in others they were married, but while the fast lasted, they abstained from all personal contact with their wives. They enjoyed much respect throughout the nation, and the chief priest (*Huillca-Uma*), who was an Inca of royal blood, and belonged to the sacerdotal society of the sun, possessed the government of the other priests of the empire. He resided in Cuzco, and extracted auguries from the flight of birds and from the entrails of the victims, in the presence of the Inca. At the solemn feasts, the king himself in person was the high priest, for which purpose he was initiated and consecrated in all the mysteries of religion.

There were virgins dedicated to the *Sun*, considered as wives of the god; these lived in cloisters or convents in the greatest retirement. The most celebrated was the *Acllahuasi*, in Cuzco, or house of the selected ones—who were made such either from their lineage or for their beauty. This contained more than one thousand virgins. Those who alone could aspire to admittance within this sacred college were the maidens of royal blood, who, from their most tender years, were taken from the bosom of their families to be enclosed within the convent, under the superintendence of ancient matrons, to whom was given the name of *mamacunas*, and who had grown gray within these walls. They were obliged to pronounce the vow of perpetual virginity and seclusion, without the slightest connection with the world, nor even with their parents; and so faithfully was this vow executed, and so closely was this seclusion observed, that not even the Peruvian monarch himself dared tread within the precincts of the monastery, a privilege which was only, by reason of their sex, enjoyed by the queen and her daughters.

Under the direction of competent mistresses, the wives of the Sun were taught the sacred duties of their office. Their occupations were spinning and weaving the garments of the Incas of the finest vicuña wool, woven in brilliant colors and enamelled with gold and stones. These sacred virgins were also obliged to weave the garments in which the Inca sacrificed to the Sun, as also to prepare the *chicha* and sacred bread of corn, called *zancus*, for the monarch and his court.

The houses which the Virgins of the Sun occupied were richly marbled and adorned with as much taste as the palaces of the Incas and the temples of the Sun, thus carrying out the policy of the Peruvian monarchs, that nothing should be wanting to make this institution flourish, as the Roman emperors heaped with honors and privileges the college of vestals, in which was concentrated the prosperity of the empire, and which in many respects bore a close resemblance to the virgins of the sun.

In the provinces were similar cloisters, but destined to another purpose. There were received maidens of all classes, noble and plebeian, provided they were possessed of personal beauty. Designed to be concubines of the monarch, those who attained to this honor were chosen and sent to Cuzco, leaving the others to remain in perpetual virginity as the spouses of the Sun. Those who had the honor of attaining to the royal bride-chamber could not return to their monastic seclusion, but remained in the palace as ladies of the queen, until they reached an advanced age, when they were permitted to return to their home and country, where, although they occupied a lower station, they received honor and respect, as the property of the Inca, leading an easy and sumptuous life in their retirement. Those who remained in the cloisters, occupied themselves, as did the virgins of the sun, in spinning and weaving, and the cloth which they wove was presented by the Inca to the Lords of his court, the princes, and other nobles who were thought worthy of the honor by the monarch.

The wife of the Inca who was convicted of adultery was subjected to the same penalty as the virgin of the Sun who proved false to her vows. If she swore that the Sun himself was the author of her pregnancy, she was allowed to live until the time was accomplished for her delivery, and was then buried alive. The fruit of her union with the Deity was reserved for the priesthood, or was destined to form a part of the sacred society of the virgins of the Sun, according to its sex.

The Moon (*quilla*), considered as the sister and wife of the Sun, was an object of profound respect, but the worship given to it was much more limited than that given to the Sun. The Moon was considered, as at Athens and Rome, to be the protecting deity of women in childbirth. In the province of *Huamantanca* existed a celebrated temple dedicated to this Deity. Very erroneous is the assertion of Garcilasso, who pretends that the ancient Peruvians had no other god than the Sun, that they did not recognize the Moon as a goddess, nor offer sacrifices to it, nor construct temples to it; and that, although they believed that it was the universal mother, and under this idea professed great veneration for it, still, beyond that, their idolatry did not go. The same author contradicts himself, inasmuch as in other parts of his Commentaries, he alludes to the several gods worshipped by the Incas; and nothing but the partiality resulting from his birth (which is particularly evident when he speaks of the worship and religious ceremonies of his ancestors) could have induced him to make an assertion so devoid of proofs, and in such direct contradiction to the other historians, whose accounts unanimously affirm the existence of a polytheistical worship in ancient Peru.

The most beautiful of all the planets, Venus (*Chhasqui Coyllur*), was worshipped as a page of the *Sun*, by which he was closely followed, when he rose and when he set. The constellation of the Pleiades (*Onccoy coyllur*) was also an object of devotion on account of the influence attributed to it in many diseases: the Hyades, for their fancied action in seed-time, and the *maman-mircuc-coyllur*, because they believed that this star, as its name would indicate, influenced some men to eat their fathers.

Among the elemental Deities, we must particularly mention the air (*Huayra*), the fire (*nina*), the lightning and thunder (*llipiac* or *illapi*), and the rainbow (*ckuichi*): these latter two were considered as servants of the *Sun*, and were consequently respected, especially the *llipiac*, to whom they sacrificed llamas.

The terrestrial Deities were very numerous; many of them had temples, and the Peruvians sacrificed to all of them, invoking their aid, especially when they found themselves in immediate contact with them. To the earth (*Mamapacha*), they offered, in the time of harvest, ground corn and *chicha*, imploring them to grant a good harvest. The hills, mountains, and snowy ridges received a worship somewhat mysterious, as did also the rocks of uncommon shape, which are sometimes observed in the Cordilleras, and appear like men converted into stone. The sea (*Mamacocha*) was piously invoked by those Indians who dwelt between the Sierra and the coast, imploring it to grant them good health, since they believed—and in this, they were not far from truth—that its vapors produced the diseases from which those suffered who lived on the plains near the sea. On the banks of rivers

(*Mayu*) they performed the ceremony called *Mayuchalla*, which consisted in taking a little water in the hollow of the hand and drinking it, invoking the God of the river to permit them to pass it* or to give them fish; and to render it propitious, they threw corn into it.†

* Even at the present day every Indian living on the Cordilleras performs this ceremony, before passing a river on foot or on horseback.

† The principal temples of the idols of the *Chibchas* were, as we have already said, the lakes, where they might make their offerings of precious things without fear of others profiting by it, because, although they had confidence in their priests, and knew that they buried them carefully in the vessels designed for that purpose, they naturally felt more certain of it when they threw them into lakes and deep rivers. The lake of *Gualavita* was the most celebrated of all these sanctuaries, and each village had a beaten footpath leading to it, by which they went and offered their sacrifices. They crossed two ropes in such a manner as to form equal angles, and to the intersection of these went the raft which conveyed the chiefs of the lake and the devotees. There they invoked the miraculous princess *Bachuc* and her daughter, who were said to live at the bottom in a delightful spot, with all conveniences, from the time when, in a hasty moment, she quarrelled with the ancient prince her husband, and was thrown into this lake, and there her offerings were made. Each lake had its tradition, and pilgrimages to these sanctuaries were very common among the *Chibchas*.

At the time that the prince of *Gualavita* was an independent chief, he made each year a solemn sacrifice, which, by its singularity, contributed to give celebrity to this lake, even through the most distant countries, and which was the origin of the belief of the *Dorado*, in search of which so many years and so much property were spent. On the appointed day, they anointed the body with turpentine, and afterward rubbed it with gold-dust. Thus gilded and resplendent, they embarked upon the rafts, surrounded by the old men, and in the midst of music and crowds of people who covered the declivities which surrounded the lake in the form of an amphitheatre. Arrived at the centre, the prince deposited the offerings of gold, emeralds, and divers precious objects, and threw himself into the waters to bathe. At this moment the neighboring mountains resounded with the applause of the people. The religious ceremony

The Historical Deities were those which initiated men into social life and civil institutions; and in almost all polytheistical religions, there attaches to each one of these a tradition, or legend, relative to its character and actions whilst it was in direct relation to man. In the Peruvian religion the greater part of these traditions have been lost, or at least a knowledge of them has not descended to Europeans, doubtless for want of an epic poem in the Quichua language. For this reason we can only cite by name some of the historical deities, with a few observations upon their figures, as they are described by ancient travellers, whose zeal induced them to burn them or break them into fragments. The greater number of these Deities were *Huacas*, that is, worshipped by one province, one town, or only one hamlet. A few of them had temples, but the Indians sacrificed to all, and celebrated in their honor several annual feasts.

The chief of these Deities, and one intimately connected with Peruvian history, was *Viracocha*, who more than once appeared in human form to the Inca of the same name, the son of *Yahuar-Huacac;* saying that he was the *son* of the *Sun*, and brother of *Manco-Capac*, and giving an account of

being over, then commenced dancing, singing, and intoxication. In these monotonous and measured songs, they always repeated the ancient history of the country, and what they knew of its gods, its heroes, battles, and other memorable events, which were thus transmitted from generation to generation. At the doors of the dwellings of the princes, who always presided at these feasts, as in all public functions, there were stationed, as long as they lasted, two naked old Indians, one on each side, playing upon the *choismia*, which is a wind instrument, sad and shrill; and covered simply with a fish-net or *atarraya*, which among the Indians is the symbol of death, because they say we should never lose sight of this, especially in times of rejoicing and feasting. There were also races and contests among the youths, the prince rewarding the most agile and skilful.—(*J. Acosta. Historical Compendium, pag*. 198, 199.)

important events which were to take place in the future. The Inca ordered to be constructed in honor of this apparition a magnificent temple at Cacha, sixteen leagues from Cuzco.

In the interior of this edifice was a species of chapel, paved with black stones, in which was a niche, the interior of which contained an immense pedestal, on which reposed the Deity, as he had appeared to the Inca. According to the description given by Garcilasso, "he was a man of good stature, with a large beard, more than an inch in length, garments long and wide, like a tunic or cassock, reaching to the feet. He held the image of an unknown animal, having lion's claws, and tied by the neck with a chain, one end of which was in the hand of the statue. All this was made of stone; and because the workmen not having seen the original, nor a copy of it, knew not how to sculpture it, as they told the Inca, he placed himself in the dress and position in which he said he had seen it. . . . The statue was similar to the images of our blessed Apostles, and more particularly resembled that of St. Bartholomew." For two centuries previous to the arrival of the Spaniards had the worship of *Viracocha* been professed.

As sons of the Supreme Divinity, the Incas enjoyed, even after death, general adoration. Their obsequies were celebrated with the greatest pomp and solemnity, and to their corpses were offered numerous sacrifices; for which reason we should consider them as Historical Gods. The deceased monarch was embalmed with so much dexterity and skill that he seemed to be living, and in this state he was preserved entire centuries. His intestines, deposited in vases of gold,* were preserved in the magnificent temple of

* A similar custom we also observe among the *Zipas* of *Bogota*, according to the account of *Acosta*. When these monarchs died, the old

Tambo, four leagues from Cuzco, where the body was seated upon a species of throne, in a natural position, before the figure of the *Sun*, in the principal temple of the capital. Very interesting are those accounts given by the early chroniclers of those mummies which they obtained a view of. Garcilasso (l. c. Book v., Chap. XXIX.) says: "In the chamber are found five bodies of the Inca sovereigns; three of men, and two of women. The first was said by the Indians to be the Inca *Viracocha*, of great age, whose hair was white as snow. The second was said to be the great *Tupac-Inca-Yupanqui*, who was the great-grand-son of *Viracocha-Inca*. The third was *Huayna-Capac*, son of *Tupac-Inca-Yupanqui*, and great-great-grand-son of the Inca *Viracocha*. The two latter had not apparently lived as long; for, although they had marks of old age, they were less than those of *Viracocha*. One of the women was the queen, *Mama-Runtu*, wife of the Inca *Viracocha*. The other was the *Coya-Mama-Ocllo*, mother of *Huayna-Capac*; and it is probable that the Indians placed them near each other, after the death of husband and wife, as they were united in life. The bodies were so entire that they lacked neither hair, eye-brows, nor eye-lashes. They were dressed in their usual habiliments, such as they wore when living, with ornaments on their heads, and without other ensign of royalty. They were seated as the Indians usually seat themselves,—their hands crossed over their breasts, the right over the left, the eyes cast down, as though they gazed upon the ground."

According to the testimony of others, *Gonzalo Pizarro*

men extracted the intestines, and filled the cavities with liquid rosin, afterward introducing the corpse into a large trunk made of palm, lined with sheets of gold within and without; and they were carried secretly, and buried in a vault already made, from the day on which they began to reign, in secret and distant provinces.

disinterred the body of the Inca *Viracocha*, in *Haquijahuana*, and ordered it to be burned. The Indians gathered together the ashes, and, placing them in a small jar of gold, made to it splendid offerings.

The body of *Huayna-Capac* was moved from *Patallacta* to *Totacacha*, where was founded the parish of *San Blas*. It was so well preserved that it seemed to be in life. The eyes were made of very thin gold, and so well-formed that they seemed natural, and the whole body was prepared with a species of bitumen. There appeared on the head the scar of a stone thrown in war, and the long hair was visible, very hoary, and perfect. He had died about eighty years previous. The Licentiate *Polo-Ondegardo*, in the vice-royalty of *D. Andres Hurtado de Mendoza*, the second Marquis of Cañete, brought this mummy, with several others of the Incas, from Cuzco to Lima. Garcillasso adds: "The bodies weighed so little that any Indian might carry them in his arms, or on his shoulders, from house to house of the gentlemen who wished to see them. They carried them, covered with white cloths, through the streets and squares, surrounded by the Indians, worshipping them with tears and groans; and many Spaniards lifted their caps as they passed, because they were the bodies of kings, which was so grateful to the Indians that they could not sufficiently express their thanks." Finally, the mortal remains of these powerful and wise monarchs were interred in a court of the Hospital of Saint Andrew, in Lima.

Besides the Incas the Peruvians adored also heroes in some of the provinces, and it seems that this worship originated before the Incas conquered those territories. In the ancient town of *Huahualla*, for instance, they sacrificed to the mummies of *Caxaparca*, and of his son, *Huaratama*, both dressed in the garb of warriors, with many feathers of divers colors; but tradition relates to us nothing concerning the deeds of these persons, who, it is probable, were distinguished commanders of the nation.

We have already said that the greater number of the historical gods were *Huacas*, or gods of towns or provinces, of which there were made figures of stone and wood. A large number of them were destroyed by the Spanish conquerors, who, in their religious zeal and national pride, disdained to preserve the laws or traditions of the Indians; and thus it is not to be wondered at that, thanks to the strange course of *Father Arriaga*, we have so slight a knowledge of their names and forms.

The most interesting of the *Huacas* which this ardent religioso destroyed was found about two leagues from the town of *Hilavi*, on an elevated summit, where were found the sepulchres of Indians, of richly sculptured stone chambers. There was here a statue, three times a man's height, and of magnificently sculptured stone, with two monstrous figures beside; one of a man who looked toward the west, and the other, with the face of a woman, on the same stone at the back of the former, who faced the east. On both might be seen serpents, which were twined from the feet to the head; and about the soles of the feet there were gathered other reptiles, like toads. In front of each one of these idols was a square stone, of a span and a half in height, which seemed to serve as an altar. In order to break in pieces so valuable a monument, the Jesuit *Arriaga* employed more than thirty persons for three days.

The *Huaca-Rimac* was also greatly celebrated. It was on the banks of a river of the same name, on which is now situated the present capital of Peru; the name of which, *Lima*, was derived from the name of the idol that was there. It had a human figure, and was found in a magnificent temple, in which oracular responses were given to all the questions put by the priests. Not only throughout the nation of the *Yuncas*, who occupied this valley, but throughout the entire surrounding country, was this idol worshipped; and even from distant provinces deputies came with questions and offerings.*

Another oracle existed in the province of *Huamanchuco*, the famous *Huaca-Catequilla*, which predicted to *Tupac-Inca-Yupanqui*, who consulted it by means of his priests concerning the result of the campaign which he was going to undertake against a brother of his, who had rebelled, that he should die in battle; and this was verified. The son of *Tupac-Inca*, irritated at the death of his father, destroyed the temple of the oracle; but the priests resolved to place the idol in safety, and carried it to Cahuana, where they built it another temple, and continued its worship.

In the province of Manta was a sumptuous temple dedicated to *Umiña*, or the God of *Health*, which contained an idol, with a face half human, made of an emerald, very precious, well guarded, and deeply venerated.

Another famous *Huaca*, worshipped by several provinces, was *Sañacmama*, which *Arriaga* found in the territory of *Chanca*. It was in the form of a large jar, and was found in the centre of eight jars of similar figure, surrounded by many other jars and pictures, and by two cups of clay, with

* Tradition relates that the celebrated temple of the idol, RIMAC, in the valley of *Huatica*, was contiguous to *Limatambo*; and that the destroyed town has passed into that of *Magdalena*. There exists a large number of *Huacas*, of different sizes, some being more than fifty yards in length, and about fifteen in height, from *Limatambo* to *Maranga*. In one of these remained for a long time the Frenchman, *Mateo-Salado*, who passed for a hermit, until he was burnt in 1573 by the horrible tribunal of the Inquisition.

which the Indians pledged the *Huaca.* They found the great jar filled with *chicha,* which age had converted into water; and near it many *cuys* (a species of small rabbit), and other sacrifices. On the day of the *Corpus Christi* the Indians hold a festival, taking the jar from its place, and covering it with clothing, similar to that used by the *Pallas.*

In the town of *Quichumarca* they worshipped the *Huaca Huari,* whom the Indians considered as the Deity who lent strength when they were about to build houses and cultivate land; and his two brothers, all of horrible aspect.

The *Huaca Choquechuco* was an object of worship in a town of the same name, as also the *Huaca-Humivillca,* and his brothers. The first, rudely sculptured in stone, of the color of liver, had a human face, and was seated on a stone mortar.

Near the town of *Tamor* they worshipped a large stone, which had been split by lightning. They called it the *Huaca Llipiac,* a name derived from the lightning, and to it was offered in sacrifice sheep, gold, and silver. The *Huacas Quenac* and *Quenac-Huillca,* with Indian forms without arms or feet, and of furious aspect, were also worshipped in several towns. In the same town of Tamor existed the *Huaca-Huayna-Yurac,* son of *Apu-Yurac,* who was venerated in the ancient town of *Hupa;* both had the form of men seated upon small plates of silver. We must also note in the town of *Chochas* the *Llaxehuillca,* in the form of an Indian seated, crestfallen, and one eye larger than the other. The race of *Sopac* worshipped the *Huaca Apu-Xillin,* and his son *Huayna-Xillin,* probably celebrated ancestors of this stock; and in the valley of *Jauja* the *Huancas* worshipped the celebrated *Huarivilca,* to whom they had constructed a sumptuous temple near a fountain of the same name. The chroniclers also mention the *Huacas Huamantuçoc* in the town of

Quepas, *Mullu-Cayan* and *Cota-Tumac* in the ruins of *Cocha-llipiac*, *Umy* in the seat of *Chincas*, *Yusca* in the town of *Cayna;* as also the *Huacas Xampay*, *Atahuanca*, *Pariacaca*, *Huanchorhuillca*, *Hananllautu*, *Quincanllautu*, *Caxaparac*, *Sian-Achcay*, *Chauca*, *Churaquella*, *Taucatanca*, and many others which it would be useless to enumerate: and it is probable that all those mentioned by authors constitute but a small fraction of the sum total of them, since each town had its protecting God, and sometimes several, as they had been more or less celebrated, and more or less venerated in the surrounding country. They generally worshipped on the islands of the coast, *Huacas*, whom they pretend to have been creators of the *huanu*, [Guano], and at the season of corn gathering they went with rafts and barges carrying *chicha*, *mullu*, *paria* and other articles of sacrifice, and asked leave to bring away the *huanu*.

We must also remark, that several nations worshipped different animals: thus the Collas rendered worship to sheep entirely white, as in *Siam* was done to elephants of the same color: the Huancas worshipped dogs, the Antis large serpents (*Amaru*), and tigers (*uturunca*), etc.

Individual and family Deities or household Gods were innumerable; each house and individual possessed its characteristic and tutelar divinity. Among the former, those deserving of special mention, were the so-called *Mallquis*, or *manaos*, which were the entire bodies of the ancestors reduced to a mummy or skeleton state, which the descendants piously preserved in the *Machays* or tombs, arranged in such a manner that they might easily see them and offer them sacrifices; at the same time, they gave them food and drink, for they interred with them vessels and dishes which they filled from time to time with food. They also placed at the side of the departed, in the sepulchres, arms, utensils, and other spoils which they had used in life; thus, if the deceased were a warrior they interred with him implements of war, if he were a workman, they buried with him signs of his trade; if a woman, they buried spindles, shuttles, cotton, wool, etc.

Each family had within its inheritance a large stone, placed on its side, in the field, which they worshipped with feasts and sacrifices: they called them *Huanca*, *chichi*, or *Chacrayoc*, that is, master of the field. Similar stones they placed in the canals of irrigation, offering sacrifice to them before and after sowing their seed, calling them *Compa*, or *Larca-huillana*.

The *household Gods*, corresponding with the *Lares* and *Penates* of the Romans, were of divers forms and material; they were made of gold, silver, copper, wood, stone, clay, etc., in imitation of a human figure, an animal, or in some capricious and extravagant form. The whole family professed the greatest respect for these Deities, which descended from father to son, and of which the eldest brother was forced to render an account to the other members of the house.

Each one might have an indefinite number of these domestic deities, a circumstance which establishes a marked difference between Peru and Mexico, where the number of *Lares* was limited, and varied according to the persons; thus the king might have six, the nobles four, and the plebeian only two.

Under the collective name of *Conopa*,* or *Chanca*, the

* The Quichua word *Conopa* or *Canopa*, by which we designate in the text private Deities, or *Lares* of the ancient Peruvians, particularly deserves the attention of learned antiquaries, by its coincidence with an Egyptian word which signifies the same object. By the word *Canopus* or *Canobus*, the Egyptians denominated a beneficent spirit or tutelar god, representing it under the form of a bird or a human head.

Peruvians designated all the minor deities worshipped by single families and individuals, excepting those already mentioned, in fields and canals. They counted several classes among them, although they applied the names above mentioned particularly to individuals. Every small stone or piece of wood of singular form was worshipped as a *Conopa.* These private Deities were buried with their owners, and generally hung to the neck of the dead. Sometimes they are found made of metal, like a human figure, or with an allusion to some event in the life of the individual who worshipped them.

The most esteemed *Conopas* were the bezoar stone (*Quicu*), and the small crystals of quartz rock (*Quispi*, or *Llaca*).

The Indians derived these idols from those events which had most influenced their course through life, and which they thus commemorated; or from such freaks of nature as impressed the imagination, and thus conduced to an idolatrous worship. Corn (*Zara*), for instance, their principal food, was the origin of the several species of *Zarapconopas.* They called *Zaramama*, certain stones cut in the shape of ears of corn, and certain vessels of white earth, or clay, with ornaments like wooden sandals or shoes. Another class of *Zaramama* consisted of a doll made of corn-stalks, clothed with *anaco* and *Chilla*, [an Indian mantle] and *topus* of silver such as are used by the Indians. The corn-stalks with many ears or with double ears, were considered as sacred things, but not as Deities; they were called by the Indians *Huantazara*

They also call *Canobus* the four vessels which are found in the four corners of the Egyptian mummies, and of which the first figure is a *bird*, the second a *baboon*, the third a *sparrow-hawk*, and the fourth a *human head.*

Canobus was also the name of an island of the *Nile*, and of an Egyptian city, disgraced by the luxury of its inhabitants.

or *Aryhuazara*, because they danced with them the dance *Arihuay*, when the corn was suspended by branches of willow; in the same way did they worship the ears, the grains of which were of various colors, (*Chuantayzara*, *Micsazara*, or *Caullazara*:) or were arranged in rows, united in the shape of a cone (*Pirhuazara*).* Of the *Quinua* and *Coca*, they made their *Conopas* in the form of puppets, as they did of maize, and called them *Quinuamama* and *Cocamama*. They also held in great veneration the knotted roots of the *papas* [a species of pignut], and from them made *Conopas* (*Axomama*). Twin children, if dying at an early age, were preserved in earthen pots, and were worshipped as sacred beings, supposing that one of them was the son of the thunder. They gave the name of *Chuchas* or *Cutis* to the corpses of such infants; and in the same way did they preserve those children who were born feet first (*Chacpas*), when they died in early youth.

Many and various *Conopas* are copied from the *Llamas*, *Alpacas*, *Vicuñas*, and *Huanacas*: and these idols are made of basalt, of black stone, of porphyry, carbonate of lime, granite, clay, silver, and even of gold. The first of these animals is represented almost invariably without feet, with a cavity in the back, wherein they placed grains of corn in sacrifice. And among the Conopas, has been found the representation of a sheep in silver, so well soldered, that with difficulty only can the union of the different parts be perceived. They also worshipped as *Conopas* other less useful animals, such as deer, monkeys, mountain cats, parrots, lizards, fishes, etc., which they made of clay and hollowed out

* Even at the present day, the grains of different colors, or of singular shape, are dedicated to the saints and hung in the niches.

in the form of small vessels, which they inter with the dead, for the purpose of pouring into them the *Chicha* of sacrifice.

The following pages contain a chapter of the "Pastoral Letter of exhortion and instruction concerning the idolatries of the Indians in the archbishopric of *Lima*, by the illustrious Doctor Don *Pedro de Villa Gomez*, archbishop of *Lima*, to his visitors of idolatries, his vicars, and curates of the doctrines of the Indians (*Lima*, 1649);" and will serve to furnish some idea of the idolatries which existed among the Indians in the seventeenth century, and which are even at the present day partly observed, as some of the curates have assured us.

Chapter 58. How to examine a wizard or other Indian who comes to show himself, and give information of the *huacas*.

"The examination will consist of the following questions. I. If the search is in a town of the *Sierra*, we must ask the Indian; if it is *Llacuaz*, or *Huari*, and if they call it *Huari* or *Llactayoc*, then all the natives of that town, and all their ancestors, have had no knowledge of having come from any place abroad; for *Llacahuaz* is the name used by those who (although natives of the town, they and their fathers, and their ancestors,) did originally come from other countries. And thus is preserved among the races this distinction in many places, and the *Llacuaces*, as foreigners, have many *huacas*, and much worship, and venerate their *Malquis*, which, as we have said, are the bodies of their ancestors. And the *Huaris*, who are the founders, have many *huacas*, and both one and the other believe and relate their stories, which throw much light upon their idolatries. For these and other reasons it is well to go among the different tribes or races, and to learn their factions and enmities. and to distinguish thereby between them: for by this means, one will come to know the huacas of one from another, and it is well to improve such an occasion whenever it offers.

In order to ascertain what stock or race the Indian belongs to, we must propose the following questions:—

II. What is the name of the principal *huaca* of this nation, which all adore?

III. Is this *huaca* some sceptre, or large rock, or small stone? Discover as far as possible all circumstances and signs connected with it.

IV. Has this *huaca* a son, who may be a stone, and a *huaca* like itself, or has it father, brother or wife? This question must be asked because the principal *huacas* always have their traditions, that they had sons, and that they were men who were converted into stones, etc.

V. Who keeps this *huaca?*

VI. What other *huacas* are worshipped by the nation?

VII. What *huaca* do they invoke for the habitations, and for the corn, or for potatoes; or what *huaca* do they invoke for the increase of gain or of the *cuyes* [a small animal like a rabbit].

VIII. Whether they have *Cocamama* or *Zaramama?*

IX. What *huacas* they invoke in their dwellings for the increase of them, whom they call *Chacrayoc?*

X. What springs or lakes they worship?

XI. What they call their little bird, and why they always worship it?

XII. What they call the *Marcayoc* or *Marcachacra?* which is, as it were, the patron and advocate of the people, and is sometimes of stone and sometimes the body of some of their progenitors, who, they suppose, was the first that peopled that land; and so we must ask whether it is a stone or a body.

XIII. How they call the *huaca* which they invoke for rain? This may sometimes be a stone, and sometimes a thunderbolt; and although they say that it is called *Liuiac* [in Peruvian, a thunderbolt], we must still ask the question, if it be a stone.

XIV. What they call the *huaca* which they invoke in order to prevent the channels for irrigation from being obstructed?

XV What *huaca* they invoke to prevent too much rain, and to secure enough?

XVI. What *huaca* they invoke that the corn may grow well? and that it may not be destroyed by worms? From what lake they draw pitchers of water, to sprinkle their dwellings and seek rain? into what lake do they throw stones that it may not dry up, and that rain may fall?

XVII. To what *huaca* do they offer twins, which they call *Chuchu* or *Curi*; or the child which is born feet first which they call *Chacpa?*

XVIII. What *huaca* belongs to the prince? which is always very celebrated.

XIX. What *huaca* they invoke when they go to pay the tax on dwellings, mansions, manufactures or mines, that they may return well and promptly, and that the Spaniards may not ill treat them? and what ceremonies do they use for all these things?

XX. We must also ask them, in speaking of the *Huaca*, where it is, and how situated; what its garments, what its ornaments, and all other circumstances relating to it, which we can, that they may not give one thing for another, and a fancied *Huaca* for one that does exist; and we must believe as truth what has been related many times, and, if possible, go at once to where it is.

XXI. What *Malquis* they worship? Whether they are

the bodies of their progenitors, and how the father is called? How many sons he had? Where they are, in what cave, or *Machay*, and in what condition?

XXII. What *Conopa* or *Chanca* they have? (Which is their household god), and whether it is *Micuy-Conopa*, or *Zarapconopa*, or *Llamaconopa*, if it is the *Conopa* of corn, or of grain, and whether all the other Indians possess them? and to this question we must urge an answer, for we have proved how much easier it is to discover general *Huacas* than private ones which each one possesses.

XXIII. In order to examine the wizard, we must ask whether he is *Villac* or *Huacahuanrimac*, which is he who speaks with the *Huaca*, and offers sacrifices to it; or whether it is *Humumaxa*, who is the most frequently consulted, or *Rapiac?* or *Socyac?* or *Pachacuc?* or *Asuac?* or *Yanapac?* or a wizard? and if he speaks with the Devil, and in what shape or form he appears to him?

XXIV. We must also ask what feasts they celebrate, at what seasons, and with what ceremonies? because they have a variety of them in different places, and particularly whether they have confessed to the witch? In the provinces of *Caxatambo* and *Guailas* may be asked: *Huchaiquita-auca-cucchucanqui?* "hast thou confessed thy sins to the witch?" and we must ask, with what ceremonies?

XXV. On what days do they drink, and what dances do they dance, and what songs do they sing during the feasts of the *Huacas*, and where they meet to confess on these days with their wizards? Whether they have appointed places for this purpose, which they call *Cayan?*

XXVI. What dead bodies of *Chuchus* [twins] or *Chacpas* [born feet first] they have in their houses, or who has any such; and whether any such, either living or dead, have been baptized, which they are not accustomed to do?

8*

XXVII. Who cut the hair of their sons? And who keeps it?

XXVIII. Whether any dead bodies have been disinterred from the churches? and whose? and where have they been placed?

XXIX. What places are those which are called *Apachita* and *Tocanca*, and where are they situated?

XXX. From what place, and at what season do they worship the sun and the thunderbolt? And what witch is the *Liuac-villac?* Who has the power of invoking him, and who is the *Malquivillac?*

XXXI. Who worships the *Sierra nevada* and the sea, when they go to the plains, drawing out their eyebrows?

XXXII. What wizards take charge of the feasts and fasts, cause the *Chicha* to be made, and teach the youths their idolatries and superstitions?

XXXIII. Who places *parianas* [a species of Flamingo] for the safety of dwellings?

XXXIV. What articles do they offer to the *huacas?* and whether they have domestic animals and dwellings? Who is the major-domo of the dwellings of the *huacas*, which are called *Pachacac?*

XXXV. The wizard must be asked, when he goes to consult the *Huaca*, what answers he gives the Indians? and how he is able to feign the speech of the *Huaca?* and if he tells you that when he speaks to the *Huaca* he becomes mad (which he will tell you many times), we must ask whether it is from the *chicha* which he drank, or from the effects of the *Demon?*

XXXVI. In the past visit, what was done against the idolatries? what idols did the Indians cease to make use of? and of those which are left, what pieces over and above are kept, and where are they now?

XXXVII. We must inquire, with modesty and prudence, if there are any persons which are not baptized, because they sometimes conceal persons, to prevent their baptism, and especially those which are born in the out stations and in the fields; and the Indian women have also been known to say, in order to get rid of their husbands, that they were never baptized. Much of this is attributable to malice and ignorance.

XXXVIII. Finally, we must ask for tne estate which the *huaca* has, and whether he has money; whether this is only in the power of him who keeps it, or in the same place with the *huaca;* and whether he has gold or silver, *Huamas*, *Chacra*, *Hincas*, or *Tincurpas*, or *Aquillas*, with which they give them to drink."

As to this résumé of the religious system of the ancient Peruvians, the reader well versed in the study of idolatrous religion will note that this deification of exterior objects, which infuses ideas of sublimity and power, is very analogous to the pantheism of oriental India, as it is understood by the populace; without doubt the worship of animals and vegetables, and above all their veneration for corpses, recalls the religion of the ancient Egyptains, fully described by *Herodotus*, *Diodorus Siculus*, and many modern authors. At the same time, the idea of motherhood (*Mama*) which is applied to terrestrial bodies, is a profoundly metaphysical and elevated idea, professed by some ancient philosophers, and especially by *Plato*, who uses the same word to designate ideas or archetypes, that is, the spiritual essence of things.

We will now pass to the examination of another question, which has attracted the attention of the learned; and it is the analogy of certain institutions and religious ceremonies of the Peruvians, with the Christian sacraments. The priests in the earlier days of the conquest, considered these coincidences as snares laid by the prince of darkness, who for the better securing of his victims copied the sacred rites of Christianity. Such is the opinion of *Acosta*, *Herrera*, and *Cieça de Leon:* the latter assures us that Satan in person appeared at the feasts of the Indians, in order to appropriate their worship. Taking a different view, other critics have explained these remarkable resemblances to the customs of evangelical religion, by considering them as the remains of the Christian worship, established primarily in these regions, and that the corruption has arisen from the influence of the neighboring or conquered nations, the emigrations of the people, or that unhappy tendency to the grossness of idolatry which is a frightful consequence of the fall of man, and which has been so strikingly exemplified in the history of the chosen people. Those who support this opinion, attribute to Saints Bartholomew and Thomas, the scattering in these distant regions the evangelical seed which the Spaniards found bearing but imperfect fruit, and which was almost choked by the weeds sown by the enemy. Finally, the rationalists speak ironically of both opinions, and consider such likenesses as coincidences partly fortuitous, and partly the necessary and natural results of the condition of man. Our intention is to describe with accuracy the Peruvian rites, declining to discuss the greater or less value of the opinions quoted, being unwilling to lose ourselves in conjectures upon the real or imaginary connection of both religions.

Baptism was general among all the Peruvian nations west of the Andes, and in some provinces took place two or three weeks after the birth. The father of the family imposed the name upon the child, with certain ceremonies, which we do not circumstantially know. In the provinces of the *South* and in *Cuzco*, the child was weaned at the age of two years and then baptized. At this ceremony were assembled all the relatives, and one of them, elected god-father, cut with a stone knife part of the hair with which the child had been born, an example which was followed by the rest of the relatives, until the head was completely shorn; then the name was given by the god-father, and each one of the witnesses offered it a present. On the day of the birth, the water in which the infant was washed was poured into a hole, excavated in the earth, in the presence of one of the minor priests, or of a wizard who pronounced cabalistic words over the newly-born, to conjure away and exorcise all future malign influence. Such are the ceremonies of the Peruvian Baptism, which, with the exception of imposing the name, has but little resemblance to the Christian sacrament.

Confirmation, which was a species of second baptism, took place when the child attained to puberty, that is, when the boy first puts on the shirt and blanket, and upon the appearance of the catamenia in the girl. This epoch was not for the family alone, but for the whole race or lineage. And there followed the ceremony, a day of feasting, celebrated with dancing and drunkenness. The chief of the race gave to the boy or girl who had reached this age a second name, distinct from the first, and the hair and finger-nails of the confirmed were cut and sacrificed to their *Conopas*, *Huacas*, or one of the greater Deities. This ceremony completed, the child was considered a man or woman.

Penance was practised among the Indians with the greatest scrupulosity. Before the principal feasts, they confessed their sins to the priests (*Aucanchic* or *Ychuris*), and they previously fasted several days. At the beginning, the priest placed a few of the ashes of the burnt sacrifices upon a stone, which the penitent blew into the air. He afterward received a small stone (*Parca*), and went to wash his head in a *Tincuna*, or place where two rivulets meet, or some other sacred place, reserved for this purpose. Presently, returning to the Priest, he said: "Hear me, high-lands, plains, condors, which fly, owls, grubs, and all animals and herbs, know that I wish to confess my sins." Upon beginning the confession the priest placed a small ball of colored clay upon the thorn of a *giganton* (Cactus); and when it was done, he transfixed the ball with the thorn until it burst and fell to the ground. If it divided into three parts, the confession was good; if into two only, it was bad, and the penitent was obliged to recommence. He, to prove that nothing had been concealed, was required to throw a handful of corn into a vessel, and if the number of the grains thrown in was even, the confession had been well made; if uneven, it was thought unavailing. The penance imposed by the priest consisted in an abstinence from salt, garlic and coition: as also in corporal punishment, such as the lash, etc. Sometimes they were forced to put on new garments, in order that the sins might be left in the old ones.

In the distribution of bread and the sacred *chicha*, made for the *Inca*, to the Lords or Nobles of the court, in the feast of *Mosoc-nina* or "renovation of the sacred fire," the Spaniards found much analogy to the sacrament of the *Eucharist*. (See chapters 6th and 8th.)

There were also certain ceremonies somewhat similar to "*Extreme Unction*," since the priests, physicians, wizards, and witches assisted the dying, muttering incantations against the power of the devil.

Holy orders, or the ceremony of the consecration of priests, was a matter of the highest importance among the ancient Peruvians, and was only conferred upon those youths who had given sufficient proof that they were worthy of being exalted to the dignity of so high an office. The priesthood contained a large number of members who, according to the

Deity they served, were found distributed among several classes. The greater respect was commanded by those of the *Sun* (*Intip-huillac*), of which we have spoken in the beginning of this chapter. In the province of the *Yungas*, those of *Pachacamac* were the chief. Each *Huaca* had its priest, who was respected in proportion as the huaca was venerated. His occupation was to take care of the Deity, watch in his temple, on the spot where his image was erected, to speak with him, and repeat his answers to the questions of the people; present their offerings, make the sacrifices, celebrate their feasts, and teach their worship. The same employments occupied the priests of the dead (*Mallquip huillac*), those of the thunder *Laipiacpa-huillac*), and those of the other Deities.

The *Conopas* had also priests, but to a certain point, each individual was his own priest: and if he wished to ask anything of these *Penates*, they were carried to the priest, called *Macsa* or *Viha*, and through him the service was performed.

The soothsayers and wizards formed a particular subdivision of the priesthood, as they were obliged to give adequate proofs of their sufficiency before entering upon the duties of the office. Those most esteemed were the *Socyac*, who predicted the future, by means of small heaps of corn; the *Paccharicuc* (*Pacchacuti* or *Pacchecuc*), who divined by means of spiders' feet, called *Pacchac*, who sought for that species of the insect which is concealed in walls, or under stones, and placing them upon a blanket, persecuted them with a straw, until they broke one or two feet, and then they predicted by those which were wanting: the *Hacaricuc* or *Cuyricuc*, who foretold by the blood and intestines of the *Cuys* or rabbits; the *Pichiuricuc*, who observed the flight of birds; the *Moscoc*, who interpreted dreams, sleeping by the head or clothes of him who consulted them, and receiving in a dream the answer. The office of this order of the priesthood, and even that of confessor, pertained in common to men and women, but the men alone could exercise the office of priest to the superior Deities.*

The priests who spoke with the *Huacas* were accustomed to put themselves into an ecstatic state, by means of a narcotic beverage, called *Tonca*, made of the fruit of a species of thorn apple, *Datura sanguinea*, or *Huacacacha*, that is, herb of *Huaca*, and in this state they received inspiration.

Very meritorious was it of the *Incas*, to have established the laws of matrimony, and to have instituted certain conditions, indispensable to the performance of the ceremony.

In the earlier times of Peru the union of the sexes was voluntary, unregulated, and accompanied by barbarous usages: many of which even at the present day exist among the uncivilized nations of South America. The *Incas* abol-

* Even at the present day some of these impostors are known in various parts of the Sierra and *Don Mariano E. de Rivero*, being prefect of the department of *Junin*, the curate of Huariaca, and many of the inhabitants related to him many curious and strange cases of witchcraft, producing lameness, sickness, and insanity by placing dolls of cloth pinned together with the thorns of the cactus within mattresses, pillows, in holes about the house, and in cellars. Of these witches some were burned on their own confessions, and by reason of this, as the common people believed, the afflicted were cured. The inhabitants of the Valley of Majes were persuaded that the *kara*, as it is called, a species of eruptive disease which shows itself in red, white and blue spots on the face, arms, and feet of the common people, is produced by a drink composed of corn placed in a pot with a large toad, which being afterwards ground and made into a beverage is drunk in pledges, by jealous women and such as are forsaken by their lovers. This disease is cured in the beginning with sudorifics and certain ptisans, which the old female quacks keep a profound secret. These spotted persons are called *Karientos*.

ished these rude customs, and fixed conditions under which matrimony might take place; which were the following: the bridegroom and bride must be of the same town or tribe, and of the same class or position; the former must be somewhat less than twenty-four years old, the latter eighteen. The consent of the parents and chiefs of the tribe was indispensable; the bridegroom must provide all that was necessary for the house, which the whole town must assist him in building; the furniture which the bride should bring to her husband was supplied by the parents; all the marriages must take place on an appointed day, and in the presence of the governor of the province. The Inca himself presided at the unions of the royal family, as monarch and high priest, and taking by the hand the different parties to be united, he gave them to each other and pronounced them to be man and wife; in the same manner did the *curacas* [princes of conquered provinces] unite the couples belonging to his class, or of other inferiors in their districts, without the intervention of the priest. They then celebrated the wedding with splendid banquets and balls, more or less luxurious, as the means of the parties permitted.

Polygamy was one of the prerogatives of the royal family and nobles, but the sovereign alone could have more than one wife and an unlimited number of concubines. Gentlemen were permitted to have some, but one proper wife only. With the permission of the governor of the province, or head of the tribe, and by means of a legal sentence, a divorce might be obtained, provided mutual consent was obtained or on account of serious charges; and it is a singular fact that the adultery of the husband was unpunished, if with a spinster, but loss of life was the penalty for all unfaithfulness committed with a married woman.

After the death of her husband, the woman might choose

widowhood or be buried alive with her husband. Among the Incas and nobles it was the custom to bury the legitimate wives, the favorite concubines, a considerable number more or less of servants, as also jewels, wrought silver, llamas, arms, provisions and clothing. Some of the persons who were to accompany the deceased monarch to the tomb, manifested repugnance at such a sacrifice; but generally the wives and servants offered themselves voluntarily, and there are even instances of wives who preferred suicide to prove their conjugal devotion, when they were prevented from descending to the grave with the body of their consort. The wife or servant who preferred life to the act of martyrdom which was to attest their fidelity, was an object of general contempt, and devoted or doomed to a life worse than death. This custom introduced by the Incas, which reminds one of the customs of the widows of Malabar, of burning themselves in the blaze which consumed the remains of their husbands, deserves the special attention of the learned and the archæologist.

Garcilasso De la Vega (Royal Comm. I., Book II. Chap. III.) relates that the Incas had in Cuzco a cross cut of white and red marble (crystallized jasper), three-quarters of a yard in length, in a sacred place (*Huaca*), which was held in great veneration;* and in the ruins of Coati are several crosses cut in a wall. It would be erroneous to deduce from these crosses any inference as to a connection between the Peruvian religion and the Christian. The cross is a figure so simply and easily represented in design and sculpture, that it exists as an ornament among almost all barbarous nations. A flute of *Pan*, found in Peru, was adorned with twelve Maltese crosses.

* See also Garcilasso, Comment., Part II., Book I. Chap. XXXII.

CHAPTER VIII.

RELIGIOUS CEREMONIES.

In each month of the year the Peruvians held feasts, but the principal ones related to the Sun, and they celebrated the four great periods of its annual progress, the solstices and the equinoxes (see Chapter VI.) The most solemn of all was the feast of *Raymi* or *Intip-Raymi*, celebrated in the summer solstice, when the Sun, having arrived at the farthest point of his meridional career, returns on his course to the north.

This feast was in token of gratitude and thankfulness for the benefits which the nation enjoyed, and for which they were indebted to the Deity, the feast of profound adoration to the supreme *Numen*, and, consequently, was solemnized with the same piety throughout all the countries governed by the sceptre of the Incas. There were assembled at it the chiefs and princes of the empire; and those who, because of their indisposition, age, or services, could not attend, sent their sons or relations, with the most noble lords of the territory. They all came in their greatest court dress, and splendid arms, each one with his national garb, rivalling each other among themselves by the blazonry of their heraldry and richness of their adornments. The multitude was innumerable, as well nobles as plebeians, who indeed assembled at the capital in such numbers, that there was no room in houses to receive the strangers, and the greater part were obliged to encamp in the public squares and in the streets. From the neighboring provinces, many women were also sent to dress the food of these multitudes, and chiefly to knead a species of cake of boiled corn, called *zancu*, and eaten only at the solemn feasts. The virgins of the Sun prepared for the Inca and the nobles of the empire this food with other dishes the night before. The feast was preceded by three days of rigorous fasting, during which time the only food consisted of a little white raw corn, and a certain herb called *Chucan;* at the same time, no fire was permitted to be kindled in any house.

In order to solemnize still further this feast, the Inca presided, accompanied by his court. In the first place, the monarch left the palace, followed by the royal family, and passed barefoot through the square *Haucaypata*, to salute the rising of the Sun. The retinue which accompanied the monarch were clothed in their best garbs, and the nobles, in ostentatious rivalry, displayed a profusion of jewels and ornaments; whilst the canopies of brilliant feathers and splendid cloths, which the servants carried to protect the heads of the Lords, caused the square and streets through which they passed to seem, as it were, covered with a magnificent awning.

Hardly had the first rays gilded the summits of the neighboring high-land, when a loud shout of joy burst from the multitude, with songs of triumph and clamorous music on rude instruments, the boisterous noise of which increased in proportion as the God, in his rising course, shed his rays on the people. The excited multitude raised their arms, kissed the air, and inhaled the delightful atmosphere impregnated with light. Then the Inca rose, took two *aquillas* (vases of gold), filled with *chicha*, prepared by the chosen virgins; sacrificed the one in the right hand to the Sun, pouring the liquor into a receptacle, from which ran a sewer cut in the rock to the temple of the divinity; and with that in the left hand he pledged his family, pouring out to each one of the members a quantity of the sacred liquor in a small vase of gold. The Curacas went to the adjoining square (*Cusipata*), and also worshipped the Sun in the East, under the direction of a priestly Inca, who distributed among them the same beverage.

Afterward, the monarch, accompanied by the royal family and the Curacas, went in procession to the temple, and there offered their golden vases to the image of the Sun. Only to the sovereign and his family, however, was an entrance into the sacred precinct permitted. All the others presented by the hands of the priests their rich and numerous sacrifices to the Deity. The offerings thus made, they all returned in the same order to the public square, to assist in the sacrifices which the High-priest (and not the Inca) offered upon a table or altar richly adorned. The first consisted generally of a young llama of a black color, and the priest, after opening the body, found in the entrails an omen for the future. They arranged the victim with the head to the east, caused him to be held by four servants of the priests, and then the sacrificer opened with the sacred knife the left side, and tore out the heart with the lungs and throat. If the auguries were not propitious, they offered another sacrifice of a male llama, and if neither were prosperous, they immolated a barren female llama, and if these predictions were not favorable, the nation was overpowered with the deepest sadness, and each one feared an unlucky future.

The augural holocaust over, the priests made a general sacrifice to the Sun, which consisted of a large quantity of llamas and alpacas, which they beheaded, offering their hearts to the Sun, and burning the entrails of the victims until they were reduced to ashes, and the flesh was roasted in the same square, and dressed with *zancu* and other food. They then began to drink the *chicha*, which they had in abundance. The king, who assisted, seated upon his golden seat, which was placed upon a solid block of the same metal, drank to his family, to some of the chiefs renowned for bravery, and to the most distinguished curacas or conquered princes. The members of the royal family then toasted each other, and the curacas did the same among themselves. By degrees the *chicha* took effect, the joy was augmented, followed by dancing, masquerades, music, singing, and general rejoicing, which lasted eight or nine days. Among the dances, the favorite one was, and is, at this day, the *cachua*, making a thousand figures with much velocity, and singing at the same time. The music of this dance, and the figures, are very similar to those of the Scotch in their national dances.

Some historians relate that the ceremony of the renewing of the sacred fire (*Mosoc-nina*) took place on the evening of the feast of Raymi; the priest kindled it by means of a metallic mirror, concave and burnished, which concentrating the rays of the sun on a quantity of dry cotton cloth, it was soon in flames; a proceeding equally in use in ancient times, and which Plutarch describes in the life of Numa. This mirror was carried by the priest, attached to a bracelet on the left hand (*Chipana*), and when the Sun was obscured, which was a bad omen, they obtained fire by means of friction. Other authors pretend, on the contrary, that the day destined to the renewing of the fire was that of the feast of the vernal equinox.

The second principal feast, called *Situa*, was solemnized at the autumnal equinox, and was preceded by a fast, which took place the day of the new moon before the feast. The night before they prepared in all the houses *zancus*, a portion of which was mixed with human blood, taken from children of five or six years old, from the root of the nose between the eyebrows, with a small sharp-pointed stone. A few hours before breakfast all those who had fasted washed themselves, and took a little of the potion mixed with blood, rubbing with it their whole body, in order to dissipate all infirmities. With the same material the head of each house rubbed the thresholds, leaving a part stuck there in commemoration. In the royal palace the oldest uncle of the king performed this ceremony, and in the temple of the Sun the High-priest, and other priests deputed for that purpose, in the other sacred houses.

Upon the rising of the Sun the people assembled in the designated squares to adore the Deity, invoking it, and entreating it to condescend to expel all evils and infirmities; and afterward they breakfasted, eating the *zancu* without blood. Then at an hour appointed on the morrow, there came out of the fortress *Sacsahuaman*, an Inca, as a messenger of the Sun, richly arrayed, his mantle girt to his body, a lance with a little banner of feathers in his hand, and ran until he reached the middle of the principal square, where he was waited for by four Incas similarly clothed. Upon reaching them, he touched their lances with his, telling them that the Sun commanded that they should expel from the city and its environs all ills and infirmities. At the same time, the four Incas departed for the four quarters of the globe, by the four royal roads which proceeded from this square, and ran a quarter of a league, to a spot where others were waiting for them, already prepared to continue the service; and in this manner, their places re-occupied by fresh substitutes, they traversed the road for six leagues beyond the city, in the four principal directions, the Incas keeping their lances in rest, as if to put an end to all the evils which they pretended to drive away. Whilst they were thus running, the whole population of the city and neighboring places came out to the doors of their houses, shaking, with loud exclamations and outcries, their clothes, and rubbing their bodies with their hands, in token that they wished to tear out all the evils and give them to the Incas to be destroyed. This ceremony was followed by a general rejoicing with music, dancing, and intoxication, which lasted through the quarter of the moon. At night, after the feast, the Indians sallied out with torches, bound around with straw (*Pancuncu*), and fastened to coarse ropes, and ran shaking them through the streets until they were out of the city, extinguishing them by throwing them into the rivulets, pretending thus to destroy all nocturnal evils.

The third feast (*Cusquic-Raymi*) was celebrated at the winter solstice, the object of which was to implore the Sun to preserve the corn that was planted from the rigor of the frost. This festivity was preceded by a day of fast, which was solemnized by sacrifices similar to those of the feast *Raymi*, by a black lamb, and a great quantity of llamas, the hearts and blood of which were burnt as offerings to the Sun, and the roasted flesh distributed to the numerous assistants who participated in the ceremonies. The feast concluded with solemn dances, which lasted three days.

Finally, the fourth principal feast of the sun, solemnized at the vernal equinox, was that of arming the knights or cavaliers, (*Huaracu.*) After having passed through most rigorous examinations in all the political and military sciences, (see the 4th chapter,) the Incas admitted to the ceremony those young men in whose honor the feast was celebrated. The nation fasted one day, and the candidates eight or ten days; then after the adoration of the Sun in the morning, and the public sacrifices as in the other feasts, the Inca sallied out accompanied by the most ancient of the royal blood to the principal square, made to the candidates a speech concerning their future duties, and this concluded, they passed one by one in front of the monarch, who pierced their ears with a golden pin. The novitiate kissed the hand of the king, and presented himself before another Inca, who took from him the *Usutas* (sandals) of rushes which are worn by all the candidates or aspirants during their examinations, and shod him with woollen sandals, very richly bordered, and kissing him on the right shoulder, said to him: "The son of the Sun, who has given such proofs of himself, deserves to be reverenced." The novitiate then entered an ornamented enclosure, where the old Incas put on him the loose drawers (*Huaracu*), as a token that he was a man, and adorned his head with chaplets composed of the flowers *Cantur* and *Chichuayhua*, and with a leaf of the herb *Uiña-huayna*. After having received all the badges of an Inca and Cavalier, the novitiates were conducted to the principal square, where the ceremony was terminated with songs and balls, which lasted several days, and were even continued in the houses of the parents of the youths.

Garcillaso de la Vega gives, in his Commentaries, a minute description of this feast, from which we have extracted the foregoing abridgment. Sometimes it is probable that they did not limit themselves to the forms which we have given of their rites and ceremonies, and that they differed somewhat from that which we have just described; nevertheless, the information here communicated seems to be accurate enough in its elements to give a correct idea of the spirit of the ceremonies.

Beside these principal feasts in honor of the Sun, there were many others which continually followed each other, so that in a word, we may say almost half the year was passed in festivities. We will relate some of the most important ones only. The first day of the moon was always celebrated with sacrifices, music, dancing, and inebriation. In the month of April came the feasts of the harvest and of the *Misac*, (see the sixth chapter); in June the military ones, preceded by exercises and parades; in August the *Yupay-Asitua*, or supplemental balls, as a continuation of the feasts of the preceding month; in September was solemnized the *Coya-raymi*, or dance of the *Coyas* [princesses], marrying on a fixed day the princesses of the royal family, and on the following, all the brides of the empire; and finally, the feast of the enumeration of the inhabitants of the state.

In October took place the feast in commemoration of the deceased; and in November, that of the termination of the year and the end of seed-time. A solemn day throughout the province of Cuzco, was one, on which the Inca with all the Cavaliers of the court went out to the camp and pierced the earth, after the manner of the Chinese emperors, with an instrument of gold which corresponded with our plough. The magnates followed the example of the emperor, and this ceremony inaugurated the cultivation of the earth.

We have already said that throughout the empire, they celebrated the feasts of the *Huacas* one or more times during the year, according to the dignity of them; but these festivities, indefinite in number, were partial only, and the entire nation participated in the four great ones only, which we have described, and but slightly in the others spoken of.

The offerings which the Indians presented to the Sun and other deities, consisted of that which was produced both by nature and art. At times, the sacrifices consisted of human victims, although Garcilasso de la Vega pretends to say several times in his Royal Commentaries that not only were the Incas opposed to so horrible a holocaust, but that they abolished it, and repressed it with zeal among all the nations whom they conquered. In this, as in many other points, Garcilasso is found directly opposed to all the historians, who accuse of falsehood this descendant of the Incas, and charge that it is not through his ignorance of the fact, but through a partiality in favcr of the prudence and humanity of the Peruvian monarchs, whose blood, although mixed, ran through his veins. The authors of the sixteenth and seventeenth centuries who make mention of human sacrifices among the ancient inhabitants of Peru, are:—*Gomara*, (Hist. of the Indies, Book IV.); *Cieça de Leon*, (Chronicle, Chap. XIX.); *Acosta*, (Natural Hist. of the Indies, Book V. Chap. XVIII.); *Tamara*, (Customs of all Nations, Book III. Pag. 298); *Levinus Apollonius*, (of the Discovery of Peru, Book I. Pag. 37); *Balboa*, (Hist. of Peru, Chap. VIII.); *Benzoni*, (Hist. of the New World, Book III. Chap. XX.); *Montesinos*, (Ancient Memorials) in several places; *Betanzos*, (quoted by Garcia, Hist. of the Indies, Pag. 198); *Herrera*, (Hist. of the Indies, Dec. V., Book IV. Chap. IV.), and according to *Prescott* (Conquest of Peru, Book I. Chap. III.), *Sarmiento* (M. S. Relation, Chap. XXII.); *Ondegardo* (Second Relation, M. S.); and the Decades of the royal audience. To these testimonies we may add that of *Jose de Arriaga*, (Extirpation of the Idolatry of the Indians of Peru, 1621.) Against so many proofs, the most of which are worthy of credit, the testimony of Garcilasso is of no value, notwithstanding the pains he takes to exculpate his ancestors from all suspicion on this point. It is true that the Peruvian priests did not proceed with the frantic ferocity of the Mexicans; nevertheless, the quantity of their victims reached a very frightful number, and consisted principally of children of tender age, which they sacrificed to the Sun, and it was no unusual thing to sacrifice two hundred at one time. On certain occasions, they also offered certain virgins to the Sun. When the Inca, or some great lord, fell sick, he was accustomed to offer one of his sons to the Deity, imploring him to take this victim, instead of the sick man. When comets appeared, or epidemics prevailed, they were accustomed to offer children to the Sun, to appease his anger. We have already seen, that at the death of an Inca or a principal Chief, they interred with the deceased his servants and women; at the same time the priests immolated other victims upon the altars. It is said that in the exequies of Huayna-Capac, more than one thousand men were thus sacrificed. This barbarous custom lasted for some time after the conquest. Cieça de Leon relates (Chronicle, Chap. LXII.) an act of this nature in these terms: "And Alaya, lord of the larger part of the valley of Xauxa, died about two years since; and the Indians say that they interred with him a large number of wives and servants alive. And if I am not deceived, they so told the president Gasca, and it was forbidden to the other lords, giving them to understand that it was a great sin which they committed, and useless as to its supposed benefits." In some provinces the offering always presented was the first-born; in others they offered one of twin sons to the Sun, or to some other Deity; and even more than fifty years after the conquest, there was immolated in a temple of the region of Hunayan, one league and a half from the City of Catas, every year, a certain number of youths and children, pretending that the idols subsisted upon human flesh.

We are not told whether, under the reign of the Incas, it was the custom to offer the prisoners of war, as in Mexico; a custom, however, which is general even at the present day among the barbarous nations of the Pampa del Sacramento, who eat the flesh of the victims of war, after burning the entrails as an offering.

The most ordinary sacrifices were of llamas, principally to the Sun. This deity had numerous flocks of these animals, and the pasturing of them was one of the occupations of the Indians of Puna. In the general sacrifices, the color of the fleece was immaterial, but for the inaugural holocaust, the law commanded a black llama without a spot of any other color. An accurate calculation demonstrates that in the single city of Cuzco, there were beheaded annually some two hundred thousand llamas in honor of the Sun. As we have already said, the flesh of the holocausts was roasted and distributed among the assistants at the feast, with the exception of the black sheep, and the blood and intestines of the others, which were reserved for the Deity and converted into ashes. From the wool of these animals the Inca ordered to be woven clothes for the soldiers.

The Alpacas, Vicuñas and huanacos were also victims offered to the Sun, or to the Huacas. The fat (*Huira*) of all these animals formed one of the most precious objects of the offering. In the present province of *Jauja*, they sacrificed dogs (*Alljo*), foxes (*Atoc*), pole-cats (*Añash*); in others small rabbits (*Cuys*), flies (*Cuspi*), hares, squirrels, (*Carachupas*), apes, deer, (*Lluchos*) and stags, (*Tarush* or *Taruco*.) Of the ferocious and noxious animals which they could not take alive for sacrifices, such as tapirs, (*Anta*) lions, (*Puma*), tigers, serpents, lizards, etc., they made figures of them in gold or silver, which they presented to the Deity; and the same proceeding was observed with the llamas by those who came from distant territories [where the animal did not range] to the feast.

The birds chiefly destined for sacrifice were the *Iriburu*

pichu (*Vultur papa*), the condor, the black *Tunqui* (*Cephalopterus ornatus*), the colored *Tunqui* (*Rupicola-peruana*), the *tornasol* (*Trogon-heliothrix*), the humming bird, long-tailed parrots, common parrots, cuckoos, flamingos, (Parra), and other birds of brilliant plumage.

They also offered several species of marine shells (Mullu), of the most beautiful colors, the bezoar stone, and honey.

Of the vegetable kingdom, the principal offering was corn, under all forms; in the ear, the grain, raw, cooked, or converted into the usual drink of the Indians, called *Acca* or *Asahua* (*Chicha*). At all the feasts they emptied, as a libation to the Deity, a small gold vase filled with chicha; and consumed, after the ceremonies were concluded, a considerable quantity of this beverage, so that each religious function was concluded with a general intoxication, and always with violent quarrels. The herb *coca* was one of the most precious offerings, especially to the *Huacas*, to whom it was offered, after having been chewed in the mouth, or mixed with fat and corn ground together under foot. They also offered many vegetable productions, such as quinua, potatoes, pineapples, plantains, May-apples, fruits similar to dried almonds, and of a strong and aromatic smell: every species of drink made of roots, and fruits, flax, cotton, etc.

The offerings taken from the mineral kingdom were the richest, as they consisted of the noble metals and precious stones, the relative value of which the Indians knew, notwithstanding their being found very rarely among them. The gold they presented to the Deities, either in dust or cast into the form of small bars, or in thin leaves, or wrought in different ways. They used also for sacrifice the dust of cinnabar (*Paria* or *Pucculllimpi*), sulphate of copper (*Pinso* or *Anas-llimpi*), sulphate of iron (*Llacsa* or *Comer-llimpi*), and pulverized pyrites (*Carhuanuqui* or *Carhua-llimpi*). Upon offering powders or dust they first marked with it the Huacas or Conopas, and afterward blew it into the air. They called this ceremony *Huatcuna*. Among the precious stones we must notice the emerald, hyacinth, topaz, opal, chrysoprase, jasper, ruby, and obsidian.* Of all these they have found specimens in the Peruvian *Huacas*, and among the emeralds some of considerable value. We must also speak of a sacrifice very common among them, and which consisted of eyelashes, which the Indians plucked out and blew into the air. This offering was very general, inasmuch as they could present it for themselves, without the intervention of the priests, necessary on other occasions.

Finally, to complete the religious ceremonies, it only remains for us to examine the manner in which the ancient Peruvians buried their dead and embalmed the corpses. In the preceding chapter we have said that the deceased kings were deposited in the principal part of the temple of the Sun, in Cuzco, embalmed, and covered with their gala dresses, with a rich sceptre in the right hand. The Coya or empress was also embalmed and deposited in that part of the temple dedicated to the Moon. The royal exequies were very imposing: they arranged the corpse with much pomp in the temple before the image of the Sun, sacrificed to it for three days the best of what they had, chiefly gold, silver, corn, and coca, and during four moons the subjects daily wept the death of the sovereign. Each quarter of the city went out to the field with flags, arms, garments, and other royal insignia, singing hymns which celebrated the deeds, wisdom, and greatness of the defunct, a ceremony which was repeated at each anniversary of his death; and also at each full and new moon, certain persons repeated,

* We have only been able to meet with the last named.

amid tears and sobs, mournful dirges and dithyrambic praises relative to the lost monarch.

The kings of *Quito*, or *Scyris*, were buried, according to Fray-Marcos de Niza (Conquest of the Province of Quito, Rites and Ceremonies of the Indians), all in a very large sepulchre, made of stones in a quadrangular and pyramidal form, so covered with pebbles and sand that it formed a miniature hill. The door looked out to the east, was closed with a double wall, and only opened upon the death of one of them. We find in them their embalmed corpses, arranged in order with their royal insignia, and the treasure which the monarch had commanded should be interred with him. Over each one of them was found a cavity or small niche, where was found a hollow figure of clay, stone or metal; within were small stones of divers colors and shapes, which denoted his age, the years and months of his reign.

The manner of burying the vassals was very different, and varied in each province. In some parts, principally at the South, the cavaliers of royal blood, curacas, and other magnates, were deposited in large vases of gold and silver, in the form of urns, hermetically sealed, which were found arranged in meadows, woods, or forests, as Gomara relates (Hist. Gen., Chap. 122). We regret that we have not met with a single one of these urns, which were found in such abundance by the Spaniards, and of which we know nothing,—not even the shape. Cieça de Leon (Chronicle, Chap. lxii.) says: "In order that the sepulchres should be made magnificent and spacious, they adorned them with pavements and vaults, and put in with the deceased all his chattels, wives and servants, and a large quantity of food, and numerous pitchers of chicha, or wine, such as they were in the habit of using; they thus give us to understand that they have a knowledge of the immortality of the soul, and that in man there is more than the mortal body." The same author also says, in the chapter quoted: "And many of his servants, that he might not fail of attendants in another world, made holes in the grounds and fields of the master, or lord, now dead, or in those places where he most enjoyed and feasted himself, and there they buried themselves, thinking that his soul passed through those places, and took them along for his future use or service. And some of his women, to give to his burial more importance, and to remain in his service, would, even before his interment, hang themselves, by their own hair, and so kill themselves."

The nation of the Chinchas, and others, of the provinces on the coast, interred their corpses (probably those of the common people) just below the surface of the earth, covering them with a light coat of sand, without the smallest elevation of the ground, indicating the spot in which the deceased were laid. These interments, at the present day, are found in rows, or spaces, one alongside of the other. On the western declivity of the Cordilleras they used sepulchres, in the form of ovens, made of adobes; and in the Sierra they were constructed of stones, square or oval, or in the form of obelisks, as in the Punas of Southern Peru, in the vicinity of the river Chucaña, and between Pisacoma and Pichu-Pichu. These obelisks have been erroneously supposed, by some travellers, to be triumphal monuments of the Inca Yupanqui.

A large number of the tombs was enclosed by flat stones, one or two yards in height. The sepulchres built of adobes, or stones, always contained the corpses of the principal families. The plebeian families were arranged in rows, or formed a semicircle in caves, fissures of rocks, or terraces formed by rocks; as, at the present day, large numbers of them are found in the departments of Junin, Ayacucho, and elsewhere. Sometimes they were buried in holes, around which the

9*

Indians heaped stones.* We have found mummies in the fissures of rocks, so narrow, that it seems incredible that they should have been able to place in them the corpses, when newly dead, and, of course, much more bulky, than the dried remains which are left; even these remains can, with difficulty, be extracted from these narrow places. Those bodies which were placed under shelter from the weather and changes of the atmosphere have been preserved; but of those subjected to exposure nothing but the skeleton remains.

In whatever way they were buried, the ancient Peruvians arranged the corpses in a drawn-up posture, the face turned toward the west, with provisions of chicha, corn, coca, deposited in round earthen pots, and other vases, that they might find food to sustain them. They placed next to the corpse small sacks full of the ears of two sorts of corn, very rare: one, the ear of which is short, dry, and a little curved at the point; the other, with the ear long, thin, with large grains, almost triangular at the point, very much turned, with the grains covering it like the tiles of a roof. The celebrated English botanist, Robert Brown, possesses one of these ears, in a state of petrifaction, which was found in a Peruvian ruin. This species (called *Zea-rostrata*, by the celebrated writer on maize, *Bonafous*,) as well as the other we have named, seems to be a native of Peru; but at the present day it is but little cultivated, and but little is seen among the numerous varieties of corn in the department of Cuzco. Grains of the *Zea-rostrata*, taken from a sepulchre, and, consequently, many centuries old, have germinated in Europe, like the wheat found in Egyptian mummies, which counts a thousand years.

In the walls of the sepulchres, which are made without

* Many of these tumuli are similar to those which are found in Asia, and in North America.

doors, are found certain holes and conduits, which lead from the surface outside to vases within; into these they empty the chicha on those feast days which they solemnize in honor of their mallquis.

The corpses, as they appear in the sepulchres, are found enveloped with much cloth, and as it were bundled up. We will describe them as we found them in more than fifty mummies which we have uncovered. At first sight we distinguished nothing more than what seems a coarse statue, seated, in which nothing is visible but a round head, two knees, and two feet of large appearance; a strong net of coarse thread, with meshes sufficiently wide, is bound closely over a coarse mat of rushes, in which the corpse is wrapped. In the sepulchres of higher Peru, are found mummies in mats of *totora*, [a particular species of rush on Lake Titicaca] in shape very similar to beehives, with a square aperture at the side of the face. Upon removing the mat you discover a large roll of cotton, which envelops the whole body from end to end, and secures two canes or reeds to the sides, and sometimes also a stick across the shoulders: after removing this roll is seen a cloth of wool, red or parti-colored, which completely envelops the mummy, at the lower part of which are one or two cloths of cotton, like sheets, fastened firmly, as the cloth is around the corpse; under these we find some small vases, ornaments, the *hualqui* with the coca, and in the greater part of the mummies a *conopa* of stone, clay, silver or gold, hanging from the neck. The internal covering is a cotton cloth, quite fine, probably white originally, but tinged with a reddish yellow by time, and sewed like the other coverings; this being removed, the corpse is seen naked, only the head enveloped in two or three rolls, the upper one of which is of a fine web, and almost always with threads of divers colors: the under one is narrower and thicker, sometimes made of rushes only, but ordinarily of a yellowish cotton.

The position of the corpse is squatting; raising the knees to the chin, the arms are crossed over the breast, or support ing the head, so that the fists touch the jaws. The hands are generally fastened, and in most of the mummies there is a coarse rope passed three or four times around the neck, and we also see a stick which passes from the ground between the legs to the throat, and which serves to support the corpse more firmly. In the mouth is always found a small disk of copper, silver or gold. The greater part of the corpses were sufficiently well preserved, but the flesh was shrivelled, and the features disfigured: the hair always perfectly preserved, that of the women artificially braided, but the black pigment or coloring matter had lost more or less of its primitive color, and had become reddish.

We now come to the interesting question, whether the ancient Peruvians embalmed their corpses, or whether they owe their good preservation to the influence of the climate which is so conducive to natural mummification.

Both opinions have their defenders, who sustain them with reasons more or less well founded. There is no doubt that the art of embalming was known to the Peruvians, but probably only to a certain class of Incas, who, holding it as a secret, exercised it upon the corpses of the kings and their legitimate wives only.

If we may rely upon the relations of Garcilasso de la Vega, and of Father Acosta, already quoted in the preceding chapter, this art had reached a degree of perfection which seems to have surpassed very much the skill of the Egyptians; since there are not known mummies belonging to any nation, in which the fleshly parts remained perfect, the skin soft an smooth, and the features of the face unaltered.

We candidly confess that the statements of the authors above named, upon this subject, seem to us inaccurate, or at least exaggerated; and all who know the inevitable changes which the smooth parts of the human body do undergo, in spite of all preservative means, as soon as vitality ceases, will participate in our opinion.

It is certain that the corpses of the kings were incomparably better preserved than the others, in consequence of a certain means used; and the assertion that this was a secret of the royal family, is founded upon the fact that there have been found no other artificial mummies than those of the kings and queens. Neither do we know what means the masters used to embalm them, nor what substances they used to avoid putrefaction and give a certain flexibility to the skin. To obtain a knowledge of this, it would be necessary to submit one of these mummies to a chemical analysis.

It is generally believed that the other mummified corpses, which are found by millions as well on the coast as on the mountains, had been also embalmed; but it is a serious error, they being only natural mummies, as we shall presently prove. The late Don Francisco Barreda published in the memoirs of natural sciences of Don M. E. de Rivero (Vol. II. page 106) a dissertation to prove that these corpses were embalmed, and describes the procedure which the embalmers used with them as follows:

"The professors of the art performed the operation in several ways. In imitation of the Egyptians, they drew out the brains through the nostrils, thus explaining the want of the small bone which separates the eyes, and the fracture made in the suture which connects this with the forehead, thus facilitating the passage to the interior of the cranium. They sometimes preserved this small bone, entirely withdrawing the brain, and yet without leaving any mark capable of manifesting the corruption which would have been produced, if they had extracted the brain in any other way; thus proving that such was their knowledge of anatomy, that they made their extractions from this organ in different ways and in different places. They drew out the eyes, as being composed of very corruptible substances, filling the orbits with cotton and other materials ingeniously arranged, which covered the deficiency when the eyelids were closed: all was neatly executed without altering the features of the face, whatever aspect it might have worn in life."

"The tongue, with all its appurtenances, was torn out, with the lungs, by a small fissure, made from the anus to the pubis. After emptying through it all the intestines, they left the lower belly and breast free from the parts which might putrefy. The vacuum of both cavities they filled with a subtile powder, the color of liver, which exhaled a slight turpentine odor the instant that it was taken out, and afterward lost it in a short time, by its contact with the open air. It absorbs humidity, and makes a slight effervescence in cold water. We presume, from these circumstances, that the compound is made of resin of the *molle* (tree of Peru), lime, and some mineral earth. They anointed the face with an oily liquid, of an orange color, covering it afterward with cotton; they joined the hands to the jaws, and the knees to the breast, fastening the different members with bandages, until they assumed the desired position."

In our opinion, this description is a mere play of fancy of Señor Barreda, composed according to the method which the Egyptians used to prepare their mummies. In none of those preserved in the national museum at Lima have they been able to discover either dust, or herbs, or other preservatives, as the distinguished director of this institution, D. Mariano D. de Rivero, has assured us in his Treatise on Peruvian Antiquities, p. 42.

We have examined hundreds of these corpses, as well in the warm regions of the coast, as in the frigid Sierra, but never did we succeed in finding a preservative in any. It is true that we found in almost all the skulls a brown or blackish mass, sometimes finely ground like dust, sometimes in small pieces, of different sizes; but the chemical and microscopical analysis which our friend, Don Julio Vogel, made of this substance has proved that the dust, as well as the pieces, was composed of cerebral fat and globules of dried blood, and that it is impossible to discover the slightest vestige of a vegetable substance; an irrefragable proof that the brains have not been extracted, as Barreda pretends. We can also assert, from our own experience, that all the mummies contain the brain and the intestines, and that in none of them can we perceive any incision in the perineum.

Among the numerous proofs which militate against an artificial mummification, we will quote a few, but those quite conclusive. In the year 1841 we found in a sepulchre of the natives the mummy of a pregnant woman, perfectly preserved, from which we extracted the fœtus, which is now in our possession, mummified, and which, according to the opinion of one of the most celebrated professors in the art of midwifery, M. D'Outrepont, had seven months of fœtal age.

A few years before there was found in *Huichay*, two leagues from Tarma, the mummy of a woman who had died in the pangs of childbirth, since only the upper part of the child's head had come to light.

In the mummy of a child of ten or twelve years, which was found by Doctor Von Tschudi, in a Huaca of the coast, and which is now in the Imperial Academy of Petersburgh, the ribs of the left side were detached from the breast-bone, and thus the concavity of the breast, and in part the concavity of the abdomen, were open; there may be distinctly seen the heart, surrounded with the pericardium, the shrivelled lungs, the diaphragm, the transverse colon, and part of the small intestines.

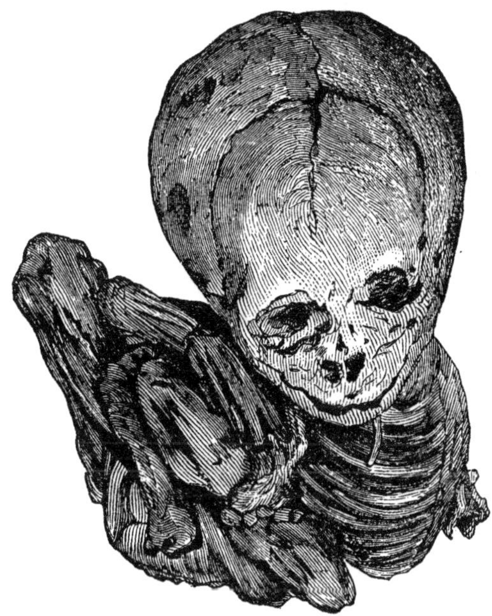

These and other facts are conclusive, and show the fallacy of the hypothesis of Señor Barreda, and of others, relative to an artificial and laborious art of enbalming.

On the coast, the heated soil and calcined sand dry the corpses; and in the interior, the pure cold air, and the dry winds, do the same thing—a phenomenon which, even at the present day, we can observe. Place, for instance, a corpse in a cave of the Sierra, or in the sandy ground of the coast, under shelter from the voracity of the birds, and, in either case, it will be found at the end of months, entire,—not corrupted, but dried; and in proof of this assertion we will cite the cemetery of Huacho, and other towns of the coast, as also the mummified animals, which are sometimes observed on the roads, even on those of the Sierra.*

In those regions in which it frequently rains, it follows naturally that the mummies must be badly preserved. In truth, such is the case; and most frequently they are seen reduced to the form of mere skeletons. But in the nitrous parts of the mountains these are preserved in a state quite fresh, for several generations, notwithstanding the humidity.

* On the roads of the coast, as from Islay to Arequipa, and from this latter to Lima, there are seen a number of these mummies of animals which serve also as landmarks, to show the road; when the wind covers it with sand.

CHAPTER IX.

STATE OF THE ARTS AMONG THE ANCIENT PERUVIANS

In studying the Peruvian works of art, from the humble vessels of clay moulded by the hands of the rustic potter, and from the rudimentary idol, the coarse attempts of the silversmith, to the wonderful monuments of an admirable architecture, in the construction of which thousands of human beings concurred, this question naturally presents itself, viz.: whether the arts had their origin in Peru, and emanated from the progressive evolution of its primitive inhabitants; or whether, proceeding from the other hemisphere, they were the fruits scattered on a new soil by the great reformer of civilization and his successors. Historians differ very materially on this point; and whilst some attribute, exclusively, the degree of artistical splendor to which ancient Peru had attained, to the seeds scattered by Manco-Capac, and to the beneficent encouragements of the Incas, others attribute to the aboriginal inhabitants no small part in the conception and execution of the monumental works and mechanical productions which excite, even at the present day, the admiration of polished Europe.

The critical examination of the ancient monuments which have escaped in whole or in part the destructive action of time, and the mad Vandalism of the conquerors, gives us more light than the incorrect and contradictory pages of authors, and indicate to us two epochs very different in the Peruvian art, at least so far as concerns architecture; one before and the other after the arrival of the first Inca. To the first period pertains the palace known under the name of ruins of the *Gran-Chimu*, in the department of Libertad; the ruins of *Huanuco el Viejo* [old Huanuco]; those of the temple of *Pachacamac*; those of the isles of the lake *Titicaca*; the formidable pyramid, colossus of stone and statues of *Tiahuanacu* on the southern shore of the lake of *Chuquito.* The second epoch comprises the remainder of the department of Cuzco, and of others which we shall speak of in this chapter.

It would be a vain undertaking to indicate the positive age of these monuments, as all certain means of investigation are wanting: the only result we can obtain is, that they are of an epoch anterior to the arrival of the first Inca; and that in Peru, as in Mexico, the people were found in a more advanced state in the arts than the greater part of the nations of Northern Europe.

With these facts before us, the assertion of Garcilasso, that before the light introduced by the first Inca the natives of Peru were little better than tame beasts, collected in groups, without the slightest aspect of towns, streets, squares, etc.; that some, through fear of war, inhabited steep rocks, valleys, natural fissures, caves, or the hollows of trees, etc., is very remarkable; an assertion which the same author contradicts when he eulogizes the admirable architectural works which the Incas met with in their conquests, in regions where the new civilization had certainly not penetrated.

In treating, in this chapter, of the cultivation of the arts among the ancient Peruvians, we must limit ourselves to an exposition of the state in which they were found upon the arrival of the Spaniards, without involving ourselves in investigations and hypotheses upon their successive steps to perfection; while nevertheless, we indicate the progress in each one of the artistic branches.

The art of working timber or manner of applying this material to common or habitual purposes, was very slightly known among the Peruvians; and it is very remarkable that they succeeded in working with more facility substances much harder, such as all kind of stones; and that although they readily invented tools to overcome their hardness, they yet could not succeed in discovering means of overcoming the fibrous tenacity of timber. They knew nothing of the saw and iron hatchet, indispensable instruments in carpentry, and with much toil they wrought out posts and beams, in limestone or marble, in place of timber. In their immense edifices, the ridge poles with their rafters only were of timber; they were made of the trunks of maguay (*Agave Americana*): the doors being of skins or linen, and even of precious metals soldered or riveted: the furniture was of stone or metal. The want of instruments adequate to cutting and smoothing the resisting fibres of the timber was the cause of the greater part of their idols being of stone; and the small quantity of timber which has come into our possession is distinguished by its coarse and clumsy work. A part of the weapons of war were made of *chonta* wood:* Such were the *chuqui* or large lance; the *tupina* or pike, the *macana* or species of sword, the *calhua* or short Turkish sword, the *huicopa* or small dart for throwing, the *huactana* or heavy club—arms all simple, and easy of construction with their instruments of stone. It is worthy of note that among the clubs there was one, the form of which is completely identical with that which is used by the inhabitants of New Zealand and other islands of the Pacific. Don Mariano E. De Rivero possesses

* The *chonta* is a very hard species of palm.—[TRANSLATOR.]

one which was probably one of the insignia of the prince of Tunga in Columbia; and Dr. Von Tschudi disinterred, in 1841, another similar to it, from a sepulchre three leagues from Huacho, together with arms of copper, and *ponchos* or outer garments adorned with flamingo plumes. There is no doubt that the Peruvians shaped their timber with instruments of stone. The chonta (*Guilielma speciosa* and *Martinezia ciliata*) and the Huayacan, the hardest which they knew, and which they preferred for their arms and idols, resist the tools of copper.

How superior, in comparison with these insignificant works, will be found the art of refining and casting metals! The Peruvians knew of gold, silver, copper, tin, and quicksilver, but iron was completely unknown to them, although very abundant in their country. The gold, although it was among them the most esteemed metal, they possessed, according to the best calculations, in a quantity greater than that of any other. Upon comparing its abundance, in the time of the Incas, with the quantity which, in the space of three centuries, the Spaniards have been able to extract from the mines and rivers, it becomes certain that the Indians had a knowledge of veins of this precious material, which the conquerors and their descendants never succeeded in discovering; and we do not believe that it would be a hazardous prognostication to predict, that the day will come when Peru will withdraw from her bosom the veil which now covers more wonderful riches than those which are offered at the present day in California.

In the second half of the sixteenth century, in the short space of twenty-five years, the Spaniards exported from Peru to the mother country more than four hundred millions of ducats of gold and silver, and we may be well assured that nine-tenths of this quantity composed the mere booty taken by the conquerors; in this computation we leave out of view the immense masses of precious metals, buried by the natives, to hide them from the avarice of the foreign invaders; as also the celebrated chain of gold (Huasca) which the Inca Huayna-Capac commanded to be made in honor of the birth of his first-born son, Inti-Cusi-Huallpa-Huasca, and which they say was thrown into the lake of Urcos;* also the eleven thousand llamas loaded with gold-dust in precious vases of this metal, with which the unfortunate Atahuallpa wished to purchase his life and liberty, and which the conductors interred in the Puna (probably on the heights of Mito in the valley of Jauja), as soon as they heard of the new punishment to which their adored monarch had been treacherously condemned.†

They called gold, "Tears which the sun shed," and they extracted it from the mines and washings of the rivers, finding at times pieces weighing from thirty-five to forty ounces, and even more. Their most abundant mines were those of Collahuya, which also yielded to the Spaniards a rich harvest. The silver they generally took from mines, not very deep (an open cut), abandoning them as soon as the hardness of the ore offered a resistance sufficient to withstand their

* It is said that this chain was of the size of a man's wrist, and had in length 350 links, which made 700 feet, and reached around two sides of the principal square of Cuzco.—*Zarrate*, Book I. Chap. XIV.

† Others infer from the abundant and large skeletons of llamas, that this wealth exists on one of the ridges near the pueblo of Junin or Reyes, having there met with some figures and small plates of gold and silver which we have seen in the hands of the commandant of said people. Many are the relations which are given, as well in Columbia as in Peru, regarding buried treasures, and in order that our readers may have some notion of them, we will insert at the end of the book that which has been communicated to us by persons of good standing, referring to documents and descriptions of subjects of which we have knowledge.

imperfect tools. The Peruvians not only knew native silver, but also its chemical combinations, such as the sulphate, antimonial silver, etc.; giving to each one of them a particular name; and they knew how to extract from these compounds the pure metal, by fusion or in portable stoves, mixing with the most refractory, lead, galena, (*Suruchec*, "that which causes to flow") or sulphur of antimony. The ovens to melt the silver, generally used in Peru at the present day, are originally from the Indians, with slight modifications.

We have no accounts of the mode of extracting the copper, which is seldom found in its native state in Peru; it is probable that the greater part was brought from Chili, since it is doubtful whether they melted the minerals of copper which abound in some Peruvian provinces. In the analyses made by Don Mariano E. de Rivero, of various instruments of copper, such as chisels, hatchets, etc., he has found *silex* in the proportion of from five to ten per cent. Whether this substance was mixed with it in order to give greater hardness to their instruments, or was accidentally added at the time of extracting the metal from the matrix, we cannot now say. If this existed in all the instruments which they made use of to work their stones and idols, it is probable that they had some knowledge of its properties or power of hardening copper; as carbon is used to form steel. As to the alloy of copper with tin which they made use of, we do not know whether they understood the combination of these metals; they never, however, employed the latter in a pure state, in their works.

By law the Incas prohibited the extracting of quicksilver, not only on account of its fatal influence upon the animal economy; but it was also considered as a useless metal, as its value was unknown. The mineral quicksilver of Huancavelica* was discovered more than twenty-five years after the conquest in 1567, by the Portuguese, Enriquez Garces. It was undoubtedly that known by the Incas, since there was found in the vicinity of the city deposits of it; and according to some authors they here obtained the *Ychma*, which is the cinnabar, and the *Llampi* (oxide of iron), which they used to paint themselves.

Another law determined that the *Ychma* should be dug up by only a limited number of Indians, destined for this task, and its use was strictly prohibited to the common class. All that these operators extracted was delivered up as the property of the Incas, and afterward distributed among the *pallas*, or women of royal blood, who used it as an ornament at the feasts, painting on themselves a line the width of a straw from the external angle of the eyes to the temples. The Indians knew very well how to extract mercury from the *Ychma* or cinnabar, and the law which prohibited the general use of this substance forbade entirely the playing with, seeking, or even naming it.

Great was the use which the Peruvians made of the precious metals. They used them as offerings to their deities, to make idols and sacred vessels, and as tributes to the Incas. They also made of them the articles which the kings used, the ornaments of their palaces, and the temples of the Sun of the first rank. The art of the silversmiths had attained to great perfection; and if similar progress had been made in the art of moulding, the works of art of the Peruvians would, perhaps, at this day have rivalled those of the most polished nations of antiquity.

The silversmiths knew how to melt the metal, to cast it

* For a history of this mine and its products, see the memoir of the rich mineral of quicksilver of Huancavelica, by Don Mariano Eduardo de Rivero, published in Lima in 1848.

in moulds, to inlay it, to solder it, and to hammer it. They used for the melting of it, as I have already said, small ovens provided with tubes of copper through which the air passed. The moulds were made of a species of clay mixed with gypsum, as has been proved by an analysis of a mould of an idol belonging to a nation of natives in the Sierra, which was taken to Europe. The moulded metals are chiselled in such perfection, that we cannot discover in them the slightest inequality resulting from the mould. In some of these moulded figures, we discover bits of copper, silver, and pure gold so well inlaid that they seem to form a whole. Much admiration has been excited also by the skill with which they made their hammered works. We do not know the method used in this art; most probably it was very similar to that of our silversmiths. There are two classes of these works: one consists of figures and animals beaten out first into thin plates of gold or silver, and afterward soldered together into the proper form; the second in open vases, on the sides of which are figures, somewhat coarse in design, hammered with the greatest skill, in such a manner that you cannot recognize the blow of the hammer. The soldering is distinguished by its solidity, all other parts breaking first, and by the perfect union of the soldered parts. Some authors have pretended that in many of the hollow idols there is no soldering, but it is a mistake, for if we examine carefully the pieces, we may still discover the points of reunion, though almost entirely effaced by the very perfect burnishing.

The art of gilding was unknown to the Peruvians, but they supplied the deficiency in a solid manner, by covering the copper or timber with very thin leaves of gold or silver, which they knew how to fasten closely even to stones. They also extracted threads from the precious metals, of admirable thinness, using them to imitate the fibres of the ears of corn, weaving them also into linen, etc.

Unfortunately, the first works of the art of the silversmith have not come down to our time, they having been destroyed by the covetousness of the invaders, and the hatred of the natives toward them. All the manufactures of gold and silver which the Spaniards met with were cast in clay, and most of them were sent to the peninsula; and the Indians, when they saw the desire which the conquerors had to possess similar objects, buried them, destroyed them, or threw them into the lakes. Those which have come down to us are objects of an inferior class, and incapable of giving one an exact idea of the perfection to which the Peruvians attained in this species of work, and we can gather the best information about them from the unanimous accounts of the ancient Spanish chroniclers who had an opportunity to see them; some of these we will here quote: "They had an artificial garden, the soil of which was made of small pieces of fine gold, and this was artificially sowed with different kinds of maize which were of gold, their stems, leaves, and ears; and they were so firmly planted, that although they had strong winds, they were not torn up. Beside all this, they had more than twenty sheep of gold with their lambs, and the shepherds with their slings and crooks guarding them, made of this metal. There was a large quantity of jars, of gold, silver, and emeralds; vases the likeness of earthen pots, and indeed all species of vessels, all of fine gold. They had also statuary and other larger objects painted; in fact, it was one of the richest temples in the world."—(*Sarmiento*, Relation MS., in Prescott's History of the Conquest of Peru, Book I. Chap. III.) Similar gardens were made in all the royal palaces and temples of the Sun. Francisco Lopez de Gomara says (Hist. Gen. Chap. 121): "All the service of his house (i. e.

the Inca's), both of table and kitchen, was of gold and silver, except a part, which was of silver and copper, for the sake of strength. He had in his withdrawing-room hollow statues of gold, which seemed gigantic; and elsewhere, figures of natural size, resembling many animals, also of birds, and of such trees and herbs as the earth yielded, and of such fishes as were found in the sea and in the waters of the kingdom. He had imitations of grass ropes, sacks, baskets, and knapsacks, all made of gold and silver; heaps of sticks of gold which were in the form of billets of wood for burning. In fact, there was nothing in the country which was not imitated in gold; and they say that the Incas had also a flower garden in an island near Puna, where they went to rest when they wanted to enjoy the sea, which possessed all kinds of herbs, trees and flowers of gold and silver; an invention and grandeur until then never seen. Beside this, they had an immense quantity of gold and silver to work in Cuzco, which was lost by the death of Huascar; where the Indians concealed it, seeing that the Spaniards would take it to send into Spain." In the palace of Tumebamba, says the Chronicler Cieça de Leon, in the XLIV. chapter: "Within the apartments were búndles of gold, straw, and on the walls were sculptured sheep and lambs of the same metal, and birds, and many other things. Beside this, they related that they had an immense amount of treasure in vessels and pots, and other things; and many rich blankets embroidered in silver and white glass beads." Garcilasso de la Vega (Com. Royal, Book VI. Chap. II.), speaking of the royal houses, expresses himself in these terms: "In all of them were gardens and orchards, where the Inca refreshed himself. They planted in them all the fine and beautiful trees and odoriferous plants which abounded in the kingdom; after which models they imitated in gold and silver, many trees and other smaller bushes most perfectly, with their leaves, flowers, and fruits; some seemed about to bud, others were half ripened or matured, and others entire and perfect in their size. Beside these and others, they made counterfeit resemblances of various species of corn most naturally, with their leaves, ear and stem, with their roots and flowers; and the fibres which are found in the ear and stem were of gold; and all the rest of silver, soldered together, and the same difference was made in the other plants, so that the flower, or whatever other part inclined to yellow, was imitated in gold, and the rest in silver. There were also to be seen animals, large and small, cast in gold and silver; such as rabbits, lizards, snakes, butterflies, foxes and mountain cats. There were to be seen birds of all descriptions, some placed in the trees, as if singing, others were flying about and sucking the honey from the flowers. There were also deer and fawns, lions and tigers, and all the other animals and birds which the country produced, each thing in its place, as true to nature as the reality. In many houses there were baths with large jars of silver and gold, from which water was brought into the baths. And where there were natural fountains of warm water, there were also baths made of great splendor and richness. Among other displays of wealth there were collections of billets of wood, imitated in gold and silver, as though they were deposited to be expended in the service of the houses." In his first chapter the same author says: "The Inca seated himself ordinarily on a seat of massive gold which they called Tiana; it was a third of a yard in height, without arms or back, and without any concavity for the sitter; they placed it upon a large square block of gold. The vessels of all the service of the house, as well of the table as of the buttery and kitchen, small and great, were of gold and silver; and there was a deposit of them made in each house, so that when the king travelled, they shouldnot be obliged to carry them from one place to another, so that everything necessary, as well on the public roads as throughout all the provinces, should be provided for the Inca when he arrived there, either travelling with his army or visiting his kingdoms. There were also to be seen in these royal houses many imitations of granaries and banks of earth, which the Indians call Pirua, made of gold and silver, not to inclose grain, but to add to the grandeur and majesty of the house and of its Lord."

These accounts of Garcilasso are confirmed by his predecessor, the Controller of Accounts, D. Agustin de Zarrate, (Conq. of Peru, Book I. Chap. XIV.) who says: "They held gold in great esteem, because out of it the king and his princes had made vases for their service, and of it they made jewels for their apparel, and they offered it in the temples; and the king possessed a block, on which he sat, of gold of sixteen carats, which was worth in good gold more than twenty-five thousand ducats; this, Don Francisco Pizarro selected for his prize at the time of the conquest, because, conformably to the capitulation, he was to have given to him a jewel or prize which he should select aside from the common store. The same Don Francisco de Pizarro wrote to the Court from Jauja, the 5th of July, 1534, that besides the large bars and vessels of gold, he had found four sheep (llamas) and ten statues of women, of the natural size, of the finest gold and also of silver, and a cistern of gold so curious, that it excited the wonder of all." And the anonymous author of the Conquest and Settlement of Peru, MS. (see Prescott,) relates as follows, speaking of the temple of the Sun: "The model of the Sun contained an immense mass of gold, and all the service of the house was of silver and gold; there were twelve receptacles or bins of silver, so large that two men, with arms extended, could not embrace them, each one being square; they were higher than a good pike or lance; in these were placed the corn which they gave the Sun."

These accounts suffice to give us an idea of the number of works of gold and silver of the ancient Peruvians, and of the singular perfection with which they accomplished them. In the histories of Cieça de Leon, Acosta, Zarrate, Levinus-Apollonius, Calancha, Garcilasso de la Vega, Gomara and Montesinos, etc., etc., etc., may be found further information upon this point.

Of copper very few manufactured articles are found; it seems that they did not know how to work this metal as perfectly as silver and gold; notwithstanding, the Museum of Lima preserves some vases of copper very thin, some idols, instruments, and two solid staves a yard long, with serpents inlaid, which were recently discovered in the department of Puno. One of the most interesting pieces of this metal which we have seen, was found in a sepulchre between Huaura and Huillcahuaura, and formed, judging from appearances, the upper part of a sceptre or staff or some badge of royalty. It is six inches in length, and one inch in diameter; an inch and a half from its lower opening is found in the interior a dividing wall, as far as which might be thrust the staff or rod which it surmounted.

Upon the upper part of this reposes a bird (its mate is broken off), which represents, judging from the beak, a flamingo, although the neck and feet are too short for a bird of this species; on the right side of the cylinder are three pairs of birds descending, and the same on the left, ascending. The first pair of these is small, large-headed, with straight, large beaks; the second, much larger, represent in a manner which cannot be mistaken, owls; the third is like the first. The lower ones of those on the left side are small, the heads large, with a crest; the following are *Yanahuicus* (Ibis. Ordi. of Bonaparte), with their beaks large and almost straight; the upper ones are large, the beaks in form of a hook; in front they have a high crest and the neck bound with a collar sufficiently wide, so that they may be easily characterized as male Condors.

No less admirable was the progress of the Peruvians in the art of weaving and dyeing. Without a loom or any other machine, but with the most simple manipulation, they knew how to fabricate finished cloths, very artificially interwoven with designs and ornaments. They wove cotton and wool; of the first, they made cloth of two kinds; the common white cotton and the brownish or color of the Vicuña, which they reared principally in the warm valleys of the eastern declivity of the Andes. The four species of the family of the American camel provided them with wool; these four were two domestic ones, the llama and the alpaca; and the two wild ones, the huanaco and the vicuña. For the coarser cloth, they used the wool of the llama and of the huanaco; for the finer, that of the alpaca and the vicuña. The common class were clothed in the first, the nobles and princes with the wool of the alpaca, and the Incas with cloth of the wool of the vicuña; with which they, at times, by way of favor and distinction, honored the noble Lords. It was the exclusive privilege of the chosen virgins and *pallas* to spin and weave the wool of the vicuña, and there is no doubt that they had attained to the greatest perfection in this art, and that their works were remarkable for their rare fineness and their beautiful designs. "The coverings of the bed were blankets, and friezes of wool of vicuña, which is so fine and so much prized, that, among other precious things from that land, they have been brought for the bed of Don Philip the 2d."—(*Garcilasso*, Com. Book VI. Chap. I.)

They possessed the secret of fixing the dye of all colors, flesh-color, yellow, gray, blue, green, black, etc., so firmly in the thread, or in the cloth already woven, that they never faded during the lapse of ages, even although exposed to the air, or buried under ground. Only the cotton ones became slightly discolored, whilst the woollen ones preserved their primitive lustre. It is a circumstance worth remarking that a chemical analysis made of pieces of cloth of all the different dyes, proves that the Indians extracted all their colors from the vegetable, and none from the mineral kindom. In fact, the inhabitants of the Peruvian mountains now use plants unknown to the Europeans; producing from them bright and lasting colors.

They were accustomed to ornament their textures by sewing upon them their leaves of gold and silver, or small pieces of mother of pearl, and bunches of feathers as a substitute for fringe: but they also made fringes, laces and tassels of wool and cotton to adorn carpets and tapestries.

All the fine textures of wool which we have had occasion to examine, are as strong as they are beautiful in color and design: those of cotton have suffered more from time, and those supplied by the Huacas are very frail, and seldom as fine as those of the wool of the Vicuña. In the provinces of the coast they use more of the cotton, and in those of the Sierra, as it is much colder, they use more of the woollen.

The Peruvians did not know the art of tanning the skins with bark. The skins of the llamas, huanacos, etc., they tanned or dressed in large vessels or in holes and folded them in rich earth, leaving them for some time with stale urine, and beating them afterward. The almost exclusive use of these tanned skins was reserved for the manufacture of the *Usutas* or *Llanquis* (sandals) of the people, and to hang up as doors.

In treating next of the works of the ancient potters, we shall begin by making some preliminary observations upon this branch, which, not having excited by its nature the rapacity of the conquerors, has been better preserved in numerous objects, some for curiosity, some for domestic use.

If we examine the principles of the plastic art among different nations, we shall see that although the artists always intended to represent a whole figure, yet, wanting in dexterity or skill and a correct execution of the exact proportions, they exaggerated the relative size of the parts. In the representation of men and animals, we generally find in excess the head or some organ belonging to it; thus we observe in the Egyptian statues the eyes fronting the observer and the face in profile; and in the Peruvian modelling, the nose and ears are above their natural size. Among the Egyptians, long figures predominate; among the Peruvians, short and bulky ones; and among them we find a greater want of proportions than in those of many other nations which we have had occasion to examine. In the most ancient specimens of the Peruvians, the head always forms the principal part, and presents a marked appearance, indicating that the artist exhausted upon it all his skill: the body forms a deformed mass, and the extremities are appendages of the least importance, having sometimes only a tenth part of the correct proportions as compared with the head. This is found as well in human figures as in animals.

It is a general observation that the most ancient monuments represent Deities; and beginning with a primitive monotheistic religion (in which all the nations of the world participated), it may be easily proved that the plastic art originated at the time when, the nations leaving their fundamental religion, became converted to polytheism. Among the Peruvians we discover in the Huacas and Conopas the beginnings of the art, and in them and the vessels destined for the sacrifice of the Deities, we may easily trace its progress.

In order to pronounce a just opinion upon this point, it is necessary to have examined a very large number of the works of art, and to have followed in this examination fixed rules, generally adopted by all critics, not allowing one's self to be carried away by secondary circumstances; among these the principal ones are the skill of the workmanship and the state of cultivation of the province where it is found.

A critical observation attests that the works of art of the province which was governed by the chief *Chimu-Canchu*, and those found in the imperial city of Cuzco and its vicinity, are much more perfect and correct than those which are seen in the Sierra and on the coast of Central Peru.

All the moulded works of the ancient Peruvians have a peculiar character which distinguishes them from those of the other American nations; a character which, by those versed in antiquities, will be recognized at first sight. Some of them bear a certain resemblance to the forms presented by the old continent; especially the most simple: such is a seated figure which has an Egyptian type; a vase which may pass for Etruscan, and a blackish vessel that has been found, seems to be identical with those of the Celtic-Germans; so perfect, indeed, is the resemblance that if mixed with the known remains of those countries, the archæologist would find no difference between them: but these works, so simple, and so easy to manufacture, cannot serve as a criterion to denote the special character of the works of art of any nation.

All the skill of the Peruvian potters was laid out upon the manufacture of the Huacas, Conopas and sacred vessels which they placed with the corpses in the sepulchres. The kitchen furniture and other vessels for domestic use are very simple, and without art. The material which they made use of was colored clay and blackish earth, which they prepared so well, that it completely resisted fire, and did not absorb liquids. It seems that they did not burn the vessels, since the substance of these differed very materially from burnt clay, and judging from appearances, they dried it in the sun, after having prepared and mixed it in a manner of which we are ignorant. At this day there exist in many houses, pitchers, large jars and earthen pots of this material, and they are generally preferred for their solidity to those which are manufactured by our own potters, a proof of their superiority. The greater part of the sacred vessels, buried with the mallquis and destined to receive the chicha of sacrifice on feast days, have an enlarged neck, placed ordinarily near the handle, with a hole to pour out the liquid, and an opposite opening, for the air to escape when the vessel is filled. Many are double, and it seems that they made them thus from preference; others are quadruple, or sextuple, or even octuple, that is, the principal vessel is surrounded with regular appendages, which communicate among themselves, and with the principal vessel. The double ones were made in such perfection, that when they were filled with a liquid, the air escaping through the opening left for that purpose, produced sounds at times very musical: these sounds sometimes imitated the voice of the animal which was represented by the principal part of the vessel, as in a beautiful specimen we have seen, which represents a cat, and which, upon receiving water through the upper opening, produces a sound similar to the mewing of that animal. We have in our possession a vessel of black clay, which perfectly imitates the whistle of the thrush, the form of which is seen on the handle. We also preserve two circular vases, which, being filled with water, through a hole in the bottom, on being turned over, lose not a single drop, the water coming out when it is wished, by simply inclining the upper part of the vase: which proves that the Peruvian artisans had perhaps some knowledge of atmospheric pressure.

On many of the sacred vessels there are designs and paintings, which, however, give an idea of the progress of the art of designing among the Peruvians. The architectural designs with straight lines are the only parts correct and even beautiful in appearance; but all the designs with curved lines, such as the representation of men and animals, are of little value. There is one worthy of notice which is seen very often, either painted on vessels of clay, or engraved on the arms, or worked in raised work in gold or silver, and represents a man with the arms open holding in his hands staves similar to lances (Chuqui), and the head covered with a broad cap. There is no doubt that these figures represent Deities (Huacas); others have long garments, and on the head a species of mitre, showing themselves also to be Huacas, as may be inferred from what Garcilasso relates (Hist. Chap. 121), saying "that the Indians, when they saw the bishop, Don F. Geronimo Loayza, asked if he were the Huaca of the Christians."

In some ancient edifices we recognize even now the remains of architectural paintings; and according to all appearances, the Peruvians know not how to paint the walls of their palaces in any other manner, leaving the art of design among themselves always in its first infancy. Neither did they attain to sculpturing light figures, or groups in relievo, in such perfection as the Mexicans, who distinguished themselves extraordinarily in this work.

The ancient historians leave us in obscurity respecting Peruvian paintings; a certain proof that they were not remarkable. Garcilasso de la Vega only (Royal Com. Book

V., Chap. XXIII.) speaks of the famous painting of the two condors, which the Inca *Viracocha* commanded to be made on a very high rock, on the spot where his father passed, when he came from Cuzco, on his return from the Chancas. Says this author, "These two birds he ordered to be painted, the one with closed wings, and the head lowered, as the birds place themselves, when they wish to hide from wild beasts, with the face toward Collasuyu, and the back toward Cuzco. The other he ordered to be painted in a contrary way, with the face turned toward the city, and ferocious, with wings extended, as if swooping to seize some prize. The Indians said that the one Condor represented his father, who had flown from Cuzco, and had gone to hide himself in Collao; and the other represented the Inca Viracocha, who had come back flying to defend the city and the whole empire. This painting existed in good order in the year 1580, and in the year 95, I asked a Creole priest who came from Peru to Spain if he had seen it, and how it appeared? He said it was very much obliterated, that scarcely anything was to be seen of it; because time with its streams, and a carelessness as to its perpetuation, as well as that of other monuments similar to it, had ruined it."

The Peruvian Indians have attained in this day to some skill in this art, principally those of Cuzco and Quito, where they are accustomed to paint in oil the portraits of the Incas and images of the saints.

It now only remains for us to speak of the art in which the ancient Peruvians excelled, that is, architecture, and its accompaniment, the art of hewing stone. In contemplating the stones artificially cut which we find in the ancient palaces, or in the form of statues, cups, vases, and rings in the sepulchres, they will suggest ideas of the most profound wonder to the thoughtful man who seeks to explain the manner in which the ancients attained to making works of such rare perfection without instruments of iron and steel. For three centuries past, wise men of all nations have attempted the solution of this problem, without having been able, up to the present day, to arrive at any positive knowledge regarding this singular manipulation. It is certain that the tools already spoken of, made of a mixture of copper and tin, or of copper and flint, were not sufficient to work upon the hardest minerals. Trials made in our day with chisels of these materials, found in the Peruvian Huacas, have proved that such tools have much less hardness than those of steel, and that, in using them upon hard stones, such as marble or granite, they soon become blunted, and useless. Nevertheless, it seems that they made some use at least of such instruments, and that they knew how to sharpen them easily. In our opinion, they used them only to break the stones and give them the first rough form, but they used other means to plane and polish them; and according to appearances they did it by means of a toilsome and slow manipulation, rubbing them, now with pieces of other stones, now with powder of the same, and now, to put the last polish upon them, with herbs which contain flint, similar to the "horse-tail," or "shave-grass" of Spain. The ancient proverb *gutta cavat lapidem*,* may here be justly applied, and the objection that it is too laborious, has its refutation in the quiet and patient disposition of the Indians, who, accustomed for generations to a daily repetition of their occupations, continued throughout entire years, with the greatest indolence, the most monotonous labor; moreover, this proceeding is the most simple and natural. After having considered with the utmost scrupulousness all the circumstances, we cannot explain in any other way the raised work on rings of emeralds, on jasper, granite, and

* "Constant dropping wears away the stone."

basalt, the cups, vases, idols of marble, porphyry, granite, and other of the hardest minerals, and in general, the finest works of stone among the ancient Peruvians.

For architectural works they ordinarily used square stones and also polygons, and sometimes of spherical shape, such as are found among the interesting ruins of the palace of *Limatambo.* The exactitude with which they formed them was such that, using them in the construction of their edifices, the fronts and angles were so closely cemented that there was but the smallest possible space existing between them. The size of these stones is very different, ordinarily from one to two yards in height, and the same in length; but we have measured some which were twelve yards in length, and eight in height.

In order to give an idea of the size of the stones, we insert here the design of a part of the fortification at the entrance to *Ollantaytambo* on the side of Cuzco.

Father Acosta (Book VI. Chap. XIV.) says: "In Tiaguanaco, I measured a stone of thirty-eight feet in length, and eighteen in width, and its thickness was six feet; and in the wall of the fortress of Cuzco, which is built without plummets, there are many stones of much greater size." The stone, causing so much labor, of which Garcilasso speaks, (Book VII. Chap. XXIX.,) surpassed all, but was not placed in the position destined for it in the fortress of Cuzco. In its transportation it overcame, according to this author, the strength of the men who were supporting it, and rolling over, killed three or four hundred Indians; this we believe to be an exaggeration, knowing as we do the timidity of these people and the caution which they use in their labors.

Here arises the question: How did they transport these heavy masses to their appointed places, and how did they raise them to the necessary height, being deficient in all that mechanical knowledge which in our days much facilitates those operations? The answer is found in the social institutions, already mentioned, among the ancient Peruvians. For the construction of private houses all the people assembled, and for the public buildings, all the able inhabitants from one or more provinces: thus they supplied by the number of people and disposable forces the want of auxiliary means.

A serious error made by the greater part of ancient and modern historians, is in the statement that the Peruvians did not use any cement or mortar in putting together stones for their edifices; for they had cements of different kinds. For the palaces, temples, baths and all the other edifices constructed of polished stones, they used instead of mortar either a clay very soluble and remarkably adherent, called *Lancac-Allpa*, or a mixture of lime, *Iscu* (which they burnt and slaked, as is done at the present day,) with a species of bitumen, the use of which has been lost, (See *Gomara*, Hist. Gen. Chap.

194); and for the buildings of less importance, constructed of rough stone, they employed a mortar made of lime (*Pachachi*), with coarse sand; as we see even now in many of the old towns among them.

Designs of all classes of Peruvian architecture, from the imposing palace to the rustic hut, have resisted the destructive tooth of time, and permitted us, aided by the relations of the contemporaneous authors of the conquest, to give a correct general idea of them.

The private houses were very simple, and according to the custom of the province, were either of stones, or of bricks, or of cane, as on the coast. The bricks, or more properly *adobes*, unbaked bricks (*Ticacuna* in the Quichua language), were made of clay mixed with the grass *Ichu*, cut somewhat fine like chaff, intimately mixed and pressed. They were made in a rectangular form, as large as the thickness of the wall which they were going to construct with them; from six to eight inches in height, and from fifteen to twenty in width: after being formed they were exposed for a year or more to the air and the sun, until they became as hard as our burnt bricks. Even at the present day the Indians make their adobes in the same way, using sometimes instead of *Ichu* the straw of cut wheat, or even dung.

The houses were small and of few rooms, not communicating with each other; each one had a door opening into the court or street; the door also answered the purpose of a window. In the more important buildings there were inter mediate doors and windows in great numbers, (notwithstand ing some authors erroneously represent the contrary) as we may still see in many ruins of palaces and temples. In the large cities, the houses touched each other and were disposed in rows, front joining front, thus forming straight streets. The general plan of all the large towns was similar to that of the greater part of those in the South of Europe and of those now in Peru: a square with the principal edifices forms the centre, from which project, in the direction of the four quarters of the world, the principal streets. In many towns of the Sierra, the dwellings were scattered and arranged without order, as the face of the ground permitted.

We have observed among the ruins of ancient towns in the departments of *Junin* and *Ayacucho* houses like towers and of a singular construction, and of considerable size. Each dwelling is square, and has a width within of six feet and an altitude of from sixteen to eighteen. The walls are a foot and a half in thickness, and in the eastern one, or in that of the south, is found the door, a foot and a half in height and two feet in width. After having passed into the lower entrance, and with some difficulty through this opening, you arrive at a species of sitting-room, five and a half or six feet in height, and as much in width. The walls were naked, but in the thickness of the walls, there are small closets which served to keep provisions, and you sometimes see in them ears of corn, coca, pots, and vessels. The roof of these apartments is made of large flat stones, leaving in the middle an aperture of two feet in diameter; mounting, not without difficulty, through this opening, you arrive at another story similar to the first, with some windows like embrasures; its roof has an opening like the ceiling of the first, through which you pass to the third compartment, the roof of which, formed of rough stones, serves as a cover to the whole dwelling. This uppermost space is somewhat lower than the two inferior ones, and was probably intended to hold the provisions. We found in one of them the mummy of a girl. The central compartment was to all appearance the dormitory, and a stone sufficiently large, which is almost always found in it, served to close the aperture of the floor; the lower one was at the same time a dwelling-room and a kitchen, and we can very easily recognize the hearth. With a large flat stone they closed, from within, the outer door of the house.

Upon digging or excavating the ground of one of these dwellings, we found, not very deeply buried, earthen pots, vessels and jars, two *Conopas* and human bones.

Among the public edifices we must consider the hostelries and royal inns, the houses of public sports, the baths, palaces, monasteries, temples and fortresses.

The *tambos*, or royal hostelries, were edifices built without the slightest architectural art, constructed of rough stone or adobes, and formed a square or rectangle, surrounding a plaza sufficiently large, in the middle of which there was a watch-tower which overlooked the edifice, little more than a fathom high. In the enclosure, cut by two entrances opposite to each other, are found very large compartments, to lodge the soldiers, and small apartments for the Inca, and the nobles or lords of his suite; the doors faced the square. These apartments for the soldiery were thirty or forty feet wide, and in length six or seven hundred or more; so that it was easy to lodge in them four or five thousand soldiers. They were constructed upon the royal road, distant five or six leagues one from the other, so that without too much fatigue one might conveniently reach in one journey one of these lodging-houses. Some authors pretend that the number of these *tambos* amounted to nine or ten thousand, which is a great exaggeration, there not having been, in truth, a third of this number.

Similar to the construction of the *tambos* was that of the royal warehouses, and instead of the watch-tower there was a small fortress in the centre of the square with a permanent garrison. Situated in the neighborhood of the seat of the chief *Curacas*, they were intended as a receptacle for the taxes of the provinces, the arms and provisions for the army. *Coptra* was the particular name given to the deposits of clothing, shoes and arms; *Pirhua-Coptra* to the granaries, where they kept the corn and *quinua;* and *Cumpi-Coptra* to the warehouses of fine wools and precious cloths, embroi dered in the monasteries of the virgins of the Sun.

The houses for play were joined to the palaces or stood alone, and were not distinguished for their architecture, but for their extent. They were edifices of four walls only with a roof, intended to serve as a square wherein to celebrate the feasts, when the rainy season did not permit them to take place on the public squares without shelter. Garcilasso de la Vega says (Com. Royal, Book VI. Chap. IV.), that he succeeded in seeing four of these halls in Cuzco; the largest was in *Cassana*, and capable of containing three thousand persons, another in *Amarucancha;* the smallest in *Collcampata*, and another was in the place where now stands the Cathedral Church. He relates that one of these *Galpones* was two hundred paces long and fifty or sixty in width. As regards its interior plan, whether it had galleries, and tribunes or other platforms, we know not; neither do we know whether there were similar edifices in other cities.

The baths or *Armanahuasi* attracted attention by a certain elegance of exterior, and by a rich internal apparatus. The fountains (*Puquio*) were carefully covered at bottom with a hydraulic mixture of small stones and a species of bitumen; and over them might be seen arranged the figure of an animal, a lion, tiger, monkey, bird or snake, of marble, basalt, or even of gold or silver, which threw water from the mouth, either in the form of a perpendicular stream, (*Huraca*) or from a horizontal conduit (*Paccha*). The flowing water was conducted through a pipe of metal or stone, into jars of gold, silver, or sculptured stone, one of which is in our possession. The small sitting-rooms which are seen in these baths, seem to have been intended as dressing-rooms, as they were ornamented with statues of stone and metal. The most celebrated baths were the hot baths in *Huamalies*, made of stone sculptured with the greatest exactitude, and internally adorned with great luxury. In the warmest fountains (*Coñic puquio*) with which the Peruvian mountains abound, even in the most efficacious ones, we do not find any traces of their having been made use of in the time of the Incas.*

The royal palaces, or *Inca-huasi*, whose number from Cuzco to Quito amounted to more than two hundred, were found not only in the capitals of provinces, and even in cities of minor importance, but also in pleasant cities, not on the royal road, and were, as to some, very sumptuous, constructed of marble or other stones highly polished; as to others, very simple, and only distinguished from the royal inns by their uses. Of the most magnificent among them we have accounts, either through tradition, or from their beautiful ruins; these are found in Tinta, Lampa, Tiahuanacu, in the neighboring islands of Hatuncolla, and of Capachica, in Paucarcolla, in Cuzco, in the beautiful valley of Yucay, in Limatambo, Huamanga, old Huanuco, Chavin,

* We will here insert the temperature of some of the hot baths, which were known to the Incas.

Baths of Caxamarca, 129.7° Fahrenheit.

Baths of Huamalies; Banos of Chavin of Huanta, 112° F., Air 52° F.

Baths of Huallanca, 123° F. and 150° F.

Vapor baths of Aguamiro, tube of 14 yards, 124° F., the second of 14 yards, 118° F., Air 70° F.

Those of Cono, distant half a league, 110° F., Air 68° F.

Yauli, in four examinations, 120° F., 114° F., 110° F., 92° F., Air 60° F., (Sulphurous).

Baths of Yura of Arequipa, in four trials, 94° F., 90° F., 89° F., 80° F., Air 68° F. (Sulphurous).

Chachapoya, etc., in Chimu, in Truxillo, and in the kingdom of Quito in Puncallacta, Callo in the province of Latacunya (Humboldt's Views of the Cordilleras, pag. 197. Ulloa, Relation Hist. of Voyage, etc., Book II. Chap. XI.), in Hatuncañar and Tomebamba, in the province of Cañar (Cieça de Leon, Chronicles, Chap. XLIV.) and others. The majority of the palaces in the north of Peru and of the ancient kingdoms of Quito, were built at the end of the fifteenth century, and at the beginning of the sixteenth, by order of the Inca Huaynacapac, who had a singular predilection for architectural works.

Viewed externally, the palaces and temples did not present as imposing an aspect as the Teocalis of Yucatan; since, although they occupied a very considerable space of ground, they were low, of two or two and a half stories in height, and disfigured by rustic roofs of straw.* The walls were at times admirable for the artificial and neat union of the hewn stones, but too simple withal, wanting columns, cornices, relievos and other architectural ornaments. The entrance to these edifices consisted of a wide aperture in the wall, facing the east; or in a portal covered on the top with beams placed as tiles, or with flag-stones, but never with arches. A general error among most historians, as well the ancient as the modern, is the opinion that the Peruvian architects had not attained to the construction of arches and vaults; for in many *Huacas* of stones we observe vaults very superiorly constructed. According to all appearances, they used the same plan in making them that the Indian masons employed

* An exception to this rule was the palace Amaracancha, built by order of the Inca Huaynacapac. Garcilasso says (Comment. Royal, II. Chap. XXXII.) that he saw it. There was a most beautiful round tower, which was in full view, before entering the house. The walls were four stories in height, and the roof was so high that it equalled in that particular any tower which he saw in Spain, that of Seville excepted !?

at the present day, do in the construction of small vaults in the smelting ovens; that is, by filling the space with materials forming a convexity, and arching them afterward with lime and stone. In some of the larger edifices you meet also with vestiges of arches, but it is certain that their application was quite limited.*

The internal architecture of the palaces offers more complication of detail and more interest. Some large saloons and a multitude of small apartments occupied the space of the building: they communicated among themselves by intermediate doors, but the majority of them had but one door opening into the court surrounding the edifice. The walls were sometimes carved, presenting architectural ornaments very well executed, and a number of large niches, and small boards in the form of shelves. In the most sumptuous palaces the walls were covered with small plates of gold and silver, and even the floors of some of the principal rooms

* Stephens, in his travels in Yucatan in 1843, says, speaking of the arch of San Francisco of Merida:

'But this convent contains one memorial far more interesting than any connected with its own ruin, one that carries the beholder back through centuries of time, and tells the story of a greater and a sadder fall.

"In one of the lower cloisters going out from the north, and under the principal dormitory, are two parallel corridors. The outer one faces the principal patio, and this corridor has that peculiar arch so often referred to in my previous volumes, two sides rising to meet each other, and covered, when within about a foot of forming an apex, by a flat layer of stones. There can be no mistake about the character of this arch; it cannot for a moment be supposed that the Spaniards constructed any thing so different from their known rules of architecture; and beyond doubt, it formed part of one of those mysterious buildings which have given rise to so much speculation, the construction of which has been ascribed to the most ancient people in the old world, and to races lost, perished and unknown."

We have copied this extract as confirmatory proof of our statement that the Indians were not ignorant of the mode of constructing the arch.

[It would rather seem to prove the reverse.—TRANSLATOR.]

were lined with these metals, which was one of the principal causes of their destruction; the Spaniards having demolished them to possess themselves of a material so much coveted. In others, you see the floor adorned with pavement of marbles of different colors like mosaic work. In the niches were found arranged statues of gold and silver, representing men and all sorts of animals. "They counterfeited herbs and plants such as grow on walls, and placed them on the walls in such way that they seemed to have grown there. They imitated on the walls also lizards and butterflies, rats, large and small snakes, which seemed to be ascending and descending upon them."—(*Garcilasso De La Vega*, Royal Com. Book VI. Chap. I.)

The monasteries of the virgins of the sun, or *Pasña-huasi*, were large edifices, similar to the royal inns, and surrounded by high walls. Their number, throughout the kingdom, amounted to twenty or twenty-five, and some contained, servants included, a thousand persons.

The temples, their most sumptuous edifices, present the best specimens of Peruvian architecture, and especially those which were dedicated to the supreme *Numen*, the Sun. These may be divided into three classes: those of the first order contained seven sections communicating internally. The principal part, with a wide door toward the East, occupying the middle of the edifice, was dedicated to the Sun or *Inti*, and was the richest in its internal decoration: the second section was dedicated to *Mama-Quilla*, or the moon: the third to the stars, or *Coyllur;* the fourth to *Illapa*, or the thunderbolt: the fifth to the rainbow, or *Ckuichi;* the sixth to *Huillac Umu*, or high priest, and to the assemblies of the Inca priests, to deliberate upon the sacrifice, and every thing concerning the service of the temple; and finally, the seventh was a large room only to lodge those entrusted with the worship which they performed by alternate weekly services. Beside these, there was a number of small sitting-rooms, for the priests and persons employed.

The temples of the second order contained only two principal parts: that of the Sun, and that of the moon; and in those of the third, there was even wanting the chapel dedicated to the moon.

In order to form an idea of the magnitude and beauty of the temples of the first order, we will give here a description of the temple of the Sun in Cuzco, availing ourselves of the accounts of the ancient Chronicles, contemporaneous with the conquest, there being left at the place (where at the present day stands the convent of the Dominican friars) only some fragments, as sad relics of one of the most beautiful architectural works of the new world.

VIEW OF PART OF THE CONVENT OF ST. DOMINGO IN CUZCO, BUILT ON THE CYCLOPEAN REMAINS OF THE TEMPLE OF THE SUN.

This temple, called *Inti-huasi*, or house of the Sun, occupied a large space: it had," says an ancient author, "a circuit of more than four hundred paces, the whole surrounded by a strong wall; the whole edifice was built of an excellent species of fine stone, very well placed and adjusted, and some of the stones were very large and lofty; they used neither earth nor lime, only the bitumen with which they made their edifices, and the stones were so well placed, that no joint or mortar was apparent."

"Throughout Spain I have seen nothing which may be compared with these walls and the laying of these stones, but the tower which is called the Callahorra, which is contiguous to the bridge of Cordova; and another work which I saw in Toledo, when I went to present the 1st part of my chronicle to the prince Don Philip."—(*Sarmiento*, Relacion MS. Chap. XXIV. in Prescott's Conquest of Peru, Book I. Chap. III.)

In the height of the wall, which did not exceed two stories, there was on the exterior a species of fillet or cornice of gold, a span and a half in width, embedded in the stones.

The principal part, dedicated to the Sun, had a large door in the eastern wall. The ceiling was covered with cotton cloth, neatly woven, embroidered with divers colors, which very beautifully concealed the internal surface of the roof of straw. A band of gold, similar to that on the external side, covered the junction of the roof with the walls. All the walls were hung with plates of gold, and tablets of the same metal served as doors. In the lower wall, in front of the portal, was placed the image of the Sun made of a large plate of gold, with a human face and many rays, richly chased, with emeralds, and other precious stones.* On both sides of

* According to Father Acosta and Father Calancha, this golden sun fell to the lot of one of the most valiant conquerors, Captain D. Mancio Sierra de Liguizano, who staked it one night and lost it before sunrise; from

the image were found corpses embalmed, of the different Incas, each one seated upon his throne of gold.

Communicating with this principal part there was a large apartment of polished stones, adorned at the top only with a fillet of gold, and which served as a vestibule to five chapels. The largest of them was dedicated to the moon, whose image of silver, represented with the face of a woman, was presented on one of the walls. The walls and door were covered with plates of silver: the mummies of the legitimate wives of the Incas were placed on both sides of the moon, as those of the Incas, their lords, were on both sides of the Sun. The second chapel dedicated to the stars, like that dedicated to the moon, had a door of gold; and on the ceiling of blue cloth, yellow needle-work in the form of stars. In the third chapel dedicated to the Yllapa, [or lightning] the walls were of gold, as in the room dedicated to the rainbow, which was painted in very brilliant colors on one of the walls. Adjoining these chapels was a chamber with the walls lined with gold, intended as a species of sacristy, to Huillac-Umu, and as a conference hall for the chief priests.

Garcilasso de la Vega, speaking as an eye-witness, says (Com. Royal, I. Book III. Chap. XXII.): "Of these five saloons there were three only which remained in their ancient state as to walls and roof. They wanted, however, the plates of gold and silver: the other two, which were the chambers of the moon and the stars, were level with the ground. In the outside of the walls of those apartments which looked into the cloister there were on each side four tabernacles or niches, finished with hewn stone, as was all the rest of the house; there were mouldings in the corners and throughout the space of the tabernacle or niche, similar to the mouldings

whence originated in Peru the ordinary proverb, when they would describe a desperate gambler: "He gambles away the Sun before he rises."

made in the wall, so that they were lined with plates of gold, not only the walls and upper part, but also the floors of the niches. The corners of the mouldings were very richly inlaid with fine stones, emeralds and turquoises, as in that country diamonds and rubies were not found. The Inca seated himself in these tabernacles on great festival days, sometimes in one apartment, sometimes in another, conformably to the season of the feast."

All the implements connected with the service of the Sun were of gold and silver, as I have previously mentioned. The dwellings of the priests, and even those of the servants, were richly ornamented with precious stones. Who can wonder that the Peruvians themselves called the place of this immense edifice, in which nearly five thousand persons employed found accommodation, *Coricancha*, or "the place of gold?"

In the provinces there were many temples, similar in their construction to that of Cuzco, but none which surpassed or even equalled it in richness. Very sumptuous were those of *Huillca*, of *Tumpez*, of *Tomepampa*, of *Hatun-Cañar*, and of *Quito*, and several others; but we have not the information which would enable us to make a comparison between them.

Of the other sanctuaries not dedicated to the tutelar Divinity, with the exception of those which we shall speak of in the following chapter, the one which for its architectural construction most deserves our attention, is that which the Inca *Viracocha* caused to be constructed, and which Garcilasso de la Vega (l. c. Book V. Chap. XXII.) describes in the following manner: "The Inca Viracocha ordered to be built in a town called *Cacha*, which is sixteen leagues south of the city of Cuzco, a temple in honor of his uncle, whose phantom or spirit had appeared to him. He commanded that the workmanship of the temple should imitate as far as it was possible the place where the spirit had appeared to him; that it should be (like the field) uncovered, without roof, that they should make a small chapel covered with stone, which should resemble the hollow of the rock against which he had leaned, that it should be one story above the ground, that the tracery and the work should be different from anything which the Indians had ever made before, or would make afterward; because they never made a house or chamber with an arched roof. The temple was one hundred and twenty feet in length, and eighty in width; it was of polished stone, beautifully cut, as is all the stone with which the Indians work. It had four doors opening upon the four different quarters of the heavens; three of them were closed, being rather imitation portals to serve as an ornament to the walls. The door which faced the east served for ingress and egress; it was in the centre of the vault, and as the Indians did not know how to make an arched vault; in order to cover it they made inner walls of the same stone, which served as beams, and were better, because they lasted longer than they would have done, made of timber; they placed them in rows, leaving seven feet of space between wall and wall, and the walls were three feet thick: thus the walls made twelve aisles. They closed them above with flag-stones ten feet in length and half a yard in height. Entering by the door of the temple, one turned to the right hand through the first aisle, until he reached the wall on the right side of the temple; he then passed to the left side, through the second aisle, until he reached the other wall. From thence he passed again to the right side, through the third aisle, and thus (as the spaces go between the lines upon this page) the tour of the temple was made through every aisle, until the twelfth or the last was reached; where was a staircase, to mount to the top of the temple."

"In front of each aisle, on both sides, were windows like

loop-holes, which gave sufficient light; under each window was a niche made in the wall, where was seated a porter, without obstructing the passage through the aisles. The staircase was made with two passages, one to ascend and one to descend; these were on different sides; the one for ascent came out in front of the high altar." Of this altar, and of the statue of the Deity, we have already spoken in the eighth chapter.

Cieça de Leon, in his Chronicle, mentions some interesting temples, dedicated to other Deities, as that one of the island *Lampuna*, consecrated to the terrible *Tumpal*, God of war, made of black stone, with its walls covered with sculptures and horrible pictures; the interior entirely obscure, with a large altar in the centre, upon which the priest offered human sacrifices. Another temple in the province of *Manta* was dedicated to the god of health, *Umiña*, and was distinguished by its architecture and richness.

The system of fortifications of the ancient Peruvians is admirable, and attests a high degree of intelligence. Throughout the empire, from the north of Quito, were innumerable fortresses or *Pucaras*, so advantageously placed that the choice of the sites where they were built would do honor to the more skilful modern engineers, (those of Pativilca, Huaraz, Conchucos, for example.) The construction was, if we consider the arms used in those days, very strong; sometimes simple, sometimes displaying much art, and always with an ingenious appropriation of the advantages offered by the ground; some were fortified with bastions, and were surrounded with ditches, while the walls were finished with parapets. The largest of all the fortresses was that of the capital of the empire, and may justly be called one of the most wonderful architectural works, attesting the physical strength of man.

Tradition relates that its construction began at the end of the fourteenth century, or at the beginning of the fifteenth, of our era, under the reign of the Inca Pachacutec, or of his son Yupanqui; and the names even of the architects are preserved, (*Apu-Huallpa-Rimachi*, *Inca-Maricanchi*, *Acahuana-Inca* and *Callacunchuy*,) who successively directed or superintended the work. It was built on a rough ridge, called *Sacsahuaman*, a little to the north of the capital; the declivity of the ridge was on one side very steep, defended only by a small wall sufficiently high, and more than a thousand feet in length; but it was toward the north that the declivity gently lost itself in the plain, and as it was the point most easily attacked, it was protected by three walls, one behind the other, and with projecting angles of more than twenty yards; these walls were semicircular and connected with the wall at the south, and were as long as that was, constructed in a Cyclopean manner, that is, of immense polyangular stones, which were perfectly fitted the one to the other, without any perceptible mortar. These huge masses were rough, except only at the joints; the edges for about the width of a hand were finely cut, so that the polished lines of the joints in the centre of the mass produced a very beautiful effect. Most wonderful is the extraordinary size of the stones which compose these walls, principally the external ones, as there were some among them which were fifty feet in length, twenty-two in height, and six in width. Each wall was at a distance of thirty feet from the next one, and the intermediate space was terraced to the top of the enclosure; almost in the centre of each was a door, with a movable flag-stone to fasten it. The first enclosure was called *Tiupuncu*, (the door of the sandy ground); that of the second, *Acahuana-puncu* (the door of the architect Acahuana); and that of the third, *Viracocha-puncu* (the door of the Inca Viracocha). A parapet half the height of a man's body, garnished each wall. In an oblong plaza enclosed by these walls, were three strong places in the form of small forts, the largest of which, in the centre, called *Moyoc Marca* (circular tower), was cylindrical, and the two on the extremities of the square, *Paucar-Marca* and *Sacllac Marca*, were squares. The *Moyoc Marca* was designed to receive the family of the Inca, and the wealth of the royal palaces, and of the temple of the Sun, in times of war, and to serve as a place of rest in certain festivals, during peace. Its internal fittings corresponded with that of the palaces, all of gold and silver. The two square fortifications were of similar construction, with many apartments in them, large and small, to lodge the garrison. These forts communicated subterraneously with each other, as also with the royal palaces, and with the temple of the Sun in the city.

These subterranean works were, according to tradition, very ingenious; they were commonly four feet wide, and a fathom high, but in certain places they were contracted, and there were in the walls sharp-pointed stones, so that a man could only pass through the centre of them; or else their height diminished so much that only on all-fours was the transit possible. All this was with a view of saving the wealth of the city in the fortress, and to prevent the pursuit of an enemy, for behind each narrow pass was a space just wide enough to defend the passage against an entire army. History records the valor and constancy with which it was defended in the time of Hernan Pizarro, and the presence of mind of a certain captain, who, with his formidable mace in hand, strode along the battlements, threatened with death every Indian who did not remain at his post, and then when all was lost, like another Numantin, threw himself headlong into the abyss, preferring to perish, rather than be a captive to the proud conqueror.

It is related that the Apostle Saint James appeared during the siege, deciding the battle; and from that time the natives held this saint in great veneration, celebrating his feasts throughout the interior of Peru.

At the present day there are on the ridge of Sacsahuaman three crosses of wood, and at a few steps distance is seen a staircase which descends to the city. A short distance from the fortress is a large piece of amphibolic rock known by the name of the smooth rolling stone, which served and still serves for diversion to the inhabitants, by rolling like a garden roller, having a sort of hollow formed in the middle through friction.*

Each fortress had its distinguishing mark: the most celebrated were those of *Calcahilares*, of *Huillcahuaman*, of old *Huanuco*, of *Chemie* in Mansiche, of *Hatun-Cañar*, of *Coranqui*, and others. The small fortress of *Huichay*, two leagues from Tarma, which defends the entrance to this valley, was of very peculiar construction. Its entrance through an opening, in which the wall was made of small stones, conducted to a gallery which led to the fortress. At the foot of the declivity was a deep ditch, and behind this a bulwark, fourteen feet high, flanked by three turrets. A wide cellar or subterraneous passage, natural in some parts, conducted from this fortress, through the centre of the ridge to Tarmatambo, where was to be seen a large palace, the ruins of which still attract the attention of the traveller. In the cellar was found an abundance of provisions, as in times of war it served as a granary, and also as dwellings to the neighboring population.

In the environs of the fort, they procure at the present day saltpetre for the manufacture of gunpowder; and consequently excavations have so far destroyed it, that in a few

* In other places they have also these rolling stones, made of smooth and very fine sand-stones.

years the site of so interesting a monument will be unknown.

"In the valley of Yucay, four leagues from Cuzco, the Incas had large edifices and a fortress between unassailable rocks; while around the ridge were terraces, where they planted corn abundantly: they had also in the walls of the edifices sculptured figures of leopards and other animals supporting the trophies of their conquests. In the mortar of the well-fitted stones is found liquid gold, and it is supposed that this was used in memory of the deeds of some prince, as was customary in the time of the Romans."

The hydraulic system among the ancient Peruvians deserves our attention as much as its architecture. They made open canals, called *Rarccac*, and subterranean aqueducts, *Pinchas* or *Huircas* of wonderful extent, overcoming, with great skill, all the obstacles which nature opposed, with a view of fertilizing their arid fields. In many territories, and principally in those where the uneven ground of the Sierra extends into the Puna, (for example, the heights beyond Tarmatambo on the road from Tarma to Jauja, and in the same region of Jauja) are found a large number of square fields, almost all of the same width, and each one surrounded with a small wall of stones. They are now covered with Puna grass, and are useless for cultivation. These were the *Topus*, which were allotted to the subjects of the immense kingdom for the support of their families. They were in that day watered by aqueducts of admirable construction, and eminently useful for agricultural purposes. But the Spaniards destroyed these channels, and the artificial passages of water having thus been dried up, the earth has become altogether sterile. As most of these narrow passages were subterranean, it is not possible to discover them, but it is known that many of them contained pipes of gold which the conquerors considered profitable booty. The largest space of these *azequias* or canals which has been preserved entire is found in the valley of *Nasca*, which owes its rare fertility in the cultivation of the vine solely to the water which was brought by the *Pinchas* of the ancients; and in the vicinity of Cajamarca is, even now, seen one of these channels excavated in the mountains, which gives outlet to the waters of a lake; and another in the plain which leads to the ridge of Pasco, having its origin in the river which is near Hullay. The subterranean aqueducts are found paved with flag-stones closely joined, from four to six feet long, and about three feet wide; their interior altitude from the floor to the roof was from six to eight feet.

Garcilasso de la Vega (Royal. Com. I. Book V. Chap. XXIV.) speaks of two azequias: one made by the Inca Viracocha, which, beginning in the heights of the Sierra between *Parco* and *Picuy*, runs as far as the *Rucanas*, more than one hundred and twenty leagues: another traverses almost the whole of *Contisuyu*, and runs from the south to the north more than one hundred and fifty leagues, along the top of the steepest Sierras, and extends to the *Quechuas*.

This author adds: "We may compare these canals to the greatest works which the world has seen, and give them the first place, considering the lofty Sierras over which they are carried, the large stones which they broke without instruments of steel or iron, and which were broke with other stones by mere force of arms; we must remember too that they knew not how to make scaffoldings with which to build the arches of bridges and span the chasms and small rivers. If they had to cross any deep river they headed its sources, thus encircling all the Sierras which presented themselves before them."

The bridges which the ancient Peruvians constructed over small streams and mighty rivers were very simple, and without architectural art, but even better adapted to the violent torrents which would not permit them to build permanent foundations or piers for arches, and which would have destroyed their most solid ones, even had they possessed the art to fix them in the bed of the stream. In the narrowest part of the rivers, they constructed on each bank a buttress of middling-sized stones, joined by a mortar of bitumen and gypsum, and fastened to them five or six very strong beams, to which they attached three strong ropes, placing over them, cross-wise, poles, and covering them with branches, small stones and sand, so as to form a solid floor: on both sides they passed from one end to the other of the bridge a rope, which served to lay hold of. They sometimes made use of stones for buttresses planted by nature, as is seen in the celebrated bridge of Apurimac.

Those which existed even at the time of the Incas, are that of the lake of Lauricocha, in the district of Junin, and that of Compuerta, in the department of Puno. Both are composed of a micaceous and calcareous rock, with broad stones of two and three yards, leaving a path about $\frac{3}{4}$ of a yard in width, and from $1\frac{1}{2}$ to 2 yards in height. The buttresses are large, broad, and without the slightest mortar.*

This class of bridges, as also those which consist of a single rope to which the traveller fastens himself and his load, in a hand-basket which hangs from a staple, and which is drawn with ropes from on side to the other, are yet in use, which proves their fitness.

We cannot do less, before concluding this chapter, than make a passing observation upon the opinion of a distinguished historian, concerning the works of art among the ancient Peruvians. The celebrated French philosopher

* The celebrated bridge of pure sand between Arequipa and Vitor, we are also assured, was constructed in the time of the Incas.

Raynal says, in his well-known work:* "It is proper to class among fables this prodigious number of cities constructed with so much care and so much expense; those majestic palaces designed to accommodate the Incas, in their places of residence and in their travels; those fortresses which are found scattered throughout the empire; those aqueducts and arcades, comparable only to the magnificence left us by antiquity; those lofty roads which made communication so easy; those bridges so massive, those wonderful attributes of the *Quipus* which supplied the art of writing, unknown among the Peruvians."

This arbitrary opinion, sustained with the vaguest reasons, cannot be characterized in any other terms than by calling it an emanation of the skepticism of a publicist who sacrificed all historical truth to the prejudices and spirit of party. The famous historian Robertson, without doubt influenced by his French predecessor, professed the same opinion, though he propounded it with less arrogance.

Fortunately, the ruins of the monuments whose marvellous records dazzle the prosaic imaginations of the authors above quoted, will prove to remote centuries the veracity of the ancient historians, and will demonstrate the empty conceit of certain self-styled philosophers, who bring historical truth down to the level of their speculative ignorance.

* Philosophical and Political History of the Settlements and of the Commerce of the Europeans in the Two Indies, by William Thomas Raynal, 1783. Book 17, pp. 310, 315.

CHAPTER X.

ANCIENT MONUMENTS.

Of all the ancient monuments whose ruins invite our attention, there are none which, by their astonishing character, their immense extent, and the seemingly impossible labor which their construction demanded, impress us more profoundly than the royal roads which traversed the entire empire from South to North: the one, over the heights of the Cordilleras, admirably surmounting the difficulties interposed by nature; the other descending from Cuzco to the coast, and following a route to the North. Travelling over some hundreds of leagues of these gigantic roads (abandoned at this day), and remembering the accounts of the authors who saw them in their perfect state immediately after the conquest, we could do no less than admire the vast plan of their originator, the constancy and power of the Incas in carrying them on to completion, and the patience of the people in supporting those fatigues and privations in their construction to which they were undoubtedly subjected. To build these roads in deserts, over shifting sands, reflecting constantly the rays of a burning sun; to break in pieces rocks, to level obstacles without iron tools, and without gunpowder; without compass, to hold on a line over a lofty mountain region, covered with eternal frost; to fill up profound chasms bordered by frightful precipices; to make a road over rivers, lakes, and morasses;—all this would be an enterprise which, even in the existing state of our knowledge and with modern instruments of labor, would be deemed worthy of the most civilized nation now on the globe.

To give an exact idea of these roads, we will avail ourselves of the descriptions of impartial authors.

Juan de Sarmiento, president of the royal council of the Indies, speaking of the road over the Cordilleras, says, in his "Relation of the Succession and Government of the Incas," preserved in manuscript in the library of the Escurial: "One of the things most wonderful, in contemplating the works of this country, was the thought how, and in what manner, they were able to make such long and superior roads as those we see; what a large force of men must have been required for their construction, and with what iron tools or other instruments they were able to level mountains, and break in pieces rocks, and to make the roads so broad and good as they are. For it seems to me if the Emperor should see fit to order the construction of another road, like that which leads from Quito to Cuzco, or that which from Cuzco goes toward Chili, I certainly think that, with all his power, he would not be able to make it; nor indeed would the strength of men accomplish it, without such complete order and arbitrary subdivision of labor, as the Incas established among their subjects who built their roads; for if it were a road of but fifty, or a hundred, or two hundred leagues, it is easy to perceive, that although the earth might be rough, still, with great diligence, it might be accomplished. But these roads were so extensive that one stretched even *eleven hundred* leagues, all made, too, over large and terrific sierras, the bases of which in some places, if one looked down, were beyond the reach of sight; while in others, the sierras were perpendicular masses of stone, the sides of which it was necessary to excavate to make the road broad and straight; while the only implements for their construction were fire and a tool of some kind for picking. Other places were so abrupt, high and rugged, that it was necessary to make steps from below to reach the summit, midway of which were cut broad platforms as resting-places for the laborers in the ascent. In other places there were frightful heaps of snow, and these of frequent occurrence, not situated as they wished, not elevated or depressed as we see it on the plains; and upon this snow, if it were necessary to fill up cavities, they were obliged to construct actual mountains of trees and turf, and over them to make a smooth paved road. Those who read this book, and who have been in Peru, may recall the road which goes from Lima to Xauxa, by the sierras of Guayacoin, and by the snowy mountains of Pavacaca, and they know that they have both seen and heard more than I have here written."

Pedro Cieça de Leon thus writes concerning the road over the sierra (Chronicles, Chapter XXXVII.): "From Ipiales there is a road leading to a small province named Guaca, and before reaching it may be seen the road of the Incas, as famous in these parts as that which Hannibal made over the Alps, when he descended upon Italy. And it may be, it is held in the more estimation as well for the grand lodging-places and depositories which are found along its whole length, as for the great difficulty of its construction over such rough and stony sierras as one cannot contemplate but with wonder." Of the road along the coast this author speaks more particularly in his seventieth chapter. "And here I will notice the great road (says he) which the Incas commanded to be made in the midst of the plains; which, although now in many places broken up and destroyed, yet furnishes evidence of how great a work it was, and of the power of those who caused it to be built. Guaynacapa, and Topaynga Yupanque his father, were those who, according to the statements of the Indians, traversed the whole coast, visiting the valleys and provinces of the Yungas; although there are some Indians who say that the Inca Yupanque, the grandfather of Guaynacapa, and father of Topaynga, was the first who descended to the coast; the Caciques and princes by his command caused a road to be made fifteen feet broad, on each side of which was a very strong wall more than a fathom in thickness, while the road was perfectly clear and smooth, and shaded by trees; and from these generally hung over the road branches loaded with fruit, while the trees were filled with parrots and various other birds. In each one of the valleys there were built grand and princely lodging-places for the Incas, and depositories for supplies of the army; for they were so timid that they did not dare go on an expedition without large supplies; and if any wrong were committed, those in default were severely punished; so that, for instance, if any of those who traversed the road dared to trespass on the fields, or intrude into the houses of the Indians, even though the damage committed might be but trifling, they were punished with death. Along this road the side walls extended from one place to another, except in those spots where, from the quantity of sand, the Indians were not able to lay it solidly in cement; and at such places, that the way might not be lost, they drove in the ground large trees properly fitted, after the manner of beams, at regular intervals; and thus they took care to make the road smooth and clear over the valleys; they renewed the walls wherever they became ruinous or injured, and perpetual watch was kept to see if any large tree, of those in the sandy places, was overturned by the wind, in which case it was immediately replaced. Thus, it will be seen, this road was certainly a great work, although not so laborious as that of the Sierra."

Don Augustin de Zarrate thus speaks of the two roads (Descubrimiento y Conquista, Lib. I. Cap. XIII.): "When Guaynacava went from the city of Cuzco with his army to conquer the province of Quito, which was about five hundred leagues distant, as he went over the Sierra he found great difficulty in the passage, by reason of the bad roads and immense chasms and precipices he encountered. And so it seemed right to the Indians to make a new road by which he might return victorious from his conquest, (for he had subdued the province) and accordingly, they built a road along the whole Cordillera, very broad and smooth, breaking and levelling rocks when necessary, and filling up to the level, with masonry, the chasms sometimes from a depth of fifteen or twenty fathoms, until they thus perfected the road for the space of five hundred leagues.

"And they say it was so level when finished, that a carriage might have gone over it; although afterward, in the wars between the Christians and the Indians, in many places the masonry over the chasms was broken up to prevent a passage of the enemy. And the difficulty of this geat work will be seen by any one who considers the labor and cost which have been expended in Spain in levelling only two leagues of the Sierra between the ridge of Segovia and Guadarrama; and that it has never been so perfectly done as to make even an ordinary way, notwithstanding the Kings of Castile pass over it continually with their households and court, every time that they go from Andalusia or Toledo to this part of the kingdom.

"And not content with making this remarkable work, when, at another time, the same Guaynacava wished to return from the province of Quito, which he much prized because he had conquered it, he returned through the low country or plains, and the Indians then made over them another road of as much difficulty as that on the Sierra: for in all the valleys refreshed by streams and forests, (which, as we have before said, commonly covered a league) they made a road almost forty feet wide, with very large adobe walls from one end to the other, and the walls were four or five adobes in height; and when they left the valleys they continued the same road over the sands, driving down trees and stakes on the line, so that no one could lose the road, nor be turned from it through its whole length, which, like that of the Sierra, was five hundred leagues. And although these trees in the sandy parts are now broken in many places, because the Spaniards, both in peace and war, used them for fuel, still the walls in the valleys are, at this day, entire in most places, by which one may judge of the former greatness of the work; and so Guaynacava went by one road and returned by the other, being covered and shaded all the way by overhanging branches and flowers of sweet odor."

Lopez de Gomara (Hist. Gen. Cap. 194) says: "There were two royal roads from the city of Quito to that of Cuzco, very costly and noble works: the one over the mountains, and the other across the plains, each extending more than a thousand miles. That which crossed the plains was walled on both sides, and was twenty-five feet broad, with ditches of water outside, and was planted with trees called *molle*. That which was on the mountains was also twenty-five feet wide, cut in some places from the living rock, and in others, made of stone and lime; for, indeed, it was necessary to cut away the rocks or fill up the valleys to bring the road to a level:—it was a work which, as all agree, exceeded the pyramids of Egypt, and the paved ways of the Romans, and, indeed, all other ancient works. Guaynacapac restored, enlarged, and completed them; but he did not build them entirely, as some pretend, nor could they have been constructed in the whole time of his life. These roads went in a direct line, without turning aside for hills, mountains, or even lakes; and for resting-places they had certain grand palaces which were called '*tambos*,' where the Court and royal army lodged: these were provided with arms, food, shoes, and clothing for the troops. The Spaniards, in their civil wars, destroyed these roads, breaking them up in many places, to impede the march of each other; and the Indians themselves demolished a part of them when they waged war and laid siege to the cities of Cuzco and Lima, where the Spaniards were."

Juan Botero Benes thus speaks: "From the city of Cuzco there are two roads or royal ways of two thousand miles in length: of which, one goes over the plains, and the other over the top of the mountains, in such manner, that to make them, it was necessary to fill up valleys, to cut away rocks, and remove the summits of mountains. They are twenty-five feet wide. Works which are, beyond comparison, greater than the monuments of Egypt or the structures of Rome."

Don Juan de Velasco, a priest of Quito, in treating of the great spaces of the upper road, very well preserved, which he examined on the mountain of *Sashuay*, thus writes (Hist. del Reyno de Quito, Tom. II. Part II. Pag. 59):

"The breadth which I measured, in a part somewhat broken, was about sixty Castilian *varas:* in another part which was perfect, it was more than seven *varas*, which is more than twenty-one feet, a space sufficient for three carriages to go side by side. It may be that the twenty-five feet of which Gomara speaks were ladies' feet; and that the fifteen of Cieça and Robertson were those of giants. The part cut out of the living rock, to equalize the surface, was covered with a cement or a mixture of lime and bitumen. The earth-supported and less firm parts were made of stone covered with the same mixture, in which might be seen very minute stones, yet much larger than coarse grains of sand. In the chasms and fissures of the mountains, the road was built up from foundations deep below, to the proper level, with large stones cemented with the same mixture. What struck me with surprise was, that where the torrents of water from the rains above had rushed down and eaten out, in the less firm parts, the portion below the surface, there was left in the air a causeway like a very firm bridge of a single stone; such was the strength of this cement or mixture."

"The difference in the extent of these roads, the only point in which the early writers differ (!), arises from the different calculations of leagues and miles, and from the different points toward the north whence they begin to compute. They did not begin at the city of Quito, as some have said, but in the province of Dehuaca, one degree further north, which is equal to one hundred miles more. From the city of Quito to Cuzco by the upper road, the shortest distance is computed at five hundred leagues of four thousand lawful paces, which makes two thousand miles; while the upper road is in truth, at the shortest, twenty-one hundred miles. The lower road is much longer."

Finally, the learned *Humboldt*, who travelled over a part of the royal road of the Incas, thus describes it (*Ansichten der Natur*. 3d Ed. Tom. II. p. 322):

"But what, above all things, relieves the severe aspect of the deserts of the Cordilleras, are the remains, as marvellous as unexpected, of a gigantic road, the work of the Incas, which, over a length of more than two hundred and fifty geographical miles, makes a communication between all the provinces of the empire. The traveller discovers at different points, and for the most part, at equal distances, edifices constructed of well-cut stone, a species of caravanseras, called *tambos*, or *inca-pilca*. Some of these edifices are found provided with fortifications; others present in their arrangements baths, with conduits of warm water; in fine, the larger ones were designed for the family of the sovereign himself. At the foot of the volcano Cotopaxi, near to Callo, I measured and made designs of some of these habitations, so well preserved, which Pedro de Cieça, in the sixteenth century, called the *apartments of Mulado*. In the pass of the Andes, between Mansi and Loxa, called *Paramo de Assuay*, at fourteen thousand five hundred and sixty-eight feet of height, (a road much frequented on the side of Cadlud, almost of the same altitude as Mont Blanc) we found on the plain of Puttal much difficulty in making a way for the mules over a marshy piece of earth, while, for more than a German mile, our sight continually rested on the superb remains of a paved road of the Incas, twenty feet wide, which we marked resting on its deep foundations, and paved with well-cut, dark porphyritic stone. This road was wonderful, and does not fall behind the most imposing Roman ways which I have seen in France, Spain and Italy. By barometrical observation, I found that this colossal work was at an elevation of twelve thousand, four hundred and forty feet, which exceeds, by more than a thousand feet, the height of the Peak of Teneriffe. At this same level there are found at Assuay the ruins of the palace of Inca Tupac-Yupanqui, known under the name of the '*Paredones del Inca*.' From here the road goes toward the south in the direction of Cuenca, and ends at Canar, a small fortress in good preservation, which probably goes back to the times of the Inca above named, or to those of his warlike son, Huayna-Capac."

"We have also seen most beautiful remains of ancient Peruvian roads between Loxa and the river Amazon, near the baths of the Incas, in the Paramo [desert or open place] of Chulucanas, not far from Guancabamba, and in the neighborhood of Ingatambo, near Pomahuaca. The remains of the road of the Incas near Pomahuaca has but little elevation, and my observations show that it is nine thousand one hundred feet lower than those of the Paramo de Assuay. According to astronomic latitudes, the distance between them in a right line is forty-six geographical miles, and the higher exceeds, by thirty-seven hundred feet, the altitude of the pass of Mount Cenis, above the lake of Como. Some of these paved roads, laid with flat stones, or, as in certain parts, covered with pebble stones and gravel [Macadamized roads], traverse the broad and arid plain between the sea-shore and the chain of the Andes; while others turn toward the Cordilleras. They have way-marks placed at regular intervals, which indicate the distances. It is also to be remarked that for passing rivers and precipices they have bridges of stone or of cords [suspension bridges], while aqueducts supply water to the small towns, and to the *tambos* or lodging-places. These two systems of roads met at Cuzco, the great central point of the empire."

The remains of the upper road, which we have measured, vary, in different places, from eighteen to twenty-five Castilian feet. The lower road is about one foot wider. The statements of all the authors cited, as to the length of these roads, are somewhat exaggerated. Cuzco, according to Pentlandt, is in S. latitude 13° 30′ 55″, and in W. longitude 74° 14′ 30″, and at a height of 10,676 feet above the level of the sea. Quito, according to Oltmanns, is in 0° 14′ 00″ S. latitude, and 81° 40′ 38″ W. longitude, which would make the distance between them, in a direct line, a little more than three hundred leagues; if to this ve add for the continuation of the road northward from Quito to Dehuaca, and for necessary turnings, one hundred leagues, we have a total of four hundred. The lower road, by reason of the two angles which it makes in descending from Cuzco to the coast, and again in ascending from the coast to Quito, was about a hundred and twenty leagues longer. What Sarmiento says of eleven hundred leagues on the Sierra is not true; but the errors of his day are more excusable, as distances were then calculated approximatively only.

In considering the most interesting monuments of architecture, we will begin at the North, with the immense ruins of the palaces of *Gran Chimu.* Don Mariano E. Rivero visited them, and thus describes them in a little work printed in Lima, in 1841, and subsequently republished in London:

"These ruins are found at the extremity of the valley of Truxillo, and at the distance of a league and a half from Huanchaco. We have no data from which to fix with certainty the period when this place was built: all we know is, that in the time of the Peruvian Inca Pachacutec, who was the ninth monarch, there reigned in these valleys as absolute sovereign *Chimu Capac*, whose proper name was *Chimu Canchu;* that the Inca's son, the prince Yupanqui, with an army of thirty thousand men, began to make war on this ruler Chimu: that Chimu's pride was subdued, and by the advice of his captains, he was induced to capitulate, offering to worship the Sun, and abandon the idols of his country, which consisted of the representations of fish and other animals. In memory of this victory, the Inca commanded certain fortresses to be built in the valley of Paramanca, the ruins of which may be seen in the neighborhood of Pativilca.

The ruins of Chimu cover a space of three-quarters of a league, exclusive of the great squares, the walls of which are of small stones joined together with mortar; and which probably were used as fields for agriculture, as the marks of the furrows are even to this day visible.

From the village of Mansiche, which is at the gates of Truxillo, we begin to see the walls of adobe, and the vestiges of this once great settlement; and at the distance of a mile from the native village just named, on the left hand of the road from Huanchaco, commence the grand squares. The dimensions of these vary from two hundred to two hundred and seventy yards in length, and from one hundred to one hundred and sixty in breadth; their number may be seven or eight: they are found on the north side of the large edifices or palaces. The walls which surround those edifices are of considerable solidity, and are formed of adobes of ten or twelve yards long, and five or six broad in the lower part of the wall, but gradually diminishing until they terminate in a breadth of one yard at the top. Some of the squares contain *Huacas*, and the walls of large apartments or halls.*

Each of the palaces was completely surrounded by an exterior wall; that of the first is plain, and double the size of that of the second. It was five yards broad at the bottom, tapered gradually to one at the top, and was fifty in height. It is constructed of stone and mortar and adobes.

In the first palace, which is the larger, there is another square in which are found apartments made of small stones and mortar, whitewashed within, with the thresholds of stone from one and a half to two yards long, and more than a third of a yard in thickness: it is supposed that these were sepulchres, or perhaps apartments for the

* The word *Huaca*, or as it is written in old Spanish, *Guaca*, is Peruvian, and properly signifies any sacred place or thing; and also sometimes any thing, whether sacred or not, that is excellent or extraordinary. It was a generic term, and was applied by the natives to their idols and places of worship. It is here applied to places of interment, large sepulchres containing many dead bodies.—[TRANSLATOR.]

concubines of Chimu. There are also several *plazas* regularly laid out by line, thus forming different streets, of varying dimensions. The large excavation in which are now growing several fig-trees was the reservoir from which the inhabitants obtained the water they needed; and was supplied by subterranean aqueducts from the river *Moche*, which is distant about two miles to the north-east. This palace had two entrances opposite to each other, and placed respectively in the middle of the longer sides. On the eastern side, and about thirty yards from the right angle formed by the walls, there was a square or enclosure of five hundred yards, by four hundred in extent, which reached to the sea: in this were found some small houses and a *Huaca* with subterranean passages in its most solid parts. Beside this, there were other squares which were enclosed for agricultural purposes.

The second palace is at a distance of one hundred and twenty-five yards east of the first, and is placed parallel to it. It contains various plazas and houses, from the regular arrangement of which result streets, though somewhat narrow. At one of the extremities is the Huaca of Misa, surrounded by a low wall. This Huaca is traversed by small alleys from three-quarters to a yard in width, and in it are also found some tolerably large chambers. In former times there have been taken from this Huaca many mummies, cloths, various pieces of silver and gold, *iron* [?] tools, and an idol of stone with small pieces of mother of pearl, which are now in the possession of Señor Condemarin.

All the walls of these interior edifices are of the mixture of which we have already spoken, or of adobes, half a yard long, and a quarter of a yard wide. We subjoin vertical sections, which will give an idea of the walls, and of the labor employed in their construction.

SECTIONS AND PORTIONS OF THE EDIFICES AT GRAN-CHIMU, IN THE VALLEY OF TRUXILLO.

Outside of these remarkable edifices there was a great number of enclosures and small houses, some round and others square, which undoubtedly were the habitations of the lower classes; and the great extent of which justify us in supposing that the population must have been very numerous.

Among these ruins there exist many small artificial eminences composed of small stones in the form of a truncated cone; these are known under the name of *Huacas;* and from these have been frequently obtained curiosities illustrative of the ancient inhabitants; and there is not the least doubt that the subterranean explorers have also sometimes found riches.

It is well known that in 1563, Don Diego Pineda being then chief magistrate, there were discovered in the sepulchres of the principal Indians considerable quantities of gold, in pieces of various forms. It appears from the books of the royal coffers of Truxillo, of 1566, that Garcia Gutierrez of Toledo, grandson of Antonio Gutierrez, gave to the king, as his fifths, on the first occasion, 85,547 castellanos of gold* from the Huaca which was known by the name of Toledo, reserving for the benefit of the Indians of the villages of Mansiche and Huaman, 39,062 dollars and four reals. In the year 1592, the work was resumed, and there was paid as the king's proportion, 47,020 castellanos, so that the monarch received in all 135,547 castellanos.†

In the year 1550, the cacique of the village of Mansiche, Don Antonio Chayque, a legitimate descendant of the ruler Chimu Canchu, showed to the Spaniards a Huaca called *Llomayoahuan*, near to the ruined palace of Chimu Canchu, upon condition that they should give a part of the treasure obtained for the relief of his Indians; and after having robbed it of great wealth, the agreement was violated by the Spaniards; the cacique then pretended that he knew of a still greater treasure which he could discover, to obtain which, they gave him 42,187 dollars, which they raised by a tax charged on the inhabitants in favor of the Indians before named; of this very little of the principal now remains,

* A castellano is about 5s. 6d. sterling.—[TRANSLATOR.]

† Nearly $170,000.

partly from the calamities of the times, and partly from the unfaithful administration of the protectors of the Indians, or the collectors of the taxes.—(*Feijoo de Sosa.*)

It is certain that there have been obtained from the Huaca of Concha, half a league from the city, considerable quantities of gold, and also some fetters, which are supposed to be of copper, and were preserved for the Bishop of Cuonca, by Don Miguel Concha y Mansuvillaga. The Huaca of the bishop, distant half a league from the one above mentioned, is the largest of all, but up to this time has yielded nothing. The Huaca of Misa, which is in the second palace, has been worked with some loss, and is traversed almost through its whole extent by small alleys more or less narrow, and white-washed; the coverings of which are of stone, from a yard and a half to two yards wide. From this have been taken various pieces of gold, many idols, mantles, and one stone idol, of which we have already spoken. From many other small Huacas have been obtained mantles well adorned with square pieces of gold; detached pieces of the same metal, and robes made with feathers of divers colors; these were found by Dr. Casaverde, and should be now in London.

It is but a short time since a company, composed of inhabitants of Truxillo, ceased to work the Huacas of Toledo and Concha; and it is even said that, in the first, has been found the great *peje*;* near to the second has been lately found very thin plates of gold about two inches broad, also instruments of stone, and mantles, all of which are in the possession of Don José Rodriguez.

* There is a tradition that in this Huaca were two treasures, known as the great and little *peje*; that the first is still buried, and that the second has been found at Toledo.

WALLED SQUARE IN PALACE OF CHIMU-CANCHU, NEAR TRUXILLO.

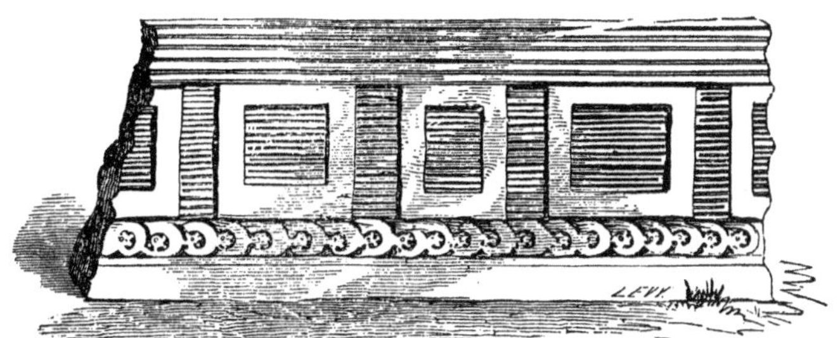

SCULPTURED PANELS ON A WALL OF PALACE AT CHIMU-CANCHU.

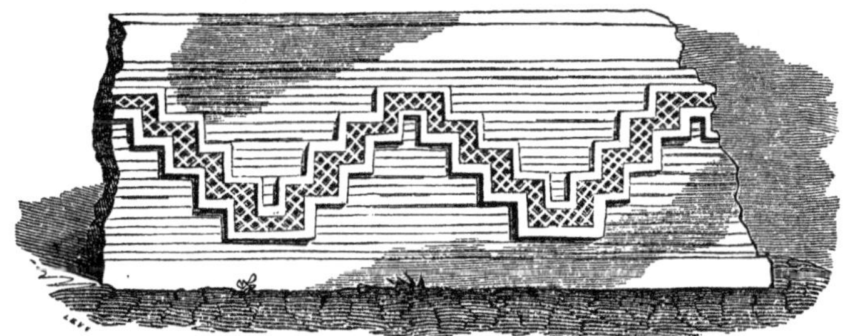

SCULPTURED ORNAMENTS ON THE WALL OF PALACE AT CHIMU-CANCHU.

To this relation we will add a short notice concerning certain curiosities, found in the Huacas of Toledo, and else where, as communicated by Don José Ignacio Lequende to the "Peruvian Mercury" (Vol. VIII. p. 80). One of these was the body of an Indian with a head-covering or veil, and a crown with four tassels, of which two hung down on the back, and the other two before, in front of the ears. On his neck was a species of broad cravat, the ends of which fell upon the breast; in one hand was something like a nail, and in the other a symbol which was unintelligible. His outer robe was a tunic terminating in points. Another was also the body of an Indian seated with his legs crossed under him, (which, by the way, is a very common posture among them,) his hands upon his knees, his temples bound with a sort of swathe or turban, the ends of which reached below his beard; two others crossed this with a skirt which fell down behind, from which came two rounded pieces to cover the shoulders; on the top of his bonnet there was a shell adorned with much beauty. Another was a model of clay, which represented an Indian with his cap stuck on one side of his head, his hair dishevelled, and hanging about his ears, and in the attitude of a toper about to drink; on his shoulder was a monkey seated by his ear. Another figure was of an Indian of very grave aspect, sitting, with a mitre on his head, which he was in the act of adjusting; certain pendants hung from each arm, and a mantle, girdled at the waist, descended and covered his feet.

The temple of the Sun was situated three-quarters of a league east of the city, and half way from the native village of *Moche:* it is found at the foot of a rock pertaining to the Cordilleras, composed of sienite, in which occur veins of a compact amphibolic rock which runs from north to south; there are also to be seen veins of feldspar; these are greatly ramified, and frequently cross each other. At the foot of this rock may be seen an edifice, with many surrounding habitations in ruins: it is almost square, having a front of one hundred and eight yards; it is surrounded by a wall four yards broad, made of adobes, as indeed is the whole edifice. It is said that here was the dwelling-place of the priests and virgins of the temple. It has a length of 150 yards, a breadth at the upper end of 125, and at the lower of 156; its height is from thirty to thirty-five yards. It is constructed in terraces of four yards each, inclining inward from the foundation, which is, of course, the broadest part. It has the shape of a [sledge] hammer, and is built of adobes; toward the centre, and in the lower part, it is traversed by a small street, which is dark and full of bats. The direction is from north to south: from this point is presented a magnificent view embracing the whole valley, the sea, and the city of Truxillo."

Worthy to be placed by the side of these wonderful ruins are those of *Cuelap*, of the district of Saint Thomas, a description of which is given by *Don Juan Crisostomo Nieto*, judge of the first tribunal, in the following official communication of the 31st of January, 1843, made to the prefect of the department of the Amazon, Don Miguel Mesia.

"Having been appointed in this territory of Cuelap to adjust the boundaries commanded to be made by the Supreme Governor of the Republic, in the course of the labor, I have encountered a work well worthy of public notice. It is a solid wall of cut stone, three thousand six hundred feet long, five hundred and seventy broad, and a hundred and fifty high: the whole structure being solid in the interior; since the whole space contained within the 5,376,000 feet (?) of circumference, having, as before said, a height of one hundred and fifty feet, is a solid mass of earth: upon this terrace there is another wall of three hundred thousand feet in circumference, being six hundred long on one side, and five hundred on the other, with the same elevation of one hundred and fifty feet that the lower wall has. This upper enclosure is also filled in with earth, like the lower. But in this upper elevation, as well as in that below, are found a multitude of habitations or chambers made of cut stone, of the size of eighteen feet by fifteen; and in these chambers, as well as in the stone work of the outer solid walls, are found niches, artificially made, of a yard or two-thirds of a yard in length, and of half a yard in width, in which are deposited the bones of those long since dead; some of these are naked, and others enveloped in cloths of cotton, very thick, and sometimes coarse; and all wrought with borders of many colors. The only difference between these niches and those of our Pantheons is in their depth; for instead of the two or three yards which we now use, to place our bodies, (as we do place them) after death in a straight position, they only used a few feet; because they so doubled them that their knees reached to the point of their beard, and their hands were twined about their legs, and the whole position resembled that of the fœtus of four months. There were three doors or openings in the solid wall, and these call for our notice; for the right side of each one of these openings is semicircular, while the left is angular; and from the base of the entrance commenced an inclined plane, which ascended, by almost imperceptible gradations, to the top of the elevation mentioned, of one hundred and fifty feet; and this, half way up, had on it a species of sentry-box, from which, as it proceeded, it diverged from its former direct course, and made a curve to the right, having also, at the upper extremity, an ingenious hiding-place, made of cut stone, from which the passage of any one from below might be effectually impeded. The entrance below commenced with a width of six feet; but in the interior, at the upper end, this was diminished to two feet, and as soon as the summit was reached, the landing was on a look-out, from which was a commanding view, not only of the plain below, and of all its roads, but even of a considerable part of the province, embracing the capital at a distance of eleven leagues.

Proceeding onward, we next came upon the entrances and inclined plane of the second wall; this wall differed from the first in length and breadth only, in height (as we have said) it was the same. Here were found other sepulchres which were built like ovens, six feet in height, and twenty-four or thirty in circumference; the floors of these were paved with flat stones, and on each rested the remains of a man or woman. Having examined these places yesterday, I and my companions paused to rest; to-day we ascended to the top of a rock which is without the walls, and a part of which, in fact, serves as a foundation for the edifices. Having, with much toil, passed over a road almost destroyed by the waters, and having subjected ourselves to the dangers of descending an almost perpendicular depth of nine hundred feet, by aiding each other, we came to a hollow or species of cavern, formed by the rocks which make the hill, in which were ten bundles of human bones, perfectly preserved, wrapped each in its mantle or covering. One of these bundles contained the remains of a man of full age, and was covered with a cloth made of hair, which, together with the skeleton it covered, is in my possession; another, probably the remains of a woman, I left, because in separating a bone from the leg, the head was broken from the trunk. This woman must have been aged when she died, since she was gray-haired; and without doubt, she was the mother of the seven children, the skeletons of which composed seven of the ten bundles we found. Of these I have two, and Don Gregorio Rodriguez also brought away two, together with a cotton mantle of various colors, and a scarf wrought in colors. We left three skeletons of children and one of an adult, because the ligaments which held the bones together were broken. All had the same posture, and the hair of the children was very fine, short, and red, and not like that of the present natives;

the females had in their ears golden ornaments, and also about the head a large twisted roll of coarse cotton.

I have since felt much regret at not having been able to pursue my examinations at this locality, as probably I might have discovered more; but we found it necessary to take a new direction to look at another spot where, we were assured, there was more to be seen. To accomplish this we descended on the north side, and afterward came to the foot of a very steep hill, which we found unusually difficult of ascent, because of the dry grass with which it was covered, causing us to slip back at every step. Having ascended some six hundred feet, we found it impossible to proceed further, because of a perpendicular rock which intercepted our approach to a stone wall containing small windows, about sixty feet above us; and for want of a ladder and time we could not see what was within the wall, which stood on an elevation commanding a view, as far as the eye could reach, to the east, north and west. We were therefore obliged to leave, regretting that we could know nothing of what this work might indicate, nor of the fossil remains and other objects of interest in the wall itself, nor of what might be contained in the space within; for the little time which I could spare from official duties did not allow me to be long absent from the capital, lest the administration of justice should suffer in my absence. These obstacles, too, were increased by the difficulty of procuring hands to undertake any work; for the natives had a great dread of this spot, on account of the mummies it contained; they supposing that it would occasion disease to touch them only, and they were frightened even by simply looking at them. But by working ourselves, and handling the bones with great freedom before the natives, the more intelligent of them lost at length a portion of the fear which their prejudice had inspired. There were also reasons why

I could not approach the wall before named on the southwest side, where I was assured there were some curiously formed trenches; for it was impossible to ascend from below, and the only mode of ascent would have been by ropes let down from the top of the wall itself. Nor could I visit a subterranean excavation which Don Gregorio, a man of character, assured me existed on the opposite bank of the river of Condechaca, and where, as he said, were many skulls, small excavations, and other objects; he had penetrated it to a distance at which the lights were extinguished for want of air, and he could proceed no further."

The ruins of old *Huanuco* are chiefly interesting from the six portals, which are well preserved one within the other, and of which it is not positively known whether they formed a part of the sumptuous palace of the Incas, or of the immense temple of the Sun which was so imposing in the reign of the sovereigns of Peru, and which "alone had room for the service of more than 30,000 Indians," (*Cieça*, Chron. Chap. LXXX.) Another object of interest is a species of look-out, the use of which in ancient times we do not know, but which was probably the place where priests offered their sacrifices to the Sun.

GATEWAYS—OLD HUANUCO.

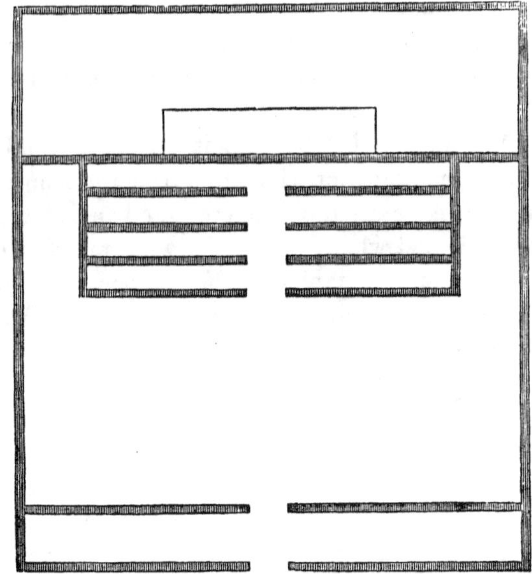

GROUND PLAN—GATEWAYS—OLD HUANUCO.

LOOK-OUT—OLD HUANUCO.

The architecture of these ruins is singularly distinct from that of the other edifices in the time of the Peruvian Emperors, and according to all appearances derives its origin from an era more remote than the dynasty of the Incas. Don

Mariano Eduardo de Rivero says: "The ruins of old Huanuco are two leagues distant from the town of Aguamiro toward the west. The Indians know the ruins under the name of *Auqui-Huanuco;* they are situated in a plain, four leagues in length and three in width, and at a height of 3600 metres above the level of the sea. This ancient settlement is converted, at the present day, into a place for herding cattle, and you meet here and there with a few Indians only, who do not understand the Spanish language. Among the ruins you notice particularly the fortress, or look-out, and the palace. The bulk of the settlement is about three-quarters of a mile from these edifices, and the look-out about a half-mile from the entrance of the palace.

The look-out is quadrilateral, fifty-six paces in length and thirty-six in width; the height of the wall is about five yards, and inclined inward from the base. It rests upon two courses of round stone about a yard and a half high. The walls are a yard and a quarter in thickness, and are of cut stone, terminating in a cornice, which is composed of a blue shell limestone: the stones are a yard and a half in length, and half a yard thick. With few exceptions, the stones which compose the walls are of equal dimensions, and are, generally speaking, very well cemented. The interior is composed of gravel and clay, but in the centre is seen a large cavity, which they assert communicates by a subterranean passage with the palace. On the southern side is a door, and instead of steps a terrace after the manner of an inclined plane, which was a contrivance much used by the Indians, judging from appearances, to raise large masses to the upper part of the edifices. At the door-way are observed two partially effaced figures, of which it is hard to say whether they were meant for monkeys or other animals. From the upper story may be distinguished the whole plain, and the gates of the famous palace.

Our design represents the six portals of the house of the Inca. Upon entering it, on the right and left hand are two saloons of more than one hundred yards in length and fourteen in width, with their corresponding doors. The walls, which are of *Pirca* (round stones mixed with clay only, without any order), one yard and a half in width, have sculptured stones in the doorways only. You next enter the first portal or gate of sculptured stone, three yards in height and one and a half in width; the opening of the door is two yards, the lintel is of one single stone four yards long, and half a yard thick. The jambs are of one single piece, and seem to be sculptured by chisel. There are to be seen two figures cut in the same piece, which seem to be monkeys.

About three yards distant, comes the second gate, constructed in the same manner, except only that it has two sculptured figures, effaced in the upper part. You enter next a spacious court, surrounded with stone of *Pirca*, of slight elevation, and three-quarters of a yard in width; in continuation and in the same line are found two other gateways of similar architecture, but of smaller dimensions.

Next comes another smaller court, and finally two other gates, still smaller, and of sculptured stone. Passing these, there are found on the left hand rooms of cut stone, five yards in length, two and a half in width, and four in height; there are also niches in the walls. There are other rooms of cut stone, through which passes an aqueduct, which is said to have been the bathing-place of the Inca.

In front of the dwellings is found an artificial terrace, sufficiently wide, and underneath a large court where it is supposed several species of animals were kept for the diversion of the monarch. In the centre was a receptacle for water; an aqueduct passes through the last gate, and very near the sculptured rooms.

In one of these is found a niche, where they assert the maids were placed in order to see whether it would contain them, and if they could get in, they were deemed fit for the service of his majesty.(?) There are also, at the first gateway, two holes, which perforate the wall, and are said to have been the place of punishment; the first is hollowed in the form of the breast, of a convenient height, and was, without doubt, intended for the women, the second being for the men.(?)

The direction of these edifices is from east to west, and the stones of which they are composed are blue lime and sand-stone.

To the south-west of the look-out, and about a quarter of a league from it, are seen houses made on the same ridges, forming a series of terraces or steps, and it is said that there they preserve the grain of seven provinces.

We must take notice that the army of Liberty, in the year 1824, marching toward the south, in the campaign against the Spaniards, encamped in the very same places where halted the army of the Inca, when he marched to the conquest of Quito.

The stones of which the palace and fortress are composed were taken from a ridge, about half a mile distant, and there is yet to be seen some lying cut in the quarry. At a short distance are to be seen the vestiges of a large settlement, which seems to have contained many thousand inhabitants; and this probably was a favorite spot, and of much importance to the Incas. All the walls are made of round stones and clay. The celebrated hot-baths of Aguamiro are two miles from this old town.

At the distance of three-quarters of a league from *Miro-huain*, is the place where criminals were interred, and which served also as a prison; it has a deep well.

Near the town of *Chupan*, and on the banks of the *Mara-*

ñon, is a tower situated on the upper part of a high ridge which overhangs the river, and rises above the road which passes by its foot; it forms a most frightful precipice, from which they threw criminals into the waters of this powerful current.

In speaking of the ruins of the district of Junin, Don Mariano E. de Rivero says:—

"At the town of *Chavinillo* begins a system of fortifications or castles, as these places are called, situated on both sides of a chasm. It has not yet been discovered what induced the Incas to construct in this part of the interior, and away from the great road which led to Quito, so many places of defence; but it is presumed to have been with a view to the invasions which they suffered from the tribes which inhabited the Pampas of the Sacramento, and the banks of the large rivers which irrigated these immense plains; and a proof of it is that the fortress of *Urpis*, which is in the interior of the mountains, about five leagues from *Tuntamayo*, on the road by *Monzon* and *Chico playa*, is the largest, the best situated and best constructed of all; almost the whole is of wrought stone.

The first castle which was built in this direction, was that of *Masor*, near *Chavinillo*, situated on an eminence, the walls of which are of micaceous slate mixed with clay. In the angles of the large square are certain round sentry-boxes, made of the same material, three yards in height, and filled with bones; outside of these are seen round rooms, and square, with cupboards; the lintels are of the same stone. There must have been water on this eminence, as there are still seen the remains of an aqueduct.

On the opposite side, and on the other bank of the river, are seen two of these castles; the first situated on the point of a steep ridge, and the other on the mountain a little above it. Between these two are small forts, which have the appearance of steps, and communicate by roads that are very plain.

Following the course of the river in the direction of *Chuquibamba*, you pass through the towns of *Cagua*, *Obas*, and *Chupan*. All along the road are found the ruins of ancient settlements and castles. Near the last there is one with a staircase leading to the top, very wide, slightly sloping, and well constructed.

On the chasm of *Chacabambá*, province of Huamalies, upon the river Marañon, and near the royal road of the Incas, by which I came from Jauja, following its track, generally nine yards in width, are found the ruins of the *tambos* of the Incas, made of small pieces, almost square, of the micaceous slate. There still exist in *Tambocancha* six sentry-boxes, and in front of them four others, from four to five yards in height, round in part, and having square doors. They are made of the same rock spoken of above, with chalky clay; in the interior they are well cemented and form a solid wall, divided by large flagging stones; they are used by the natives at the present day to keep their potatoes and corn. The whole of the precincts are surrounded by a wall of stone and clay, and many human remains are found, as also walls of houses, some round, some square.

In the province of *Conchucos-Alto* is found the town of *Chavin de Huanta*, situated on a narrow piece of uneven ground, which runs from north to south. Its inhabitants, numbering eight hundred, enjoy a mild temperature and sulphur waters, which spring from a sandy rock, very near the river Marias. The temperature of the water by the thermometer of Fahrenheit is 112 degrees, the atmosphere being at 52°. A few squares from the town are found the remains of ancient edifices almost destroyed, and covered with vegetable earth. The outer walls are of stone, made of different shapes and laid without any mortar, but in the interior they are discovered to be of round stone and clay.

Being desirous of examining the interior of this castle, I entered with several persons who accompanied me through an opening rather narrow, and by the aid of lighted candles which were constantly extinguished by the multitude of bats which flew out very swiftly, with much inconvenience and difficulty, we arrived at a passage two yards in width, and three in height. The roof of this is made of pieces of sand-stone roughly cut, a little more than four yards in length. On both sides of this passage are rooms a little more than four yards wide roofed with large blocks of sand-stone half a yard thick, and from two and a half to three-quarters of a yard wide. Its walls are two yards in thickness, and contain some apertures which are supposed to have been left for the admission of air and light. In the floor of one of these is the entrance to a very narrow subterranean way, which, we have been informed by some persons who have explored it with a light for a considerable distance, leads under the river to the opposite bank. From this passage-way they have extracted several small idols, vases of stone, instruments of copper and silver, and the skeleton of an Indian sitting. The direction is from east to west.

At the distance of a quarter of a league west of the town and on the summit of a mountain called *Posoc*, which signifies a "thing which is ripe," is found another ruined castle which externally presents what seems a mass of rubbish, but we are assured that in the interior are found saloons and a subterranean way which communicates with the castle mentioned in the last paragraph. It is asserted that a Spaniard obtained from it a treasure with which he went to the capital, and before dying in the hospital of Lima, gave up a journal of his doings, which has passed through many hands. Some persons made an attempt to enter the passage, but were prevented by the jutting out of a stone which impeded the passage. The majority of the houses of *Chavin* and its environs are constructed over aqueducts. The bridge which must be crossed in order to reach the castles is made of three stones of wrought granite, each one of which is eight yards in length, three-quarters wide, and half a yard thick, all taken from these fortresses. In the house of the curate are two figures cut in sand-stone; they are two yards in length, and a half in height, are arranged on each side of the street door, and were brought from the castle for this purpose.

Fatigued, and at the same time pleased with my laborious investigation, I rested myself upon some blocks of granite more than three yards in length, which had engraved upon them certain characters or designs which I could not decipher, but which were identical with those which I met with at the entrance of the subterranean passage near the river. As I sat there my imagination rapidly called up all the ancient places I had visited, and the great events which took place at the time of the conquest. With saddened feelings I lifted my eyes toward the ruins of this silent spot, and saw the deplorable relics of the depredations committed by our ancient oppressors.

Three centuries have not been sufficient to efface from memory the infinite evils sustained by the peaceable and simple inhabitants of the Andes, and even then I almost seemed to see the waters of the small torrent dyed with the blood of the victims; I could imâgine the rubbish on the banks to be but heaps of corpses, upon which fanaticism seated itself, and erected its throne to tyranny, and from whence it thanked God that it had accomplished the work of destruction.

Carried away by such sad meditations, and compassionating the unhappy fate of a nation so laborious and wise, I could fancy that I heard from the bottom of the subterranean passage, as it were, a voice which said to me: 'Traveller, what motives induce you to wander over these silent spots, to remove rubbish, and to tread upon ashes which time has respected, notwithstanding men are pleased to depreciate them? Are not the facts furnished by history sufficient to prove to you our greatness, simplicity, hospitality, and love of labor? Perchance, better witnesses of the opulence of our ancestors will be found in the remains of monuments that escaped the bloody sword of the inhuman conqueror, than can be seen in the theft of our wealth, the plunder of our cities, the treachery to, and death of our adored Incas, of our wise men, and of our nobles! He who denies the persecutions and torments which we endured, the evil which was done to our country, to arts and humanity, may as well assert that the Sun, our father, does not contribute, with his reviving heat, to the development of moving life, and that the high and majestic Cordillera does not enclose within its bosom the mighty veins of precious metals, which were the primal cause of our ruin.'

The history of the conquest of Peru presents to us nothing but sad details of vengeance, of sordid passions, and a propensity to destroy all which might illustrate our story to future generations; so that although we have consulted several authors of different epochs, they either repeat what others have said, or pass over in silence the most remarkable events; and as shortly before the arrival of the Spaniards the Inca Huascar perished at the hands of Atahuallpa, and also almost all the nobility who, as we have already said, were the only ones who were learned in the history of the country and in the reading of the *Quippos*, we are left in complete ignorance of the origin of these nations, and of the great conqueror and legislator, *Manco-Capac*.

Let us profit by this example: we will strive at least for the preservation as far as is possible of the precious relics of our ancestors. We will not be accused by future generations of indolence, destruction and ignorance.

Near the present pueblo, *La Fortaliza*, to the north of the gate of *Pativillca*, are found the ruins of *Paramanca*. Dr. Unanue (Nuevo dia del Peru, Trujillo, 1824), differing in opinion from Garcilasso de la Vega, thinks that the edifices of *Paramanca* should not be called fortresses, because their construction does not warrant the title; neither in his opinion were they erected to perpetuate the pride and pomp of Yupanqui and humiliation of Chimu, but simply to preserve the memory of both chiefs, the most powerful of Peru, who met here, to celebrate the peace and bind more closely their friendship; for which reason, one of these edifices is erected toward the east, being the most elevated, indicating the dignity and extension of the empire; the other toward the west, but more humble in appearance, indicating the districts of Chimu.

This interpretation seems to us erroneous. Not only the construction of these edifices, which pertains undoubtedly to fortifications, but also their situation, is opposed to the opinion of the learned *Unanue*. If the larger had betokened the empire of the Incas, its direction would have been toward the south, and that of the smaller toward the north. The only high road the whole length of the coast, leads between the two fortified eminences; by means of them the entrance to the kingdom of Chimu might be closed. The Incas knew from long experience, that the conquered nations were easily excited, and therefore always held themselves in readiness against them. Very distrustful might *Capac-Yupanqui* well be of an enemy so fearful and obstinate as *Chimu-Canchu*, who had only surrendered after a long-continued resistance, and it is very probable that that cautious general caused these edifices to be constructed as fortresses, in order to curb the nations recently subjugated, and not as monuments of victory; which, according to the custom of the Incas, were always erected in the capital of the empire. In the opinion of some authors *Chimu-Canchu* erected these edifices as frontier posts, which is very probable, since the king *Canchu*, long before he was attacked by *Capac-Yupanqui*, was engaged in a cruel war with *Cuyz Mancu*, chief of *Pachacamac*, and *Chuquiz Mancu*, chief of *Runahuanac*. In the valley of *Paramanca*, took place the first but indecisive battle between *Chimu* and *Capac-Yupanqui*. The etymology of the name, Paramanca, gives us no clue to the nature of these edifices. There are authors who write *Parumonga*, others *Paramanca:* but in our opinion, Paramanca is the true name. Let us hear the words of an author in favor of the opinion we express: "At the entrance to *Patavillca*, on one side, exist the fortresses ordered to be constructed by Inca Yupanqui, which sufficiently mark the extensive knowledge of the Indians in military architecture. On a small mountain contiguous to the mountain of *Vendebarato*, is seen a quadrilateral fortress, with three enclosures of walls commanding the interior: the longer is three hundred yards, and the shorter two hundred. Within the innermost enclosure are several dwelling-houses, separated by narrow passages and streets. About thirty yards from each angle of the inner enclosure are found some bastions, which flank the curtains. There is also seen on the side a high escarpment, facing the sea, in which are three semicircular walls, which are called the gallows, and were used as a prison for delinquents."

Toward the south, two leagues from *Chancay*, near the farm of *Chancaylla*, are ruins of subterranean depositories, which according to tradition were erected by the Incas during the campaign of *Capac-Yupanqui*, against Chimu, to keep an abundant supply of provisions for the army, which counted in its three divisions one hundred and twenty thousand men.

The ruins of Pachacamac, seven leagues from the capital of Lima, in the vicinity of the pleasant town of Lurin, are very much dilapidated, and present but little interesting in their architecture; though they are interesting in their extent, and in the particulars of their history.

On the conical elevation near the bank of the sea, four hundred and fifty-eight feet above its level, are found the ruins of the ancient temple of *Pachacamac.* At the foot of this hill are seen, at the present day, the decayed walls of the edifices which were intended to receive the strangers who came on pilgrimage from the most distant provinces of the empire, to present their offerings to the Deity. The whole was surrounded by a wall of adobes, nine feet in width, and probably of considerable height, for some parts of it are twelve feet in height, although in its average extent it is not more than four or five. The material throughout the whole fabric is not hewn stone, as in the edifices of Cuzco, but adobes, easily crumbled. The upper part of the high-land or ridge, which is about one hundred feet high, is artificially formed by walls, each one thirty-two feet in height, and from seven to eight wide. In the most elevated parts is seen the temple, with the sanctuary of the Deity on the side toward the sea. Its door was of gold, richly inlaid with precious stones and coral; but the interior was obscure and dirty, this being the spot chosen by the priests for their bloody sacrifices before the idol of wood, placed at the bottom of the enclosure, the worship of which succeeded the pure and abstract worship of the invisible Pachacamac. At present there remain of this temple some niches only, which, according to the testimony of Cieça de Leon, con-

PRESENT STATE OF THE RUINS OF PACHACAMAC; INCLUDING THE TEMPLE OF THE SUN, THE HOUSE OF THE VESTAL VIRGINS, THE PALACE OF THE INCAS, AND THE ANCIENT SETTLEMENT IN THE VALLEY OF PACHACAMAC. THE SMALL ISLANDS BEYOND ARE SANTO DOMINGO, FARRALLONES, AND PACHACAMAC.

tained representations of several wild beasts; and we have detached fragments of paintings of animals, made on the wall, upon the whitewashed clay. We can, however, still distinguish the place of the sanctuary, according to the description of the early chroniclers. The opinion is erroneous which deems these the ruins of the temple of the Sun; it is one, however, which has been adopted by almost all modern authors, although diametrically opposed to that of the historians contemporaneous with the conquest, as well as to the account given by Hernando Pizarro, brother of Francisco, and destroyer of the temple.

Outside of this edifice there were in Pachacamac a temple of the Sun, a royal palace, and a house of virgins; monuments erected by the Incas Pachacutec and Yupanqui. According to our investigations, the temple of the Sun extended from the foot of the mountain, on which was situated the temple of Pachacamac, toward the north-east; on the side toward the north-west, as far as the lake of sweet water, and at the foot of the mountain, from the south-east of the temple of *Pachacamac*, to the house of the chosen virgins. The settlement is found all around these edifices from the side of the estate of San Pedro, of the deserted San Juan, and of the existing town of Lurin. Near the latter we notice the ancient cemetery, which attests better than any other proof how thickly populated in ancient times was the valley of *Pachacamac*, in the neighborhood of the temple. The treasures with which this edifice abounded were such that according to one author, the value of the nails only by which they affixed to the walls the plates of gold, amounted to four thousand marks; which as an insignificant trifle, Pizarro gave to his pilot, Quintero. On the haciendas of Lomo and Nieveria, and on the brow of contiguous mountains, are seen ruins of vast extent with saloons twenty or twenty-five yards in length, and six or eight in width, of mud walls, forming narrow streets; indicating that here was once a large population, and the palaces of their princes or other great nobles.

Some two miles from the shore of the sea, are found the small islands known under the names of the *Farrallones*, *Santo Domingo* and *Pachacamac;* and in the latter were found by us in 1842, vestiges of an edifice of considerable extent. These barren islands formed part of the continent as promontories, and were separated by the terrible earthquake of 1586, which made such ravages on the Peruvian coast.

The account of Cieça de Leon is the only one which contains much relating to New Cuzco, which the Incas caused to be constructed in the valley of *Huarco*, and which was connected with the immense fortress of Huarco, built upon a high hill, with large square flag-stones, and with a stone staircase, descending to the sea.* The same authority informs us of the temple of *Guarivilca* in the valley of *Jauja*, consecrated to the god *Ticeviracocha*, chief divinity of the *Huancas;* whose singular worship reminds one of the mythology of the northern countries of Europe. Notwithstanding the most scrupulous investigations, it has been impossible to find any vestiges of the ruins of this temple.

Cieça de Leon (Chronicles, Chap. LXXXVII. and Chap. LXXXIX.) makes mention, in few words, of the ruins of the very ancient and large edifices on the banks of the river *Vinaque* near *Huamanga*, which, according to tradition, were

* In lower Chincha we are assured was a temple of the Sun in the same situation, where at present the convent of *Santo-Domingo* stands, and in the vicinities of the town of *Huancay*, district of Pisco, even yet may be seen the ruins of a so-called palace; but in truth of a red Tambo, so named from its walls having preserved this color.

built by bearded white people, who, a long time before the reign of the Incas, came to these parts, and made this their home; and also of the edifices of *Vilcas* built by order of the *Inca Yupanqui*.

The *Chulpas* which are seen upon the hill which is bathed by the lake of *Clustoni*, in the department of Puno, present a particular construction, and we know not whether they

HILL OF CLUSTONI AND HATUN-COLLA.

were dwellings, or served to keep the grain and potatoes; or perhaps they were used as sepulchres, (which seems to us the most probable), since they also bore the name of *Huacas*. All those which we have examined are built of lime or sandstone, mixed with pieces of micaceous slate, with little windows of one foot in height, and divided in the centre with stone slabs, and covered with straw or pieces of stone, similar to those of Huamalies.*

Among the ruins of *Hatun-colla* are observed remains of

* There are also to be seen, on the road from Lampa to Puno, towers of similar construction.

monuments, and it is said that here was the residence of a prince, whose palaces and town were covered by the waters of the lake, although history is silent as to any such event. Here is also found a chair of stone, (a species of lava), with its back made of a single piece, which is said to have been the throne of the Lord of the place. The Inca *Lloque Yupanqui*, after having subjugated the *Canas* and *Ayahuiris*, passed without permission to *Hatuncolla* and *Paucarcolla*, districts governed by *Apus* or Lords, who nevertheless allowed him to construct a temple to the Sun, a house of virgins, and royal palaces, distributing among them garments and rich cloths.

We have already spoken of the baths of the *Huamalies*, and of the palace of *Limatambo*: it now remains to say something of the ancient monuments which exist four leagues from the bank of the lake of Titicaca; and without doubt, those which count more centuries than any other remains of Peruvian antiquity, are the ruins of Tiahuanaco,* which, according to history, were erected in one single night, by an invisible hand.

RUINS AT TIAHUANACO—STONES ABOUT SIX OR SEVEN YARDS HIGH—PARTLY CUT—PARTLY ROUGH—PLACED IN LINES, AT REGULAR DISTANCES.

* Tiahuanaco signifies in the Quichua language "the resting-place, Huanaco," and is a name which, according to tradition, was given to it by the *Inca Yupanqui*, upon the conquest of the nation of Aymara; on account of the swiftness with which his *Chasqui* or courier ran to the place.

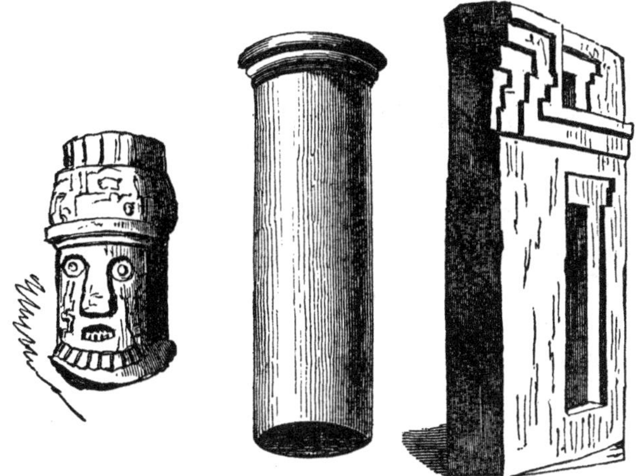

FRAGMENTS FROM TIAHUANACO.

ENLARGED VIEW OF MONOLYTHIC GATEWAY IN THE DRAWING ABOVE.

At the present day these edifices are destroyed, and even before the arrival of the Spaniards they were very much dilapidated. Indeed, it is probable that they were never completed, but remained abandoned in consequence of the new worship introduced by the Incas; since there is no doubt that they went back to an epoch anterior to the establishment of the Peruvian dynasty. Most worthy of notice among the ruins, are the fragments of the statues of stone, of which, says *Cieça de Leon*, Chap. C. V.: "In front of this hill are two idols of stone, cut in the human form, very excellently done, and formed so well, that it seems they must have come from the hands of great artificers or masters. They are so large that they seem like small giants, and it is plain that they have a species of large garment, different from that which we now see among the natives of these provinces. Their heads seemed to contain their chief ornament." In the head of one of these statues, the length, from the point of the beard to the upper part of the ornament of the head, is three feet and six inches: its greatest width from the extremity of the nose to the corresponding part of the occiput is two feet and seven inches. It is adorned with a species of round cap, one foot seven inches in height, and two feet five inches in width. In the upper part are seen certain wide and vertical bands; in the lower are symbolical figures with human faces. From the eyes, which are large and round, project to the chin two wide bands, each one with three double circles. From the outer part of each eye descends a band adorned with two squares, one vertical rectangle and two horizontal lines, terminating in a serpent, similar to that on the monuments. The nose is slightly prominent, surrounded on the lower side by a wide band semicircular, and terminating toward the inner side of the eyes in two corners. The mouth forms a transversal oval, garnished with sixteen teeth. From the under lip projects, in the form of a beard, six bands, toward the edge of the chin. The ear is represented by a semilunar figure in a square, and in the fore-part of it is a vertical band with three squares, terminating in the head of a wild beast. On the top of the occiput are squares forming bands, and on the neck are distinguished many human figures. The sculpture of this head is very remarkable, and bears no resemblance whatever to what is known of other nations.

No less worthy of attention is the monolythic doorway of stand-stone, sufficiently well preserved, the height of which is ten feet, and the width thirteen.* In this block is found cut a door, six feet four inches high, and three feet two inches wide. It presents, on its eastern side, a cornice, in the middle of which is observed a human figure somewhat similar to those which we have mentioned in the preceding paragraph. The head is almost square, and there proceed from it several rays, among which are distinguished four snakes. The arms are open, and each hand holds a snake with a crowned head. The body is covered with an embroidered garment, and the short feet repose upon a pedestal, also ornamented with symbolical figures. On each side of this figure is seen in the cornice a certain number of small squares, in rows, each one containing a human figure in profile, in the position of going, with a species of walking-stick in the hand; those of the middle row differ from those of the upper and lower ones. The other ruins present no interesting particular, but the great size of the sculptured stones with which they are constructed is very remarkable.

In the year 1846, General Ballivian being President, and Don Manuel Guerra, Prefect of la Paz, several excavations were made, in order to disinter, or seek for, what was remarkable, and all that was found were some idols,† and some sculptured masses of large dimensions which have served to

* Another monolythical door, smaller, seven feet in height, is drawn upon the ground. (See the same plate.)

† An idol of stone which was brought from Tiahuanaco to the city of la Paz, in the year 1842, is 3½ yards in length, and half a yard in width.

make stones for grinding chocolate; thus destroying monuments which ought to be preserved as relics of antiquity. These large masses were ten yards in length, six in width, and of the thickness of more than two yards, and were so cut, that, when resting on each other, their junction formed a channel between them. There are other masses of stone, in the direction of the lake, which have remained in the road for reasons which we know not.

RUIN ON THE ISLAND OF TITICACA, IN LAKE TITICACA.

On the island of Titicaca, in the lake of the same name, where, according to tradition, fell the first rays of the Sun to illuminate the world after the deluge, and where the beneficent orb sent his favorite children, *Manco-Capac* and *Mama Ocllo*, to civilize the barbarous hordes of Peru, the Incas introduced a worship to the protecting Deity; the ruins, though not very imposing, are found at the present day well preserved. They are all made of hewn stone, with windows and doors, with posts and thresholds of hewn stone also, these being wider below than above.

The architecture is inferior to that of the ruins of the edifice more nearly destroyed, in the island of Coati, in the same lake; whether it were a palace or a temple, we cannot decide. Its interior decorations seem to have been similar to those seen at Cuzco. The quantity of offerings of gold and silver, piled up in the island, was such, that the traditions of the Indians on this point exceed the limits of probability. In treating of this subject, *Father Blas Valero* tells us, such was the richness of the temple, that, according to the account of the *Mitimacos* or transplanted Indians who live in Capucabana, of what remained in gold and silver might have been constructed another temple from the foundation to the top, and without mixture of any other material; and also that these treasures the Indians threw into the lake, as soon as they knew of the arrival of the Spaniards, and their thirst for gold. (Garcilasso De La Vega, I. Royal Com. Book III. Chap. XXV.)

INTERIOR OF AN APARTMENT IN THE EDIFICE ON THE ISLAND OF COATI, LAKE TITICACA.

In vain have we scanned the writings of all the ancient Peruvian Chroniclers, to obtain particulars respecting the fortress and palace of *Ollantay-Tambo*, ten leagues distant to the north of the capital of the empire, and situated in a narrow tract on the banks of the river *Urubamba*.

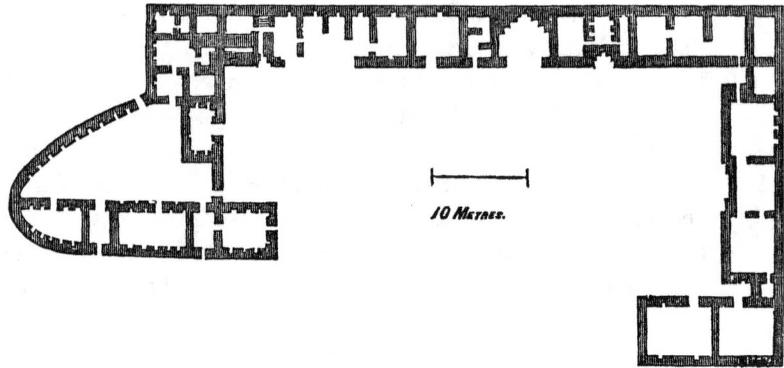

GROUND PLAN OF THE TEMPLE REPRESENTED IN THE FRONTISPIECE.

This strong defence might well have been considered by the Incas as very important, not only on account of its imposing position, being as it were the key to the *Antis*, *Pillcopatos* and *Tonos* nations, who inhabited, as we know, the valleys of *Paucartambo* and *Santana;* but also on account of its singular construction, which differed from the edifices of Cuzco, and of all other parts of the empire; which induces us to suppose that it dates its origin from remote centuries, and that the prince or lord of this territory was independent of, and contemporaneous with the first founder, and was not conquered until the latter reigns of the Incas.

They relate several traditions respecting this personage, one of which we have mentioned as forming the subject of the drama mentioned in a previous page. Others tell us that *Ollantay* being surprised in the house of the virgins of the Sun, a crime punishable with death, the penalty was commuted to degradation from his high rank.

Being after some time restored to his fortress, he rebelled against the Inca Yupanqui, who not being able to conquer him, notwithstanding the men and time which he sacrificed, adopted a plan suggested by a chief; viz.: that they should punish him (the chief) publicly, thereby giving him sufficient inducement to pass over to the enemy, and that they should be unsuspicious of any stratagem; that once

THE TOWN AND FORTRESS OF OLLANTAY-TAMBO.

admitted, he should endeavor to inspire the rebel with confidence, communicating to him certain secrets and measures which they thought of taking, in order to attack him anew;

that by this means the spy should attain a correct knowledge of the place, and of the intentions and projects of Ollantay; that finally, upon the anniversary of the birthday of Ollantay, when they gave themselves up to all sorts of diversions and disorders, he should plead to be appointed chief of one of the gates, and upon a concerted signal, should open it for the entrance of the imperial troops.

THE WALL WHICH SHUTS IN THE FORTRESS ABOVE, SHOWING ALSO THE GALLERIES OR TERRACES WHICH LEAD TO THE TOP OF THE CASTLE, OLLANTAY-TAMBO.

Such an iniquitous plan having been accepted by the Inca, he gave orders for everything requisite to its execution, and thus at last, as proposed, they entered the fortress, killing and destroying all whom they met in their passage, but were unable to take Ollantay, who defended himself with gallantry, preferring to cast himself from the steepest part of the rock, sooner than give himself up to his enemies.

The silence which Garcilasso maintains upon this event, the little confidence which would be felt in any chief punished by the intrepid and sagacious Yupanqui, in order that he might gain the fortress, give us cause to suspect, and not without reason, that this is a story very much disfigured, and that there were other causes for the war which was declared. We know that *Yahuar-Huaccac*, son of Inca *Rocca*, conquered, by order of his father, the provinces beyond the Andes, passing over this and other fortified points in his march, which is a proof that they were already under the dominion of the Incas.

The fortress is constructed upon a steep eminence. A stone staircase leads to terraces, which you pass by narrow ways, until you reach the top, where may be seen tables of stone more than four yards in height, and set on end.

A part of this hill or ridge seems to have been made by hand, presenting a precipice on the side of the river, into which, we are informed, criminals were thrown. Before entering the town, which lies at the foot of the fortress, you pass through a portal, joined to large walls built of enormous masses of hewn stone; on these walls are seen many sentry-boxes, which face the south.

These relics we believe to be, as we have already said, anterior to those of Cuzco.

Among the many remains of antiquity which even yet exist in the city of Cuzco,* we distinguish those of the street

* Some authors, ancient as well as modern, are accustomed to use the article in speaking of the city of Cuzco, without doubt resting on the very problematical etymology given by Garcilasso de la Vega, who pretends that the word Cuzco, in the private language of the Incas, meant

of *Triunfo*, where is seen part of the wall of the ancient house of the virgins of the Sun, constructed in a Cyclopean manner. In it is found a very large stone, known under the name of the "stone of the twelve corners," and it is in reality so shaped that it presents twelve distinct angles.

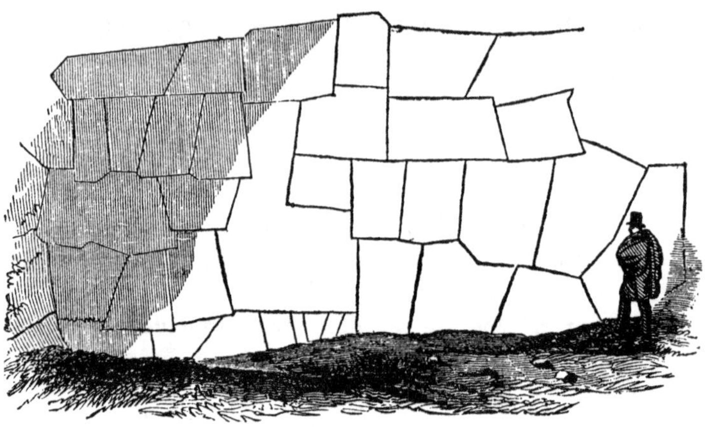

In many parts of the city may be seen remains, more or less considerable, of ancient walls and other architectural monuments.

Among the most celebrated and interesting of these are

"navel;" other authors do not use the article, and in our work we have followed their example, as being more correct and conformable to the grammatical rules of the Castilian language, although the general use is in favor of the article.

We have also preferred to write Cuzco instead of Cozco, as is done by the greater part of the old chroniclers.

the ruins of the supposed palace of *Manco-Capac*, on the declivity of the hill of *Sacsahuaman*, upon a sort of level, where is also found the church of *San-Cristoval*, which conceals a part of these ruins. This extensive edifice, constructed, according to tradition, by the first Inca, had terraces with walls three and a half or four yards high, and long in proportion. They were reached by a staircase passing through a narrow opening, until it came out on an extensive enclosure, the wall of which was some yards high, and contained niches or cupboards, narrower above than below, but for what purpose designed we know not. On this same terrace are seen, even at the present day, the remains of edifices which must have been large, and of which there is preserved but one window. There are also seen the remains of transverse walls laid upon terraces. The material of these walls is a dirty white limestone.

Over the fortress and in front of those interesting relics of antiquity are found arranged three crosses as a substitute for the banners which in remote centuries floated there, indicating the residences of the children of the Sun. These are the symbols of Christianity which have taken place of the signs and idols of heliacal worship; and although their planting cost immense sacrifices and many victims, the benign institutions of Christianity, founded upon the word of the true God, have scattered rich fruits in the depressed minds of this poor nation, and on its pure and humanizing worship alone can national prosperity be founded.

Here concludes our volume, in which, moved by respect for the public, to whom we have addressed ourselves, and by our love for Peruvian antiquity, we have spared neither time nor fatigue, neither travels, reading, nor experience, nor, in one word, anything which might tend to the success of our undertaking. We have gathered all the materials which we have been able to meet with, have classified the curiosities of all kinds which it has been possible for us to collect, and have endeavored to illustrate them by the aid of the pencil.

We have described, under its different aspects, the nation, perhaps the most refined in the New World, and certainly the most distinguished in character, the most surprising in customs and records, the most attractive to an imaginative temperament, on account of the medium in which it is, as it were, enveloped—a medium misty, and on which the dawn is just breaking, showing the effect of the struggle between the opening light of civilization and the darkness of ignorance. If liberty, the idol of our fathers, was almost unknown to the vassals of the Incas, it is also certain that there reigned among them almost an equality, a spirit of fraternity, a sincere love for their sovereigns, bound to their subjects by innumerable and reciprocal benefits, which formed the basis of peace and concord, and the link between the monarch and the nation. If our forefathers, in the country which we adore, were found unable to rival refined Europe in the splendor of science, the luxurious display of the arts, and superior tactics in war; we must nevertheless acknowledge that as little were they found infested with the leprosy of pauperism, the corroding ulcer of prostitution, with the many evils which desolate transatlantic countries. Religion, policy, agriculture formed a whole in those regions, whose inhabitants fell in hecatombs under the ever-reeking sword of insatiable avarice and implacable fanaticism. The policy of the Incas had solved many problems which still engage the attention of the most vigorous European intellects.

May this publication arouse from its lethargy Peruvian youth, may our disclosures quicken its enthusiasm, and make them understand that the very dust they tread on, palpitated, lived, felt, thought in olden times; that justice must be awarded sooner or later to each individual, each nation; that Babylon, Egypt, Greece and Rome are not the only empires which serve as food to a generous imagination; that at their feet lies stretched a shipwrecked civilization; that their footsteps are disturbing an archæological mine, no less rich and opulent than the most celebrated mines of gold and silver of their own country, and like them, too, scarce covered with a light coat of sand; that a thousand remembered lyrics, and innumerable dramatic scenes, that the wisest political and moral counsels ought to bud forth from a world which, though dead, yet may be galvanized into life, by study and artistic enthusiasm. Above all, may it communicate its ardor to and govern public opinion, that queen of the world, that impetuous current which should draw into its stream alike governors and governed, so that by moral authority, and innumerable other resources, they might undertake the gigantic work of the regeneration of the past.

Happy indeed should we esteem ourselves, if our labors might be crowned by seeing the wise and the skilful associated under the direction of an intelligent, active and paternal government, like that of those children of the Sun, the Incas; and under its auspices, Peruvian civilization rising from the dust which covers it, as Pompeii and Herculaneum, in these latter days, have come forth from the lava which for centuries has entombed them.

www.ingramcontent.com/pod-product-compliance
Lightning Source LLC
LaVergne TN
LVHW020219110826
845151LV00003B/757

9781425533274